The Christians
and
the Roman Empire

THE CHRISTIANS AND THE ROMAN EMPIRE

Marta Sordi

Translated by Annabel Bedini

London and New York

First published in the UK in 1988
by Croom Helm
First published in paperback in 1994
by Routledge
11 New Fetter Lane, London EC4P 4EE

© 1983, 1994 Editoriale Jaca Book SpA

Printed in England by Clays Ltd, St Ives plc

British Library Cataloguing in Publication Data

A catalogue record for this book is available from the British Library

ISBN 0-415-09815-7

Contents

. . . the time is coming when anyone who puts you to death will claim that he is performing an act of worship to God;

John 16:2

Part One
The Christians and Political Power

Introduction

During the three centuries which separate the first appearance of Christianity in the Roman Empire from Constantine's final acceptance of the sect, the relationship between the new religion and the ruling powers went through a great many different phases. Because of the complexity of this relationship, we should not attempt to generalise on the subject, either by suggesting (as used to be the case) that the three centuries were characterised by constant and systematic persecution of the Christians, or by following the more recent trend, which tends to minimise the range and importance of the persecutions while at the same time maintaining that confrontation was, after all, inevitable, given that Christianity and Power are by their very natures bound to be in opposition to each other.

Thanks to the progress made in the field of hagiography, we have known for some time to what extent the stories of many of the martyrs are in fact legendary, having been elaborated long after the events they describe. Likewise, the modern approach to the study of history itself allows us to make a clear distinction between the very rare cases of general persecution organised by the ruling powers throughout the empire, the small, localised persecutions fomented and often carried out directly by the mob, and the long periods of tolerance and even friendship which also occurred during these three centuries. Be this as it may, the average layman is still convinced that the Christians were 'wanted', outlaws in constant conflict with a state apparatus intent on wiping them out, a kind of subversive, if non-violent, underground organisation.

Not only is this picture historically false in itself, it also helps to falsify the way in which we see the relationship between Christianity and the state, a question as relevant today as it has been throughout history. It is directly related to the fact that all modern revolutionary ideologies see Power in general, and institutionalised Power in particular, in negative terms. It is also closely connected with the conviction, prevalent in post-war Italian thinking, that ancient Rome embodied a particularly malignant form of Power or, more precisely, of institutionalised Power. This idea must be attributed in part to the unpleasant after-taste left by the Fascists' rhetorical evocations of Imperial Rome, and to a widespread ignorance of the real history of ancient Rome, which was reduced during that period to a simple record of the city's imperialistic undertakings.

As a consequence of this misrepresentation of the facts, many people still believe that the persecution of the Christians represents either evidence of the Christians' indomitable opposition to the state as such, in their role as social and political champions of the oppressed, or, alternatively, action taken by the state which, while no doubt deplorable by our more tolerant standards, was necessary and inevitable in view of the political realities of the times. Thus we find two opposing ideological positions actually collaborating to keep alive the myths of continuous persecution and the inevitability of political confrontation between the Christians and the Roman Empire.

But when we reconstruct the relationship between the two on the basis of contemporary sources and authentic documents (imperial edicts and records of the deeds of the non-legendary martyrs), we see precisely how misleading this preconceived idea actually is. In saying this, I do not mean to imply that persecutions did not take place, or to minimise their importance by reducing the number of martyrs of the first centuries to a few hundred, as some historians have attempted to do. The Christians were persecuted and a great many people did lose their lives; but the point I wish to make is that the conflict was almost never a political one, either on the part of the Christians (who actually continued to profess their loyalty to the Roman State and to call themselves good Roman citizens even during periods of persecution), or on the part of the government itself, which almost never thought of the Christians in terms of a security threat to the state and which often found itself acting simply as the secular arm of the religious fanaticism of the crowd in periods of social and cultural intolerance.

At the beginning of my book *Il cristianesimo e Roma (Christianity and Rome)* (1965), I put forward the proposition that the conflict between Rome and Christianity was ethical and religious, ideological and emotional, but was not, at least on its deepest level, a political conflict at all. The persecution of the Christians was, I suggested, religious rather than political in character. During the course of the book I myself then examined in turn many of the questions which could be raised by this affirmation, in the multiplicity and complexity of its historical connections, but I found nothing to make me change my mind. Nor have I found anything to make me change it since, despite the ambiguities and difficulties this interpretation can cause, and, indeed, has already caused. I do, however, consider it necessary to clarify as far as possible the misunderstandings which have arisen, as they can turn out to be simply a question of using different terms to describe the same idea.

It has, for example, been objected that the so-called 'religious' conflict was in fact political as far as the imperial authorities were concerned, because religion was of interest to the rulers only in so far as it influenced political and social life. We are reminded that according to the religion of Rome, the prosperity and fortunes of the state depended not only upon the industry, worth and wisdom of the citizens and their law-givers, but also upon the protection of particular deities, so that a public policy which did not take religion into consideration was as unthinkable as a national religion without political aims. In this case, the aim was that of maintaining the *pax deorum* without which the empire itself would collapse.

In fact, the two propositions contained in this objection represent two contradictory concepts. For the first, religion is only an *instrumentum regni*, covering various different roles (social and political), whereas for the second, religion is the foundation on which the state is built and the moving force behind its policy-making. In this second case, it makes very little difference whether we use the word 'political' or 'religious' to describe the persecution of a group which the state saw as a threat to the *pax deorum*. I personally prefer the term 'religious', but I am quite prepared to accept 'political' as long as it can be agreed, once and for all, that we are talking about what I shall call 'deity-orientated politics'. Seen from this point of view, it is clear that the persecuted group is considered dangerous only in its capacity to offend the gods and bring their wrath down upon the nation. If, on the other hand, the persecuted group is considered dangerous inasmuch as it is organised in cells whose intentions are prejudicial to public well-being, who intend to undermine the structure of society, who incite to civil disobedience or who deny the sovereignty of the emperor, then the persecution is without doubt political in nature, even in cases where the group has some kind of religious affiliation.

Now, I believe that it can be shown historically that only during the reign of Marcus Aurelius was Christianity seen as a threat of this second kind, that is when Montanism encouraged many of the Christians to acts of open and hostile rejection of the state as such. During this period Montanism was confused with Christianity, even by the Emperor, but the confusion was short-lived, thanks to the

Christians themselves who, between the years 175 and 177, produced the four *apologiae* (those of Melito, Athenagoras, Apollinaris and Miltiades) which cleared up the misunderstanding. Possibly under Marcus Aurelius himself, certainly under Commodus and the Severi, a compromise was reached which gave some 50 years of *de facto* tolerance.

The persecutions which took place under Valerian and Diocletian (the only real, large-scale persecutions suffered by the Christians under the Roman Empire), together with the many demands for persecution made by the public and some sectors of the pagan establishment, were inspired by a different motive. In these cases the Christians were considered dangerous because their 'impiety' would, it was thought, undermine the *pax deorum* and cause the gods to withdraw their protection precisely in the empire's hour of greatest need. Gallienus, after the capture of his father and co-regent Valerian, immediately called an end to the persecution; Diocletian, despite his great disliking for the Christians, hesitated at length before giving orders for their persecution; both believed that persecutions were politically dangerous and likely to disturb seriously the 'terrestrial' peace of the empire. The persecutions carried out by Valerian and Diocletian were prompted by religious necessity, the desire to re-establish the *pax deorum* threatened by the 'impiety' of the Christians and to ensure divine protection for the empire; Constantine's choice of Christianity as the new religion for the empire was motivated by the desire to form an alliance with the strongest God of all.

1 The Political Authorities and Christian Preaching in Palestine from the Trial of Christ to 62 AD

As we all know, the Christian religion and the political authorities of the Roman Empire first met face to face at the trial of Jesus of Nazareth. There is absolutely no doubt that Jesus was put to death — even Tacitus refers to it in his *Annals* (xv.44.5) — or that this took place some time around the year 30 or 31 AD, under Pontius Pilate (and incidentally, an inscription found in Caesarea 20 years ago confirms that Pilate was not, as Tacitus states, Procurator, but Prefect of Judaea[1]). For the purpose of this work, we do not, at this stage, need to go into the technical aspects of the trial itself — the legal significance of whether the Sanhedrin met to consult once or several times and what decisions they reached, or the formal procedures followed by the Roman governor — but rather to examine the political initiatives which gave rise to it. It has been fashionable in some academic circles since the beginning of the century (and particularly in recent years) to overturn the Gospel version of the trial of Christ and claim that the original initiative was taken by the Romans rather than the Jews. It must immediately be said that, from a scientific point of view, the arguments used to support this theory are extremely flimsy and easily refuted. They have, however, gained a certain credence among the public and have fostered an entirely fictitious image of Jesus the revolutionary, the political reformer, who would inevitably be an enemy to, and of, the Roman state.

Bearing this situation in mind, I believe it is essential to examine briefly the whole question of Christ's trial.

In the controversy between the traditional and modern interpretations of the trial of Christ, the whole debate hinges, either explicitly or implicitly, on the exchange reported by St John between Pilate and envoys of Caiaphas and the Sanhedrin who take Jesus before him. Pilate says, 'Take him yourselves and judge him according to your own law', and the Jews answer, 'We have no power to put any man to death'. While each gospel provides a slightly different version of the story, all four Evangelists agree that Jesus actually underwent two trials: the first before the Sanhedrin, charged with blasphemy for claiming to be the Son of God, and capable of destroying the temple and rebuilding it within three days, and the second before the Roman governor, accused of *lèse-majesté* for having called himself the King of the Jews and (according to Luke 23:3) of having stirred up the people and obstructed the payment of tribute to Caesar. All four gospels also agree that, while the Sanhedrin found Jesus guilty of blasphemy and worthy of the death penalty, Pilate considered the political accusations to be unfounded and only passed a political sentence (the *titulus* on the cross was 'King of the Jews') in order to placate the crowd.[2] As far as the Gospels are concerned, then, the proceedings against Jesus were initiated by the Jews, even if the actual sentence was carried out by the Romans. The apparent incongruity of this situation can only be explained if we refer to the passage from St John's gospel quoted above. The Jews, that is, were allowed to try and convict their own criminals within certain limits, but they did not have the right to condemn to death. Any crime which by Jewish law carried the death penalty had to be brought before the Roman tribunal for judgment.

Now, while students of Roman law have never raised any objection to this version of the events, students of Jewish law have. They tend to base their arguments on two opposing premisses: some claim that the Sanhedrin did not have the right to pass any kind of sentence, while others maintain that, on the contrary, the Sanhedrin had full powers and could without doubt also pass the death sentence.[3] This second view is held for the most part by those who contest the Gospel version of the trial. In actual fact, as far as the trial of Jesus is concerned, the result is the same in either case: if the sentence was carried out by the Romans, the initial step must have been taken by them too. Logically then (and not all those who adhere to this theory have been fully aware of all its consequences), it follows that Jesus was put on trial for political crimes which the Evangelists preferred to conceal, both because they were conditioned by their pro-Roman, anti-Jewish attitude and because it would have been dangerous for a church living and expanding in a Roman world to admit that its founder had been (or had been taken to be) a political agitator, condemned to death by the Roman authorities.

In fact, neither of these hypotheses stands up to serious historical scrutiny, as I intend to show in the brief analysis which follows. My analysis will be conducted from the following three points of view:

1. Responsibility for the trial of Christ according to New Testament and non-Christian sources;
2. the trial of Christ in relation to the laws governing Roman provinces (such as Palestine) and the rights usually allowed to local authorities by the Romans;
3. consistency of Roman policy from the trial of Christ to that of James the Less in 62 AD.

(1) Responsibility for the trial of Christ from original sources. It is not surprising that the main source of evidence on this subject is the New Testament. We know how much importance the early followers of Christ attributed to the eyewitness accounts of those who were with him 'from the time when John was baptised to the day when he, Jesus, was taken from us' (Acts 1: 21). What is surprising, as I have already pointed out, is the degree of agreement which exists in all four versions as far as the main themes of the trial are concerned. There are, of course, some variations, such as the number of times the Sanhedrin met, Herod's part in the proceedings, Barabbas and the release of a prisoner for the Passover, and so on. But apart from these, the basic account is the same, both in the earliest versions (those collected in the gospels of Matthew and Mark) and in the later ones (Luke and John).[4] In all four gospels we find the Jews' responsibility to be the decisive factor, with Pilate's role reduced to a reluctant bowing to the will of the Chief Priests and the people. It is interesting to note in this context that even St John's gospel agrees on this point, even though it was written at a time when the Christians had already suffered from Roman persecution and no longer had any reason to maintain a prudent silence.

The speeches of the Acts of the Apostles repeat the same version of the events and, incidentally, give us examples of early Christian preaching,[5] discernible behind the typical oratorical re-elaboration to which speeches were always subjected in the classical world. In all the discourses reported in the Acts, the recurrent theme is the same: the Jews take the initiative and Pilate does his best to resist. It is worth adding that this theme is reinforced when we pass from the canonical gospels to the Apocrypha, in which Pilate and the Romans are completely exonerated from any responsibility for the death of Jesus. In the Gospel of Nicodemus (originating, we believe, in the Hebrew–Christian community of Egypt, and written in Coptic), even Pilate's hand-washing becomes proof of his innocence: 'You see, therefore — said Joseph of Aramathea — how he who was not circumcised in the flesh but in his heart, took water in the light of the day, washed his hands and said "I am innocent of the blood of this just man".'[6]

The claim that Pilate was circumcised in his heart probably ties up with the legend of Pilate's conversion which was circulating in the second century (Tertullian refers to it: 'Pilatus et ipse iam pro sua conscientia Christianus' (*Apologeticum*, XXI. 24)). In the Coptic Church, this legend is taken still further, with Pilate actually dying a martyr's death, while the Ethiopian Church includes his name in its calendar of saints. Only in the fourth century did the legend of Pilate's punishment and suicide take root, becoming extremely fashionable in the Middle Ages and still surviving in the present day.[7]

Some explanation is needed for the consistency with which, right up to the fourth century, the early church insists on minimising or even totally denying Pilate's responsibility for the death of Christ. I personally believe it is overly simplistic to attribute this uniformity of opinion merely to the fear of possible Roman reprisals. It is true that the early Christians were living within the Roman empire and needed to be on good terms with their rulers, but it is also true that the apologists of the second and early third centuries were perfectly prepared to launch bitter accusations against this or that provincial governor for the cruelty of his persecution. They simply made it clear that their accusations were not levelled at the empire itself, which, on the contrary, they tended to clear of any kind of blame. In fact, this technique was used against Pilate himself by the first-century Hebrew writers, from Philo to Flavius Josephus. We should also bear in mind that in the year 37 AD Pilate's rule in Judaea ended in the dismissal from which he was, apparently, never rehabilitated.[8] All things considered, then, we cannot explain the Christian authors' unanimous interpretation of Pilate's attitude in terms of a simple twisting of the truth to serve some other end.

We should ask ourselves, instead, whether the explanation might not lie in the fact that the Christians were, quite simply, recording the facts as they happened and that the Romans were genuinely not responsible for promoting the trial. But we can examine this subject later, after we have looked at the non-Christian evidence, and seen to what extent the trial as it was reported actually corresponds to the laws in force in Judaea during the reign of Tiberius.

In fact, only three non-Christian sources survive on the subject of Christ's trial, dating from the first and early second centuries: the passage from Tacitus already quoted (*Annals*, XV. 44.5), in which we are told only of the execution of Jesus at the hands of Pontius Pilate; the much-debated *testimonium Flavianum (Jewish Antiquities,* XVIII. 64, taken now to be authentic apart from some glosses of probable Christian origin interpolated into the text[9]) in which we are told that 'on charges brought by our authorities, Pilate condemned him [Jesus] to be crucified'; and the letter of the Syrian Stoic Mara Bar Serapion, dating from some time between 73 and 160 AD, in which mention is made of a 'wise king executed by the Jews'.[10] The apparent contradictions in these sources, particularly between Tacitus (sentence and execution carried out by Pilate) and Mara Bar Serapion (sentence and execution carried out by the Jews), can only be reconciled in the light of the fuller version of the events given in the Gospels, which also, of course, corresponds to Flavius Josephus' account (execution carried out by Pilate on charges brought by the Jews).

Non-Christian sources do not, as we see, give us any historically preferable alternatives to the gospel version of the events.

(2) The trial in relation to the laws governing Roman Palestine. In their account of Christ's trial, the Evangelists, like other non-expert writers, recorded the events as faithfully as they could, given that they were not qualified to provide detailed technical explanations of the workings of the law. For this reason, it is particularly interesting to see how closely their version of the complexities of the trial corresponds to the political and legal procedures in force in Roman provinces at that period. Thus, we see a certain amount of autonomy allowed to the local authorities (in this case the Sanhedrin, which takes independent action in bringing charges against Jesus), but the line is drawn at the death penalty, which has to be pronounced by the Roman governor. The edicts of Cyrene confirm this situation. Referring to a province and a period (that of Augustus), close to those of the trial of Christ, they confirm the right of local authorities to conduct their own trials and pass sentences in all cases except those carrying the death penalty. Moreover, this sanction applies not only to Roman citizens, but also to the native population of the province.[11] From a rescript of

Hadrian and an edict of Antoninus Pius (*Digest* 48. 3. 6 ff.) we find that the same conditions held in the province of Asia. Ulpian, writing during the Severan age (*Digest*, 1. 18) says that, in the provinces, the power to condemn to death, like that of condemning to the mines (a kind of maximum punishment), belonged exclusively to the governor of the province. Thus, the statement St John puts into the mouths of the spokesmen of the Sanhedrin — 'We are not permitted to put any man to death' — coincides exactly with what was the normal legal practice in the Roman provinces. At this stage, it would be interesting to ask ourselves to what extent Juster's[12] slip in calling Judaea an 'autonomous region' [?] (and it is the only occasion in his work that he forgets Judaea's provincial status at the time of Christ), has influenced the arguments put forward by those who maintain that the Sanhedrin also had the power to condemn to death. In fact, of course, rabbinical tradition itself confirms that the Jews were deprived of this right under Roman rule.[13]

There were, inevitably, exceptions to this rule. Clandestine strangling and public stoning are two examples which were in use up to the year 70 AD.[14] The right summarily to execute any foreigner found within the temple at Jerusalem is attested both by Flavius Josephus and by an inscription[15] (this was not actually considered to be a legal right, but rather an instance in which the authorities were prepared to turn a blind eye[16]). In any case, these exceptions are not central to our theme and can safely be left out of our analysis of the legal situation. The only exception which is really worthy of our attention is, in my opinion, the stoning of St Stephen, which took place while Pilate was still governor of Judaea, some time around 34 AD.[17] For those who claim that the Sanhedrin had the right to condemn to death, this episode is taken as irrefutable evidence in their favour.[18] Those who deny it — and rightly so, in my opinion — mostly try to dismiss the episode by calling it a public lynching, as in the case of a violation of the sanctity of the temple in Jerusalem; that is one of those acts of 'brutal popular justice which were un-authorised but which the Roman authorities could not always prevent'.[19]

As I have written elsewhere,[20] it seems to me that, if we take seriously the only account we have of Stephen's stoning (that in the Acts), it is difficult to deny that the proceedings against Stephen did have something of a legitimate trial about them. They began with the Sanhedrin hearing the charges brought against him by witnesses, went on with the accused gaining permission from the Chief Priest to speak in his own defence (Acts 6: 11 ff.) and ended with the Sanhedrin's unanimous verdict in favour of the death sentence (Acts 7: 57), which was then carried out by the witnesses themselves, in accordance with the ancient Hebrew law against blasphemers. This impression of a 'regular' trial is reinforced further in another passage from the Acts (26: 10), in which St Paul looks back on the part he himself played in the persecution of Stephen and the Christian community, and tells of casting his vote in favour of sentencing 'the saints' to death. Now, while doubtless 'regular' from the point of view of Jewish Law, the Sanhedrin's behaviour in 34 AD was certainly irregular as far as the Romans were concerned. And even those who maintain that Stephen's death was a simple case of public stoning are prepared to concede the irregularity of the stoning of James the Less and the other Christians in Jerusalem in 62 AD on the orders of the Chief Priest and the Sanhedrin. These last, in fact, took advantage of the fact that the governorship was temporarily vacant, Porcius Festus having died and the new governor, Albinus, having not yet arrived.[21] There is no doubt that Ananias's behaviour in convening the Sanhedrin and passing the death sentence exceeded the powers of his office and offended against Roman law (Josephus underlines the absence of a governor as the decisive factor in Ananias's decision to act); and the fact that he was considered guilty of an abuse of power is clear from the immediate reaction of Agrippa II, who punished him by dismissing him from office (Flav. Jos., *Jew. Ant.* xx. 1. 9. 199 ff.).

(3) The consistency of Roman policy from the time of the trial of Christ to 62 AD. The events of the year 62 are useful to us for various reasons. To begin with, they constitute the clearest possible evidence of the limits imposed on the Sanhedrin, and thereby confirm what is explicitly claimed by St John and implied by the other Evangelists. At the same time, they corroborate the Evangelists' description of Roman policy, which was evidently the same in the year 62 as it had been at the time of the trial of Christ. What is more, the evidence can be considered particularly reliable because it comes from a Jewish source. Now, if in the year 62 the Chief Priest and the Sanhedrin took the absence of the Roman governor as an 'auspicious moment' for proceeding against Christ's followers, this must mean that in the preceding years the Romans had made it clear that they had no intention of ever giving way again

to the pressures of the Jewish authorities, as they had done at the time of the trial of Christ. The Romans, that is, were not prepared to become the secular arm of the Sanhedrin in a controversy which they considered was, and should remain, purely religious and which as far as they were concerned had no political implications.

It is worthwhile that we should ask ourselves at what point the Romans first adopted this policy. It was already in evidence in 51 AD when the local synagogue brought St Paul before Gallio in Corinth (Acts 18: 12) and we see it in action in Judaea when the Jewish authorities in Jerusalem accused Paul before Antonius Felix and Porcius Festus (Acts 21 and, in particular, 23: 28–9 and 25: 19). In all these cases, the answer of the Roman authorities is the same: the controversy between Christians and Jews belongs strictly to Jewish Law and both the proconsul of Achaea and the procurator of Judaea declare that they do not wish to be involved in it in any way. In fact, of course, this was also Pilate's original reaction at the time of the trial of Christ, although he later gave way to the pressure brought to bear by the Jewish leaders, fearing that they would refer the case to Rome as an infringement of their laws (John 19: 7–13). The accusations brought by the Chief Priests were, in fact, extremely clever, playing as they did on the ambiguous theme of the expectation of the Messiah (much feared by the Romans) and combining charges of violation of the Jewish Law (Jesus' claim to be the Son of God) and the Roman law (his claim to be King of the Jews) at one and the same time.[22] Even before the year 31 when the anti-Jewish Sejanus fell from power,[23] Pilate would have had good reason to think that an appeal to the Emperor would be given a favourable hearing, given the fact that Tiberius was known to want to keep the peace at all costs in such a 'difficult' province as Judaea. The likelihood of an appeal to Tiberius being successful against a governor who had committed a violation, real or presumed, of local laws, can be judged by another episode under the same governor. At some stage — possibly but not necessarily after the trial of Christ — Pilate was forced by Tiberius to revoke a decision he had made, after an appeal made to the Emperor by the Jewish leaders. Pilate had wanted to put on display, during a festival in Jerusalem, the gilded shields he had dedicated to Tiberius in Herod's palace; out of respect for the traditions of the Jewish people the Emperor ordered Pilate to remove them.[24] The fear St John attributes to Pilate thus seems to have been perfectly legitimate.

At this point, we come back to my original question: how and when did Pilate's successors come to the conclusion that, as far as the Christians were concerned, appeals to Rome by the Jewish authorities would not be given a favourable hearing? And, as a corollary, at what stage did the Romans decide on such a strict policy of non-intervention (compare the events of 62) that they ended up protecting the followers of Christ from the persecution of the Jews?

I believe that when Tiberius' envoy, the legate to Syria L. Vitellius,[25] deposed Caiaphas in 36 or 37 AD on one of his trips to Jerusalem, Caiaphas was being punished for the crime of executing Stephen, just as Ananias was deposed in 62 AD as a direct consequence of his abuse of power in the case of James the Less. I am confirmed in this view by a remark made in the Acts (9: 33); apparently, immediately after Peter and Paul met in Jerusalem (that is in the same year, 36 AD[26]), 'the church enjoyed peace' throughout Judaea, Galilee and Samaria. The fact that these three regions are mentioned by name is important, because they were the only three to be under Roman rule at that time. We know that in Damascus during the same period the Christians were being persecuted both by the Jews and by the ruler, Aretas, who was at war with Rome at the time (Acts 9: 23 ff.; 2 Corinthians 11: 32). Vitellius' deposition of Caiaphas in the year 36 and Agrippa the Second's of Ananias in 62 had the same effect — that of putting an end to the anti-Christian action of the Sanhedrin. The fact that the deposition of Caiaphas corresponds with a period of peace for the church in Judaea cannot be purely coincidental; and, indeed, we have indirect but significant evidence of a Syrian legate's having intervened in Christian affairs some time before 42 AD. We know that in Antioch, seat of the Syrian legate, the disciples adopted the name 'Christian' for the first time some time around the year 42, and that this was the name given them in the official language of government circles.[27] Vitellius' intervention in Jerusalem in the year 36/7 would seem to be the most probable (and, unless new information comes to light, the only possible) occasion for this name to have become known to the Roman authorities in Syria.

We might ask why it was that, while Ananias's abuse of power was punished immediately, in 62 AD, that of Caiaphas was postponed until the year 36 or 37. This delay can probably be explained by the good relationship which, as various people have emphasised recently, existed between Caiaphas and Pilate. To accuse of an abuse of power the very authorities with whom he had to collaborate to maintain peace in the province would have been difficult, not to say embarrassing, for Pilate.[28]

Writing in the second century, Justin (Martyr) (*I Apologia* 35 and 48) and Tertullian (*Apol.* v. 2 and xxi. 24) both mention a report sent to Tiberius by Pilate on the subject of the spread of the belief in Christ's divinity throughout the whole of Palestine. Chroniclers in the Eusebian tradition dated the arrival of this document in Rome to the year 35.[29] We should not, as has often over-hastily been done, confuse this report with the legendary forgeries written much later, and still extant; in fact, the document probably provides the missing link between the abuses of Caiaphas and the Sanhedrin in 34 and the punishment meted out in 36/7. While Pilate had seen no reason to inform his emperor of the trial of Jesus which had ended in a perfectly legal, if unjust, sentence, he did have to inform him when, with the new religion spreading throughout the province, he found himself having to deal with illegal trials and executions organised by the firmly intransigent Sanhedrin. There was, at this stage, a very real risk that a large percentage of the population of Judaea and surrounding districts would become involved. We have already seen that, during the trial of Jesus, Pilate had become convinced that the political accusations brought against him were unfounded and that he was innocent (all the arguments used to contradict this fact have been proved to be without foundation and we can safely accept the traditional evangelical interpretation as valid). It is, therefore, highly probable that the report quoted by the second-century writers was actually favourable to the Christians and gave the view that the new religion did not in any way constitute a political danger to the state. Tertullian's 'Pilate who was already Christian in his conscience' (*Apol.* xxi. 24) can perhaps be explained in this light, without having to presume Pilate's actual conversion. In any case, having been informed of the developments in Judaea, Tiberius decided to intervene; and in fact, of course, the arrival on the scene of a new Jewish 'sect' could not but interest him. Here was a sect opposed by the Jewish establishment but fast gaining popularity among the people, a sect which eliminated the politically violent, anti-Roman elements from the Messianic tradition, accentuating moral and religious ideals in their place. It was an ideal opportunity for the Emperor to put into practice his main political ambition — that of solving problems with 'consiliis et astu', diplomacy and astuteness, rather than with arms and repression (Tacitus *Ann.* vi. 32. 1, on the year 35).

In the year 35, Vitellius was sent from Rome to the East, not simply as legate of Syria, but as Tiberius' special envoy, with the task of finding solutions to the unsettled situation in the area: 'cunctis quae apud Orientem parabantur L. Vitellium praefecit' (Tacitus, *Ann*. vi. 38. 5). The question of the Armenian succession and relations with the Parthians and Iberians were the principal problems, but he was also to look into the situation both at Damascus (where the Ethnarch Aretas had escaped Roman domination), and at Jerusalem, which he visited two if not three times to implement Tiberius' instructions for the area.[30] Vitellius sent Pilate back to Rome after a protest had been filed against him by the Samaritans,[31] and his place was temporarily filled by a friend, Marcellus (Flav. Jos., *Jew. Ant* xviii. 89). The protection given indirectly to the Christians with the deposition of Caiaphas must have been intended by Tiberius and Vitellius as a peacemaking gesture. It is also interesting to note in Josephus' account that, together with the dismissal of Caiaphas, various decidedly friendly gestures were made towards the Hebrew religion and culture. The office of Chief Priest was restored, some taxes were eliminated and Vitellius himself offered sacrifice in the temple at Jerusalem. From this time on, until the year 62, all the governors of Judaea followed the guidelines set down by Vitellius according to the will of Tiberius.

Different accounts of Tiberius' intervention were given by the Christians of the East and the West. Writing in the fifth century, but using much older sources, Moses of Khoren refers in the second book of his *History of Greater Armenia* to an exchange of letters between Tiberius and Abgar, Toparch of Edessa between the years 13 and 50 AD. Abgar informs Tiberius of the death and resurrection of Christ, and suggests that the Emperor should punish the Jews. Tiberius answers that he has every intention of doing so as soon as he has put a stop to the Iberian rebellion, and that he has already dismissed Pilate. Here, we have an unmistakable reference to Vitellius' mission, including the mention of Iberians[32] as well as the punishment of the Jews and Pilate. It is also interesting to see how the Armenian Church kept alive the tradition of Vitellius' mission as having been in favour of the Christians.

The earliest source in the Western tradition tells a different story. It comes to us in the famous passage from Tertullian's *Apologeticum*, (v. 2), in which he tells how Tiberius, having received Pilate's report, proposed to the senate that Christ should be recognised as a god. The proposal having been refused, and the

Christian religion having been declared a *superstitio illicita* as far as
the state was concerned, Tiberius went on to impose a veto on any
accusations being brought against the Christians in the future. Now,
while most modern historians reject this account as an apologetic
invention, I personally believe it is a record of what actually
happened. I will not repeat here all the arguments I have used on
other occasions to support this theory,[33] suffice it to say that to
reject it out of hand with such remarks as 'highly unlikely' or 'too
good to be true' is not, in my opinion, in keeping with serious
methods of historical research. However, I will limit myself at this
stage to repeating only the points which seem to me particularly
worthy of our attention.

1. Tertullian's passage has, even recently,[34] been rejected as an
apologetic invention on the grounds that 'Tertullian emphasises not
so much the refusal of the senate but the benevolence of Tiberius
who threatens those who want to proceed against the Christians.'
This seems to me to isolate Tertullian's words from their context.
He is addressing the 'Romani imperii antistites' of the dedication
who, in answer to his defence of the Christian religion according to
reason and justice, have quoted the authority of the law: 'It is not
lawful for you to exist' (*Apol.* IV. 3). Tertullian, at this point, is
trying to explain that laws may be unjust and should in that case be
modified (ibid. 13). It is for this reason alone that he is trying to
discover the origin of the anti-Christian laws (ibid. V. 1), and he
finds it in the refusal of the senate to agree to Tiberius' proposal. An
explicit refusal on the part of the senate, turning the Christian
religion into a *superstitio illicita* (Tertullian is trying to explain the
phrase 'it is not lawful for you to exist'), was certainly not something
the Christians would have wanted to emphasise (in their apologiae),
seeing it in their best interests to put the blame for persecution on
individual, evil emperors rather than on the senate. And indeed,
Tertullian makes no further reference to Tiberius or the senate, but
goes on to remind his readers that it was Nero who first put anti-
Christian legislation into practice.

2. The *senatus consultum* quoted by Tertullian was not an
invention of the African apologist. It came to him through the Acts
of the trial of Apollonius (a Roman senator, according to Jerome),
which took place in Rome during the reign of Commodus, between
the year 183 and the year 185. Eusebius, who was in possession of
the ancient Acts, tells us (*Historia ecclesiastica*, V. 21. 4) that

Apollonius was condemned to death for being a Christian 'on the grounds of a *senatus consultum*' whose contents, according to the Greek Acts in our possession, correspond precisely with the 'non licet esse vos' which Tertullian attributes to Tiberius' *senatus consultum* (Lazzati, p. 171: 'the *senatus consultum* says it is not lawful to be Christian'). Tertullian's information thus comes directly from the *authentic* proceedings of the trial (and I underline the fact that the *senatus consultum* is quoted by Eusebius and not only in the later Acts with their interpolations); his source, in other words, is the official record of a trial which actually took place in Rome, before the praetorian prefect Tigidius Perennius and which includes Apollonius' defence of his own case[35] — according to tradition, the first Christian *apologia* in Latin. If we accept, as I believe we must, the authenticity of these records, the hypothesis of a Christian invention collapses completely.

3. The *argumentum e silentio*, weak at the best of times, is in this case non-existent. The fact that Tacitus does not mention the *senatus consultum* is explained very simply by Tacitus himself; on his own admission he only dealt with foreign affairs during the year 35, 'to rest my soul from the ills of home' (*Ann.* VI. 38. 1). Tiberius, not in Capri during this period but at the gates of Rome (ibid. 45. 2), was, however, in constant contact with the senate over affairs of state, either in person or by correspondence.

4. Far from being 'highly unlikely', the behaviour which Tertullian attributes to Tiberius (in making the proposal which led to the *senatus consultum*), would be in perfect keeping with the policy the Emperor appears to have been following in Palestine when he sent Vitellius there as his envoy. By proposing that the cult of Christ should be recognised officially, Tiberius' intention was to give the new Jewish sect the same legal standing that the Jewish religion had enjoyed since the time of Caesar. He hoped in this way to deliver the followers of the new cult from the authority and oppression of the Sanhedrin in Judaea (in 35 AD the new religion was, obviously, confined to that area), and in so doing, he was only following in the footsteps of his predecesors. At the time of the creation of the province of Palestine, the Romans had allowed the Samaritans their independence from Jewish religious control and had thereby also guaranteed Samaritan loyalty to Rome.[36] Tiberius, who preferred diplomacy and craft to arms when it came to solving problems, no doubt hoped to obtain similar results with the Christians.

Failing to obtain what he wanted from the senate, Tiberius took direct action by sending his legate to Palestine.

Some of the scepticism felt by many modern historians regarding Tertullian's account must arise, I believe, from their failure to realise that Tiberius' proposal concerned Judaea and not Rome. In the year 35, Tiberius could not possibly have forseen that the new religion would eventually make far more converts outside Judaea than the Jewish religion he had so feared in 19 AD. Tiberius' proposal in 35 was a political proposal, closely linked with the whole policy of pacification which he was pursuing in a province with an exceptionally complicated religious structure.

From this period until the reign of Nero, the governors of Judaea had clear guidelines on how to deal with the 'Christian question', and the Roman presence in the province actually worked as a safeguard for the followers of the new faith. Only when the province regained its autonomy under Agrippa I (from 41 to 44 AD) did legal persecution of the Christians become possible once more, leading to the execution of James and the imprisonment of Peter.

Notes

1. The inscription was published in *RIL* 95 (1961), p. 49f., by A. Frova. See also C. Gatti, 'A proposito di una rilettura dell'epigrafe di Ponzio Pilato', *Aevum* 55 (1981), p. 13 ff. J. P. Lemonon, *Pilate et le gouvernement de la Judée* (Paris, 1981), p. 23 ff.; L. Prandi, 'Una nuova ipotesi sull'iscrizione di Ponzio Pilato', *Civiltà Classica e Cristiana*, 2 (1981), p. 25 ff.

On the question of the authenticity of the passage of Tacitus, see H. Fuchs 'Tacitus über die Christen', *Vigiliae Christianae*, 4 (1950), p. 65 ff. and also Lemonon, *Pilate et le gouvernement*, p. 173–4.

On the probable date of Christ's trial, 7 April of the year 30, see J. Blinzler, *The Trial of Jesus*, trans. by I. and F. McHugh (Westm., Md., 1959); cf. Lemonon, *Pilate et le gouvernement*, p. 133 (7 April 30 or 27 April 31).

2. For a reconstruction of Christ's double trial, once before the Sanhedrin and once before the Roman governor, I refer readers to Blinzler's *The Trial*, and to Lemonon, *Pilate et le gouvernement*, pp. 173 ff.

3. For the first opinion, see in particular E. Bickerman, 'Trajan, Hadrian and the Christians', *Rivista di Filologia e d'Istruzione Classica* 94 (1968); for the second, see J. Juster, *Les Juifs dans l'Empire Romain* (Paris, 1914), pp. 127 ff.; H. Lietzmann, *Kleine Schriften* (Berlin, 1958), pp. 251 ff. and 269 ff.; P. Winter *On the Trial of Jesus* (Berlin, 1961, 2nd edn revised and edited by T.A. Burkill and G. Vermes, Berlin, 1974). Burkill in fact takes a less clearly defined position in *Vigiliae Christianae*, 10 (1956), pp. 80 ff., as does E. M. Smallwood in *The Jews under Roman Rule*, (Leiden, 1976), pp. 140 ff.

4. For a more detailed analysis of the New Testament accounts of the trial, I refer readers to Lemonon's study *Pilate et le gouvernement*, pp. 177–89.

5. The Acts of the Apostles 2: 23 ff.; 3: 13; 7: 52 ff.; 13: 27–9.

6. Gospel of Nicodemus, IX. 125.

7. Lemonon, *Pilate et le gouvernement*, pp. 265 ff.

8. Ibid., pp. 217 ff. and 245.

9. Cf. A. Pelletier, 'L'originalité du temoignage de Flavius Josèph' *Recherches des Sciences Réligieuses (RSR)*, 52 (1964) pp. 177 ff; Lemonon, *Pilate et le gouvernement*, pp. 174 ff. L. Préchac makes claims for the authenticity of the text in his 'Réflexions sur le testimonium Flavianum', *Bibl. de l'Association Budé* (1969), pp. 101 ff.

10. On the subject of Mara Bar Serapion's letter, see Blinzler, *The Trial*, who dates it as having been written shortly after 73 AD.

11. The IVth Edict of Cyrene is particularly interesting on this point. For an examination of the questions and problems raised by a comparison of the Ist and IVth Edicts, see F. De Visscher, *Les Édits de Cyrene* (Osnabruck, 1965) pp. 16 ff. and 68; cf. Lemonon, *Pilate et le gouvernement*, p. 77.

12. Juster, *Les Juifs*, p. 135.

13. Cf. Lemonon's recent analysis in *Pilate et le gouvernement*, pp. 81 ff.

14. P. Winter, 'Marginal Notes etc.', *Zeitschrift für die neutestamentliche Wissenschaft und die Kond der alteren Kirche (ZNW)* 50, (Berlin, 1959), pp. 22 ff. Blinzler, *The Trial*, refutes this hypothesis.

15. Flavius Josephus *History of the Jewish War*, VI, 126; *Jewish Antiquities*, XV. 417. The inscription, published in the *Rev. Arch.* (1872), p. 220 states that anyone found within the temple 'will himself be the cause of his own death'.

16. An example of this practice occurred when (Acts 21: 27 ff.), St Paul was seen in the temple with some pagans. He risked stoning and was only saved at the last moment by the Roman authorities.

17. The date is calculated on the basis of Galatians 1: 15–24, which puts Paul's meeting with the Apostles in Jerusalem as happening in 36 AD, which would be 14 years before 49 AD (including the two years in the count), three years after Paul's conversion and the death of St Stephen: cf. M. Sordi in *Studi Romani*, 8 (1960), pp. 393 ff. For S. Dockx ('Date de la morte d'etienne', *Biblica* 55 (1974), pp. 65 ff.), Stephen's death took place in the year 36.,

18. F. Parente in *Rivista di Filologia Classica*, 94 (1968), p. 77.

19. Thus, Blinzler, *The Trial* (with previous bibliography). See also Lemonon, *Pilate et le gouvernement*, pp. 92 ff.

20. M.Sordi, *Il cristianesimo e Roma* (Bologna, 1965), pp. 23 ff.

21. Flavius Josephus, *Jew. Ant.*, XX. 91 (200); cf. Blinzler, *The Trial*; Lemonon, *Pilate et le gouvernement*, p. 90, For those who believe the Sanhedrin had the power to pass the death sentence, the abuse perpetrated by Ananias was that of convening the Sanhedrin without Roman authorisation (see Smallwood's *The Jews*, pp. 149 ff). My refutation of this interpretation first appeared in *RFIC* 98 (1970), pp. 309 ff. and has since been confirmed by Lemonon, *Pilate et le gouvernement*, p. 91 and n.129.

22. Lemonon, (*Pilate et le gouvernement* p. 188 and n.202) has underlined precisely how clever the accusations of the High Priests actually were.

23. Sejanus' attack is mentioned by Philo (*Legatio ad Gaium*, 159–61; *In Flaccum*, 1) and Smallwood (*Latomus*, 15 (1956) pp. 322 ff.) dates it some time around 28–31 AD. Tiberius had indeed shown himself to be hostile to Jewish proselytism in 19 AD (Tacitus, *Ann.* II. 85. 4; Suetonius, *Tiberius*, 36 etc.) but his disapproval referred only to proselytism in Rome itself and had no bearing on the legitimacy of the Jewish religion itself or, even less, on the respect owed to the religion in its home country.

24. Philo, *Legatio ad Gaium*, 299 ff.; cf. Lemonon, *Pilate et le gouvernement*, pp. 205 ff., who puts the event after the year 31 (the year of Sejanus' fall): cf. pp. 133–4 (with bibliography n. 20) and pp. 223 ff.

25. Flavius Josephus, *Jew. Ant.* XV. 405; XVIII. 90 ff., 122 ff. According to Smallwood (*The Jews*, pp. 171 ff.) there were two visits, one in 36 AD, the other in 37. Lemonon believes there were three, one in 36 and two in 37 (*Pilate et le gouvernement*, pp. 242 ff.).

26. See note 17.
27. Acts 11: 26. On the Roman and official origin of the name 'Christian', see R. Paribeni in *Atti Rendiconti dell'Accademia Nazionale dei Lincei* (1927), p. 685; E. Peterson in *Miscellanea G. Mercati* (Vatican City, 1946), p. 362; M. Sordi, *Il cristianesimo*, pp. 30 and 456–7; and now G. Scarpat, *Il pensiero religioso di Seneca e l'ambiente Ebraico e Cristiano* (Brescia, 1977), p. 134 n.8.
28. Lemonon, *Pilate et le gouvernement*, pp. 274 ff.; Lemonon, like Smallwood (*Journal of Theological Studies*, 13 (1962) pp. 14ff.), believes that Caiaphas was demoted precisely because of his relationship with Pilate.
29. The *Chronicon Hieronymis* (Helm, pp. 176–7) and the *Chronicon Paschale* (p. 430) give the date as 35 AD; Tertullian (*Apol., v.* 2) and Eusebius (*Historia ecclesiastica*, II, 2, 1) do not give a precise date but seem to imply that Christianity had already spread throughout Palestine (which would bring us back to the dispersion of the Apostles throughout Judaea and Samaria after the lapidation of Stephen (Acts 8: 1 ff.).
30. Flavius Josephus, *Jew. Ant.* XV. 405 (Vitellius writes to Tiberius); XVIII. 90 (Vitellius goes to Jerusalem with Tiberius' answer: it was during this visit that he dismissed Caiaphas).
31. Flavius Josephus, XVIII. 85 ff. On the Mount Garizim episode, see Lemonon, *Pilate et le gouvernement*, p. 230.
32. These were the Caucasian Iberians (*Tac. Ann.* VI. 32. 5; 33. 1) rather than the Spanish ones, and Vitellius did have dealings with them. See M. Sordi on these references in 'I primi rapporti fra lo stato romano e il cristianesimo', *Rendiconti dell'Accademia dei Lincei*, 12 (1957) pp. 81 ff.
33. M. Sordi, 'I primi rapporti', pp. 59 ff.; 'L'apologia del martire Apollonio', *Rivista di Storia della Chiesa in Italia*, 18 (1964), pp. 169 ff., and *Il cristianesimo*, pp. 25 ff. and *passim*.
34. Lemonon, *Pilate et le gouvernement*, pp. 254–5.
35. If Tertullian's source was Apollonius (a senator, according to St Jerome), two problems immediately find a solution: (1) how the apologist came to know the contents of a document kept in the archives of the senate and only available to senators and, (2) the use of the term 'Syria Palaestina' for Judaea, a designation which was current at the time of Apollonius.
36. Flavius Josephus, *Jew. Ant.* XVIII. 29–30; cf. Lemonon, *Pilate et le gouvernement*, p. 238.

2 From Toleration to Open Persecution: Nero

It had not taken long for the Roman government to recognise the followers of Christ as being one of the various sects into which Palestinian Jewry was divided, and, as we have seen, they were already called 'Christians' in the year of Vitellius' mission (if not even earlier, at the time of the debate in the senate in 35 AD). These 'Christians' were regarded with a certain favour by the rulers, both in Judaea and in the regions where a Jewish diaspora existed, and, until 62 AD, the Roman governors made it clear that they had no intention of allowing the Christians to become the victims of any kind of attack. This attitude can probably be explained by the fact that the rulers saw the kind of non-political Messianism preached by the Apostles as being useful in keeping the peace in Palestine, where revolutionary and openly anti-Roman Messianic movements had been a constant source of trouble.[1]

In Judaea the only 'state' persecution suffered by the church between the time of Stephen's death and the year 62 occurred when Rome handed over the government of the province to a local king, Herod Agrippa I, for the years between 41 and 44 AD. Taking advantage of the situation, the King put James the brother of John to the sword and, 'seeing that this pleased the Jews', went on to arrest St Peter (Acts 12: 1–3). The Acts then go on to tell how St Peter, miraculously released from prison, 'went away to another place' (Acts 12: 17) and a tradition, which probably grew up in the second century, suggests that it was now (at the beginning of Claudius' reign) that St Peter made his first visit to Rome.[2] After Agrippa's death in 44 AD, when Judaea was restored to the status of a Roman province, the church was once again left in peace to preach the gospel (Acts 12: 24). Paul's arrest during the feast of Pentecost in the last years of Antonius Felix's procuratorship (presumably in the late spring of 54 AD[3]) turned out after an initial misunderstanding (Acts 21: 38) to be a protective measure, taken to save him from a public lynching. The account then goes on to tell how Paul, after being questioned by Porcius Festus (who, being new to Judaea, called in Agrippa II and his sister Bernice to advise him), appealed to Caesar and was sent to Rome (chaps 25, 26).

The Roman attitude to Christian preaching in the Jewish diaspora of the eastern Mediterranean was, in other words, generally neutral and sometimes even benevolent. The only exception was at Philippi, where the magistrates of the local Roman colony flogged Paul and Silas and imprisoned them for a day, after they had been accused of being Jewish propagandists, preaching anti-Roman customs (Acts 16: 20–21). They were, however, released the next day without trial. In all other cases, the Roman magistrates seem to have been well disposed towards the Christians and determined to protect them from the various accusations brought against them by the Jews, on one side, and the pagans, on the other. In Corinth, for example, when the chief of the synagogue attempted to bring charges against Paul, he was brusquely interrupted by the proconsul Gallio before he had time to finish his accusations, because, Gallio said, he had no intention of judging questions of Hebrew law (Acts 18: 12–18). Pagan accusations of rabble-rousing were treated in the same way, as the incident at Ephesus shows (Acts 19: 23–40): when the silversmiths of the city rose up against Paul and his friends and a riotous public assembly was convened, the *grammateus* of the *boulé* (in agreement with Paul's Asiarch friends) put an end to the proceedings, first by claiming the innocence of the accused and then by reminding the crowd that the Romans were likely to look on the assembly as seditious and therefore punishable by law. It is significant that here, as in the year 62, the presence or absence of the Romans is clearly the decisive factor when anti-Christian action is being contemplated. Flavius Josephus tells us that Ananias took advantage of the absence of the Roman governor to put James the Less on trial and to condemn him to death; the Acts of the Apostles tell us that the town clerk of Ephesus (certainly a pagan) found a reminder of the presence of the Romans was enough to put the mob off any idea of taking violent action against the Christians.

The most interesting case of all, however is that of Sergius Paulus, proconsul of Cyprus in the years 46 to 48 AD. He was so interested in the new faith that he asked Paul and Barnabas to preach before him and consequently 'learned to believe' (Acts 13: 12). Not only did he himself become a Christian and a personal friend of Paul; he also converted the whole of his family to the Christian faith.[4]

In Rome itself, there is equally no evidence for there having been any kind of official opposition to the Christian religion up to the year 62. The only mention of a possibly hostile act is the interpretation Orosius gives (VII. 6. 15–16) of Suetonius' brief and obscure account of the expulsion of the Jews from the city (*Claud.* 25.4). However, this passage has been contested, and rightly so. In it, Orosius quotes a lost passage of Flavius Josephus, according to which in the 'nono anno' of Claudius' reign (that is, in 49 AD) the Jews were expelled from Rome. He adds: 'sed me magis Suetonius movet, qui ait hoc modo: Claudius Judaeos impulsore Christo adsidue tumultuantes Roma expulit', declaring immediately afterwards that he cannot make up his mind whether the Jews were being punished for rioting against the Christians, or whether, together with the Jews, Claudius was trying to rid himself of the Christians too. In reality, the passage quoted by Orosius does not contain the name 'Christo' but 'Chresto'. Now, the 'vast majority of critics'[5] has agreed that the figure to whom Suetonius was referring was Jesus Christ, and that the celebrated Roman biographer had made the mistake of thinking that Jesus was at that time (49 AD) living in Rome, confusing 'Christians' with 'Christ'. But when correct historical methods have been applied, not even the weight of the 'vast majority' is sufficient to prove that 'there can be no doubts as to the significance of the name Chrestus'. In reality, the use of the name 'Chrestus' was widespread in antiquity and, given its meaning ('chrestòs' means 'good' in Greek), it was undoubtedly very popular among the Jews, who liked to use names of this kind (e.g. Justus).

It is true, however, that in the second century, and possibly earlier, the Christians were often called 'Chrestiani'[6] (because of an error in pronunciation, according to Tertullian (*Apol.* I. 3.5) and, if we are to accept the reading 'Chrestianos' in the *Annals* (XV. 44. 4), Tacitus, too, knew of this popular name (which he attributed to an ironic deformation of the *vulgus*). But it is also true that Tacitus (ibid.) and Pliny (*Ep.* x. 96) writing before Suetonius, were both well aware that the founder of the new sect was not Chrestus but Christ, executed in Judaea under Pilate during the reign of Tiberius (*Ann.* XV. 44.4) and honoured 'as a god' (Pliny *Ep.* x. 96) by his followers.

In reality, apart from Orosius' interpretation, we have no evidence that the expulsion of the Jews from Rome reported by Suetonius had anything to do with a conflict between the Jews and the Christians. Flavius Josephus' account only comes to us via Orosius and cannot be taken as reliable (even if the date, 49 AD, is generally accepted as accurate). Luke's account in the Acts (18: 2) certainly tells of the expulsion of the Jews some time around the year 49, but there is no mention of its having had any implication for the Christians (Aquila and Priscilla, who arrived in Corinth from Rome and met St Paul there, were not yet Christians). We also know that, as early as the year 41, Claudius had wanted to expel the Jews because they had grown too numerous since the last expulsion under Tiberius (Dio Cassius, LX. 6. 6). His only reason for not carrying out the plan was that it would have been particularly difficult to move such a large number of people without causing serious disorders, and in the end he limited himself to forbidding them to hold mass meetings.[7] They were, however, allowed to continue to live according to their own customs. Everyone agrees that the Christians cannot have been involved in the plan of 41 AD; the expulsion recorded by Suetonius seems simply to have been the fulfilment of a plan Claudius had had in mind since the beginning of his reign but had not put into action before for fear of public disorders. Like Tiberius in the year 19, Claudius feared the proselytising tendency of the Jews and, above all (as we see from his letter to the Alexandrians in the same year), the growth in the large cities of close-knit ethnic minority groups which refused to be influenced by, or assimilated into, the local culture, and which therefore constituted the kind of united front which might prove very difficult to control.

Up to the year 62, then, the Christians in Rome continued to be left in peace, even under Nero's administration. Indeed, it was during this period that St Paul was acquitted at his first trial.[8] Having appealed to Caesar, Paul was certainly kept in custody by the army, but he was allowed complete freedom to preach the gospel (Luke emphasises this with some satisfaction in the closing words of the Acts), and he made use of his long stay in Rome to teach the Christian religion 'throughout the praetorium' and even to 'the Emperor's household' (Philippians 1: 13 and 4: 22). In the year 57, shortly before Paul's first trial came to an end, another trial was reaching a similarly peaceful conclusion. It was the trial of a woman of the senatorial class, Pomponia Graecina who, according to Tacitus (*Ann.* XIII. 32. 3 ff.) was accused of practising 'foreign superstition'. She was judged 'according to an ancient custom' by her husband Plautius, the ex-consul who had in his time been honoured with an ovation for his victory in Britain. According to Tacitus, in front of all their assembled relations, Plautius declared his wife to be innocent. After her trial, Pomponia did not change her way of living which, Tacitus tells us, continued to be marked by great austerity. In fact, we know that in the second century the family of the Pomponii Graecini were practising Christians (a member of the family is buried in the catacomb of St Callistus). It is highly probable, therefore, that such an anachronistic custom as the family tribunal was only revived on this occasion in order to guarantee absolution for the accused, thereby avoiding the scandal and gossip which would certainly have surrounded such an 'illustrious woman' had she been convicted for following a *superstitio illicita*.[9]

The protection enjoyed by the Christians in Judaea thus seems to have extended to the rest of the empire. In Judaea itself, the absence of the Romans gave the High Priest his opportunity to strike at the followers of the new faith; in other parts of the empire, the effect is the same, whether the accusers are Jewish or pagan. In Rome itself, the situation is no different and the new religion even seems to have found sympathisers among the members of the ruling classes.

At this point we come up against the much-debated question of the origins of the Christian community in Rome. From St Paul's Epistle to the Romans, it would appear to have been in existence already in 53/4 AD (using my calculations for the date of the arrest of Paul in Jerusalem) or in 56/7 if we accept current chronology. From St Paul's words in the Epistle, various conjectures have been made on the actual composition of the community, some seeing signs of a predominantly pagan–Christian presence and others of a predominantly Jewish–Christian presence.[10] In fact, from what Paul himself says, it seems clear that both elements were present in the church in Rome. The description Luke gives in the Acts of Paul's meeting with the local Jewish leaders (Acts 28: 17 ff. and in particular 22), shows that, whatever its conformation, the Christian community kept itself well apart from the Jewish community and behaved with great circumspection and prudence even where preaching the gospel was concerned. This state of affairs appears to be confirmed by what Paul says in his Epistle to the Philippians (1: 12–14), when he tells of the added impetus and enthusiasm which his arrival in Rome had given the Christian cause.[11]

Based on the Acts of St Peter[12] (written in the second century and so possibly containing some authentic material), and on later legends, tradition has it that some senatorial families — those of Marcellus and Pudens — actually gave St Peter their support and even, perhaps, their hospitality when the Apostle was in Rome.

Excavations under the church of Santa Pudenziana have uncovered what appears to have been an aristocratic home, built in the later years of the republic. It would seem to have survived Nero's reign, after which its place would have been taken first by public baths and then, in the fourth century, by a church. It is, however, impossible to establish any definite connections.[13] In any case, I do not believe we should discard out of hand the possibility that some families of the senatorial class were connected with the Christian community from earliest times. The accounts which come to us in the later legends, however vague and fanciful they may be, do in fact coincide with what we know, for example, of Pomponia Graecina's conversion, as far back as 42 AD, and we must remember that Pomponia Graecina herself had ties with the Julio-Claudian family (the Plautii were related to Tiberius and Claudius through Livia's friendship with the Tarquinian Urgulania). Equally, we must remember the conversion of Sergius Paulus; at the time of his son — the end of the first century and the beginning of the second — his *domus* housed a 'collegium' which would seem to have all the characteristics of a domestic chapel.[14]

As Tertullian was to point out later, the ancient Roman spirit, *naturaliter* stoic with a moral, political and non-philosophical Stoicism, could easily become *naturaliter christiana*. In fact, as we shall see during the autocratic rules of Nero and Domitian, the stoic aristocracy and the Christians were actually accused of the same crimes and persecuted for the same reasons. For the present, however, suffice it to say that we know from reliable sources that there were Christians among the aristocracy in the second half of the first century (Acilius Glabrio and the Christian Flavians) and that it seems probable that the same can be said for the first half of the same century, before Paul's arrival in Rome. This situation would throw light on various questions, among which is the support Christianity seems to have had from the government organs, at least up to the time of Nero's volte-face.[15] It would explain why the Christian community kept itself at a distance from the local synagogue (at least until 56 AD) despite the number of Jewish Christians among its members. It would also explain why the Christians were not involved in the expulsion of Jews from the city in 49 AD and why, when the Jewish colony was re-established, there seems to have been very little friction between the two (as we see in Acts 28: 22). The Roman Christians met for worship in the houses of patricians who were either converts to the new religion, or who in any case felt friendly towards it. St Paul himself (Romans 1: 8), writing before his arrival in the city, praises them for their faith 'so renowned throughout the world' and their good will and knowledge (ibid. 15: 14). These Christians had avoided any kind of conflict with the local Jewish community, but it appears from the passage from the Epistle to the Philippians quoted above, they had also avoided propagating the faith to any great extent among the Jewish and pagan masses. In my opinion, we can probably take Pomponia Graecina as the epitome of the behaviour of the early Christians in Rome: courageous to the point of defying Messalina's anger (and thereby winning Tacitus' admiration) but reserved to the point of choosing to protect her faith from indiscreet eyes by explaining her way of life during the 40 years she was a Christian as being 'in mourning for a friend'. This, I believe, is the style of the community which had learned of the death and resurrection of Christ through various channels, which had received instruction from St Peter, perhaps, in 42 AD[16] and to which Paul had written from far away to express his respect, apologising for having 'written to you here and there somewhat freely, by way of refreshing your memory' (Romans 15: 15), but which, seen from close, he considered over-cautious in spreading the gospel.

The end of the year 62 and the beginning of 63 saw a turning-point, not only in the relations between the Roman authorities and the Christian religion, but in the Emperor Nero's whole political outlook. To this period belong the possibly unnatural death of the Praetorian Prefect Afranius Burrus, the retirement of Seneca from public life, Nero's repudiation of Claudius' daughter Octavia in favour of Poppaea, his total departure from the Julio-Claudian tradition of the *Princeps* in favour of theocratic and oriental form of *dominatio* and his break with the stoic elements of the senate. Nero's change of attitude towards the Christians coincides with his general change of policy, and the coincidence is not merely chronological. Neither is it merely fortuitous that we find the stoic members of the ruling classes being tried and condemned in 65–6 AD, so soon after the persecution of the Christians. In the same way, Domitian's trend towards a theocratic and autocratic form of government was to give rise (in 93 AD) to the persecution of the Stoics first, and the Christians shortly afterwards.

When, how and why Nero should suddenly have decided to incriminate the Christians is still a much debated question. Tacitus (*Ann*. xv 44. 4–9) is the only author to have connected the Christians with the great fire of Rome in the summer of 64, and on the subject of this passage I must emphasise that stylistic analysis has proved its authenticity beyond any doubt. Equally, both in the past and more recently, attempts have been made to separate the mention of the Christians from that of the fire, but the arguments used seem to me far more complicated and unlikely than the mystery they were originally intended to solve. the silence of Suetonius and the Christian sources.[17]

Suetonius does in fact write about measures taken against the Christians in his life of Nero, and he also writes about the fire, but they are not mentioned as being connected. In Chapter 38 he refers to the fire, openly accusing Nero of having started it himself (and thereby agreeing with Pliny the Elder); in Chapter 16 he refers to steps taken against the Christians together with various other measures (*instituta*) for safeguarding public order and morals (measures were taken against the licentious behaviour of the charioteers, the fighting between factions of the pantomimists, the excessive spending on luxuries and the abuses of public banqueting). Chapter 16.2 ' reads: 'afflicti suppliciis Christiani, genus hominum superstitionis novae et maleficae.' In other words, the accusation against the Christians, as far as Suetonius is concerned, is limited to that of *superstitio*, the same as that brought against Pomponia Graecina. She was judged *insontem* by her husband's tribunal, but Suetonius is nevertheless convinced that this *superstitio* is in itself *malefica* and automatically implies the performance of evil deeds, the famous *flagitia*.

Of the Christian writers, Melito (see Eusebius, *Hist. eccl.* IV. 26. 9), Tertullian (*Ad nationes*, I. 7. 13–14; *Apol.* V. 1) Lactantius (*De mortibus persecutorum*, II. 6) and later, Jerome, Rufinus and Orosius all refer to Nero as the first persecutor of the Christians ('dedicator damnationis nostrae' says Tertullian in his *Apologeticum*), but none of them mentions the fire as a reason for the persecution. Lactantius, who does give a reason, agrees with Suetonius that it was a question of religion, 'the defection from the worship of the idols to a new religion' of a 'vast number of people' (*De mort.* II. 6). Orosius also agrees with Suetonius, as far as the fire is concerned (VII. 7. 4 ff.) and refers to the persecution of the Christians further on in his work, combining Suetonius' version with the Christian traditions 'indeed, his was the first attack on the Christians in Rome, afflicting on them sufferings and death, and he ordered the persecution to be carried out likewise in all the provinces' (vii. 7. 10).

Suetonius and the Christian authors all agree, therefore, that Nero's reasons for persecuting the Christians were of a general kind and could equally be applied to all parts of the empire rather than just to the capital. The motivation is fundamentally religious (*superstitio nova—religio nova*), even if at that period it would have been taken for granted that the practice of a forbidden religion automatically implied moral and behavioural deviations — the 'flagitia cohaerentia nomini' of which Pliny writes in his letter to Trajan. Tacitus is well aware of this motivation. So much so, indeed, that, while he considers the accusation of incendiarism to be unfounded, he is convinced that the Christians are guilty of 'exitiabilis superstitio' (xv. 44. 5) and hatred of mankind (ibid. 6). He also mentions the 'flagitia' which, he says, cause the 'vulgus' to hate the Christians (ibid. 4). In fact, to go back to the original question, the contradiction between Tacitus' version and that of Suetonius and the Christians only exists when it is taken for granted that they are all referring to the same measures taken against the Christians. But Tacitus does not actually state that the accusation of arson in the summer of 64 AD was the first or only occasion on which Nero took action against the Christians. On the contrary, it would seem from his account that even before the fire they had already been singled out as objects of mass hatred ('quos per flagitia invisos vulgus chrestianos appellabat') and could already be brought before the tribunal on charges of *superstitio illicita* ('exitiabilis superstitio').

In my opinion, Tacitus' account completes the picture given by the other authors, giving an account of a dramatic but limited incident that none of the others happened to mention: Nero, wanting to silence the rumours that accused him of starting the fire himself, decided to incriminate the Christians. He had in any case previously decided that accusations of *superstitio illicita* could be freely brought against them, and their general unpopularity made them the perfect candidates for the role of scapegoats and presumed incendiaries.

At this stage, we can leave the episode of the fire, which so struck Tacitus by the theatrical cruelty of the punishments inflicted[18] on what he calls a 'multitudo ingens' (and a few hundred victims would justify the use of this term, given the horror of what happened). The question we must now try to answer is when and why Nero took the decision to give free rein to accusations of *superstitio illicita*. It is this decision, and this alone, which constitutes the 'institutum neronianum' reported by Tertullian (*Ad nat.* I. 13–14) and Suetonius (*Nero*, 16. 1). The legal precedent already existed, but, whereas in the past the government had discouraged its application both in Rome (see the case of Pomponia Graecina) and in the provinces (see Ananias's punishment in 62 AD), now charges of *superstitio illicita* began to be brought against the Christians in the tribunals. The *terminus post quem* is, as we have seen, the year 62, when the intention of the Emperor not to persecute the Christians was well known to Ananias, Agrippa and Albinus; the *terminus ante quem* is, in my opinion, Juiy of the year 64, and I choose this date because the very fact that the Christians were accused of starting the fire means that they were already recognised as a separate category, the followers of a new and pernicious superstition.

On the subject of this period, it seems to me that the First Epistle of St Peter is a source of fundamental historical importance and its contents and sense of immediacy induce me to believe in the traditional theories as to its date rather than in the widespread, but by no means new, tendency to attribute it to a later period. The situation is, in fact, unique in the history of the relationship between Christianity and the Roman Empire and never again would a similar state of affairs be possible: the Christians were being slandered on all sides (2: 12 and 15; 3: 16) and public opinion was ready to explode into violence against them (4: 12), but the Emperor had not yet decided to give free reign to accusations brought against them and he was still trusted by the Christians themselves. In I Peter, we see the situation outlined above on the verge of precipitating. The Christians are warned not to be surprised by the 'great fire' which has been lit against them and they are told to be prepared to face trial for adhering to the Christian faith. Chapter 4: 15-16 reads 'Let none of you put yourselves in the position of being accused of murder or theft or of working evil deeds or for meddling in the affairs of others: but if you should be punished for being a Christian, do not be ashamed, but praise God in this name.'

Tacitus says the Christians were hated for their crimes ('flagitia') and Suetonius speaks of 'superstitio malefica'. Peter uses the same words when writing of the slanders used against the Christians: 'they speak ill of you as workers of evil deeds' (I Peter 2: 12). We know what these 'evil deeds' were from the writers of the second century. The most important were infanticide (the pagan interpretation of the Eucharist) and incest (the pagan interpretation of the Christians' custom of calling each other Brother and Sister). Beyond these atrocious and fanciful accusations was the more general, all-embracing one of being 'haters of mankind', an accusation which had in the past also been levelled at the Jews ('adversus omnes alios hostile odium' (Tac. *Histories*, v. 5. 1)). It is interesting to note that, during Nero's reign, this charge is also brought against the Stoics of the ruling classes. Tacitus himself (*Ann.* xvi. 28. 3), referring to the trial of Thrasea Paetus, says that his accusers called him 'bonis publicis maestum'.

As others have already pointed out, the trial of Thrasea Paetus (Tac. *Ann.* xvi. 21 ff.) has a lot in common with the trials of the Christians and indeed in the picture painted by Tacitus (curiously similar to the ones given later in the Acts of the Martyrs), the only difference is that he is not accused of practising the Christian religion.[19] Apart from that, all the ingredients are there: the refusal to practise the state religion, retirement from political life ('inertia'), disloyalty to the 'coerimoniae maiorum'; and the 'tristitia and 'maestitia' with which the Christian Pomponia Graecina had been reproached. Moral austerity and abstention from the dissolute living of Nero's court had contributed to making Thrasea and the Stoics of his group both suspect and unpopular ('rigidi et tristes quo . . . lasciviam exprobent (Tac. *Ann.* xvi. 22. 2)). During the same period, according to I Peter (4:4), the pagans thought it strange that the Christians no longer participated in 'lawless disorders' and 'slandered' them for not doing so. When we compare a graffito written in Pompeii before the earthquake of 62 AD, with the satire written by Persius (a Stoic and relative of Thrasea's) before that year, we find further confirmation of the similarity between the accusations brought against the Christians and the Stoics, and of the general cultural climate in which the first persecutions were beginning to mature. In the graffito, the Christians are described as 'saevi solones'; in the satire, Persius writes of 'aerumnosi solones', the epithet given the Stoics by the ignorant masses, who found the morality and religious austerity of Stoicism very hard to tolerate.[20] In Persius' satire, it is the Stoics (and the philosphers in general, the 'dark-faced know-alls') who are the butt of the ignorant populace; in the graffiti at Pompeii, as in I Peter, the objects of ridicule are the Christians — often confused with philosophers in general and in particular with those philosophers who disapproved of the 'lawless disorders'. Stoics and Christians were equally unpopular. They were also equally opposed to the autocratic and theocratic direction in which Nero was moving in 62 AD.[21] By striking a blow at them,

Nero simultaneously eliminated the elements who were most opposed to his new policies and at the same time humoured the masses with a fine demagogical gesture. The Stoics of the ruling classes (senators and knights) were accused of political crimes and their trials followed the form for crimes of *lèse-majesté*; the Christians were for the most part simple people, often with neither Roman citizenship nor even freedom on their side, and they were, as we have seen, accused of the religious crime of *superstitio illicita*.

In Rome, the first illustrious victim of Nero's new policy was St Paul himself, already well known in imperial circles through his first trial and now arrested for a second time. This is, I believe, the situation as it appears in Paul's second letter to Timothy, which probably pre-dates the I Peter by a few months (it was probably written in the late summer or autumn — anyway before the winter — of what might be the year 63).[22] In this letter the Apostle is certainly in chains and awaiting a trial which he forsees will end with the death penalty. In the meantime, however, he is enjoying the sort of treatment, and a degree of liberty, which would be completely impossible if the situation was as Tacitus describes it for the year 64. St Paul had Luke with him and wants Mark to come and join them because he is 'useful in the ministry'. He asks for books and a cloak. When, in 64 AD, the heavy charge of arson was brought against them, the Christians were arrested *en masse*, given a summary trial and executed immediately. From the second letter to Timothy, it not only seems quite clear that arson was not among the charges brought against Paul, but also that Paul's trial took place before any such accusations were brought against the Christians at all. On the eve of his second appearance before the imperial tribunal, Paul is only thinking of his previous experience and of the fact that the Christians of Rome had abandoned him on that occasion (2 Timothy 4: 10; 14: 16). The fact that he makes no reference to the far more dramatic outcome of the trials of the summer of 64, when a 'multitudo ingens' of Christians met their death for Christ, must surely mean that, when Paul was writing his second letter to Timothy, the massacre of 64 had not yet taken place.

Paul was tried and convicted before the great fire took place, and he was convicted on the grounds of the measures referred to by Suetonius. Later, in the chaos of the summary trials which followed the fire, St Peter was arrested and convicted along with 'many other' Roman Christians (and here the 'poly plethos' of Clement in his first letter to the Corinthians agrees with the 'multitudo ingens' of Tacitus).[23]

Whatever the actual extent of the massacre of the Christians of Rome, the fact remains that it was an isolated incident. Far more serious was the fact that the decision had been taken to allow the Christians to be accused of *superstitio illicita*, so that from now onwards they could be incriminated for their religious persuasion alone. Again far more serious was the fact that the state authorities had allowed and even encouraged the spreading of slanderous rumour against the Christians and had chosen to punish them in ways specifically designed to humiliate them in the eyes of the public. The *de facto* precedent for persecution had been established, and not even the abolition of Nero's acts would change the legal position of the Christians. Christianity was a 'religio illicita' and only an explicit act of official recognition would have been able to save its members from all the accusations to which they could be subjected.

Notes

1. On the subject of the difference between Zealots and Sicarii and the rise of the two movements, see G. Iossa, *Giudei, Pagani e Cristiani* (Naples, 1977), pp. 11–80.

2. Eusebius, *Hist. eccl.* ii. 14. 6; cf. *Chronicon Hieronymis* (Helm) p. 179. M. Simon (in his 'Remarques sur les origines de la Chretienté Romaine', *Religion et culture dans la cité italienne* (Strasbourg, 1981), p. 47) believes this information to be purely legendary.

3. The date of Paul's arrest depends on the interpretation given to the two-year period of Acts 24: 27. Some believe this refers to the time spent by Paul in prison; others, rightly in my opinion, take it as referring to the duration of Antonius Felix's governorship in Judaea. Felix arrived in Judaea from Samaria in 52 AD (Flav. Jos. *Jew. Ant.* xx. 137). At the end of his term of office (ibid. 182) he was accused by the Jews and only escaped punishment through the intervention of his brother Pallas. As Pallas himself fell from grace at the beginning of 55 (Tac. *Ann.* xiii. 14. 2), Felix must have ended his rule in Judaea some time around the end of 54 AD. It must have been at this period, or at the beginning of 55, that Porcius Festus succeeded him. On this question, see M. Sordi in *Studi Romani*, 8 (1960), pp. 401 ff.

4. On the subject of the *collegium* (probably a domestic chapel) 'quod est in domo Sergiae L. filiae Paulinae', see below, p. 185 f.

5. Cf. Simon, 'Remarques', pp. 42 ff. In opposition to Simon, see M. Sordi, *Il cristianesimo e Roma* (Bologna, 1965), pp. 63 ff. O. Montevecchi has recently made some important observations on the subject of the use of the *cognomen* 'Chrestu'(more than 100 in *CIL* vi alone): O. Montevecchi, 'Nomen Christianum' in *Paradoxos Politeia, Studi patristici in onore di G. Lazzati* (Milan, 1979), pp. 491 ff.

6. On the widespread use of 'Chrestianus' for 'Christianus' in papyri and epigraphs, see Montevecchi, 'Nomen', pp. 483 ff.

7. The same year 41 saw Claudius' letter to the Alexandrians, in which he makes clear his worry about the Jewish problem in that city, too. This cannot be explained by the presence of the Christians: cf. Sordi, *Il cristianesimo*, pp. 61 ff. Simon 'Remarques' p. 43) admits a connection between the measures mentioned by Dio and the letter to the Alexandrians, but he still maintains that it is 'certain' ('assuré') that the expulsion of 49 was due to Christian preaching. It is far from clear to me on what foundations he has based his 'certainty' on this point.

8. The year 58 according to the chronology suggested by me (see above, n. 3); the year 62 according to traditional chronology. Having appealed to Caesar, Paul was judged, if not by Nero himself, then by his praetorian prefect Afranius Burrus, or by the urban prefect (a post filled some years later — 64 AD — by Flavius Sabinus).

9. It is worth noting that Pomponia Graecina's changed way of life (and presumably, her conversion) first began in 42 AD when Messalina caused the death of Julia, daughter of Drusus and grand-daughter of Tiberius (*Ann.* XIII. 32. 4). According to tradition, this was the year in which St Peter arrived in Rome. On the subject of Pomponia's faith, see G. Scarpat, *Il pensiero religioso di seneca e l'ambiente ebraica e cristiana* (Brescia, 1977), pp. 130 ff. However, unlike Scarpat, I myself do not believe that Pomponia was acquitted because she abjured her faith. Tacitus simply says that her husband found her innocent and that she continued to live with the same austerity she had adopted after Julia's death, for the rest of her life.

10. H. Lietzmann (*Geschichte der alten Kierche*, I (Berlin–Leipzig, 1932), p. 134) believes in the presence of a pagan majority in the community of Rome. O. Cullman (*The New Testament: an Introduction for the General Reader*, trans. D. Pardee (London, 1968)) believes there was a majority of Jews. On the same questions see also Simon, 'Remarques', pp. 40 ff. On the question of the Epistle to the Romans, see A. Feuillet, 'Saint Paul et L'eglise de Rome' in *Petrus et Paulus martyres* (Milan, 1969), pp. 102 ff. On the questions raised by Chapter 16 of the Epistle, which some see as a note destined for one of the Asian churches, see Simon, 'Remarques', p. 50 n. 10; Feuillet, 'Saint Paul', p. 104.

11. Simon's doubts on the historicity of Paul's meeting with the Jews of Rome ('Remarques', pp. 44 ff.) can be dismissed with the interpretation of Suetonius' 'impulsore Chresto' (*Claudius*, 25. 4) which gave rise to them. Simon ('Remarques', pp. 45–6) uses the late references of the Ambrosiaster to support the theory that the earliest church in Rome was tendentially Hebrewistic, later brought back to a more orthodox position. On this subject, see Feuillet, 'Saint Paul' p. 98.

12. On the Acts of St Peter, see M. Vouaux, *Les actes de Pierre* (Paris, 1922).

13. Marcellus was the name of L. Vitellius' friend, sent by him to Jerusalem in 36 AD. On the excavations under the church of Santa Pudenziana, see M. Cagiano de Azevedo, 'Le memorie archeologiche di Pietro e Paolo' in *Petrus et Paulus Martyres*, pp. 35–6.

14. See below, pp. 185 ff.

15. On the question of contact between St Paul and Seneca, see below.

16. That St Peter went to Rome and died there is no longer seriously doubted by anyone. Tradition has it that he was in Rome in the year 42 (before his visit to Antioch: Galatians 2: 11 ff.) but there is no definite evidence either for or against this hypothesis.

17. On the authenticity of this passage from Tacitus, see H. Fuchs, 'Tacitus über die Christen', *Vigiliae Christianae*, 4 (1950), pp. 65 ff. J.P. Lemonon in *Pilate et le gouvernement de la Judeé* (Paris, 1981), gives a bibliography of publications on this subject (pp. 173 ff.). I find Rougé's hypothesis on the subject ('L'Incendie de Rome etc.' in *Mélanges d'histoire ancienne offertes à W. Seston* (Paris, 1974), pp. 433 ff.) both unacceptable and uselessly complicated. He refers to a suggestion made by C. Saumagne ('Tacite et St Paul', *Rev. Hist.* 232 (1964), pp. 67 ff.) and claims that the passage in question actually fuses a passage from the *Annals* (in which punishment is

mentioned for the incendiaries, but the Christians are not specifically named) with a passage from the *Histories* (in which the Christians are mentioned). This fusion would have been the work of a copyist of the fourth century who saw parallels between the fire of Rome in 64 and that of Nicomedia in 313.

18. The Roman church kept alive the memory of this massacre, as we see in Clement's Epistle to the Corinthians (Chapter 6) with its reports of terrible and dramatic sufferings inflicted on Christian women ('in the guise of Danaids and Dirces'). This reference follows immediately the account of the sufferings of Peter and Paul (Chapter 5).

19. See Saumagne's 'La Passion de Thrasea' in *Revue des Études Latines*', 33 (Paris, 1955), pp. 241 ff. Saumagne comes to the conclusion (erroneously, I believe) that the Christians were condemned like Thrasea and the Stoics, for *lèse-majesté*. But in the case of the Christians, Suetonius, Tacitus and Pliny all talk of 'superstitio'.

20. See M. Sordi, 'Aerumnosi Solones' in *Aquileia Nostra*, 45–6 (1974/1975), pp. 278 ff. Cf. Montevecchi, 'Nomen', p. 494.

21. The concept of *libertas* within the bounds of obedience to the Law, is no different from the ideal of the stoics, or the concept found in I Peter (Chapter 2) and the thirteenth chapter of Paul's Epistle to the Romans.

22. I personally disagree with current opinions on this subject and believe that traditional dating of the I Peter and the 2 Timothy are historically acceptable. That the latter was written first is clear from the fact that, in 2 Tim. 4: 11 Paul is expecting the arrival of Mark, while in I Peter 5: 15 he is already in Rome. For the mention of winter, 2 Tim. 4: 21.

23. M. Guarducci ('La data del martirio di Pietro', *La Parola del Passato*, 118 (1968), pp. 81 ff.) puts the date of Peter's death as 13 October 64 AD. On the question of the choice between September and October, see also Scarpat, 'Il pensiero religioso di Seneca', p. 136.

3   Christianity and the Flavians

The death of Nero, the civil wars of the year of the four emperors and the arrival on the scene of the Flavians put a temporary stop to any kind of anti-Christian action. The new dynasty first made the acquaintance of Christianity in Palestine during the war in Judaea and, until the last years of Domitian's reign, we find no traces of hostility towards the new religion.

The Flavians and Christianity in Judaea

The only reference we have to direct contact between Vespasian and the Christian religion comes to us in the writings of the late Byzantine chronicler Georgius Sincellus (*CSB* i. 646). According to him, having left the siege of Jerusalem in the hands of Titus, Vespasian joined up with Apollonius of Tyana on the latter's return to Egypt from his meeting with the Indians, Brahmins and Gymnosophists. From Apollonius, Vespasian would have heard of the kingdom of Christ.

This piece of news can only be a Christian misreading of Philostratus (*Life of Apollonius of Tyana*, v. 27 ff.), according to whom Vespasian heard of the coming of the kingdom from Apollonius in 69 AD, during the siege of Jerusalem. This unlikely report would actually seem to derive from a much earlier account, in which Vespasian and (as we shall see) one of his sons had been in contact with some Jewish Christians in Palestine, members of the family of Jesus, and had questioned them on the subject of Christ's kingdom.[1]

Our next reference comes from the Palestinian, Hegesippus, of whom we know that he was in Rome at the time of Pope Anicetus, during the last half of the second century (Eusebius, *Hist. eccl.*, IV. 22) and that he studied the apostolic succession in the various churches, including that of Jerusalem. (Eusebius quotes him on the subject of the succession in 62 AD, when Simeon, son of Clopas and brother of Joseph, took over the government of the church from James.) According to Hegesippus, then, after the fall of Jerusalem, Vespasian ordered that all the descendants of the House of David should be searched out so that 'none of the descendants of the tribe of the king should survive among the Jews' (ibid. IV 12).

As Eusebius tells us explicitly (ibid. 17) that 'Vespasian never planned any action against the Christians', this search cannot have had any very severe consequences for them. They must, however, have been involved to some extent, as two Christians, relations of Jesus and 'nephews of Judas and called according to the flesh brothers of the Lord', were arrested during the time of Domitian (according to Hegesippus — see Eusebius (ibid. 19–20)), having been denounced to the authorities by some 'heretics' as being descendants of David. Hegesippus gives us an ample account of the interrogation before 'Caesar Domitian' of these Christians, who, incidentally, appear to have survived until the reign of Trajan (ibid. 20. 6), and we are also given precise details of their poor economic condition. He tells us that the prisoners were questioned on Christ and his kingdom, what it was and when it was going to manifest itself. They were released when they made it clear that the kingdom of Christ was not of this world nor, indeed, was it in any way an earthly kingdom, but rather a heavenly and angelic one, which would only come into being at the end of time.

We can be sure of the authenticity of at least the central nucleus of this story (that is, that the descendants of the house of David were searched out under the Flavians and that some Christians of the family of Jesus were arrested) and it is worth paying it some attention. Not only does it throw an interesting light on the situation in Judaea at the time of the Jewish revolt and the Roman victory of 70 AD; we also hear echoes of it, and the misunderstandings to which it gave rise, in later periods of Christian tradition.

The revolt of 66 AD was, in fact, fuelled by political interpretations of the great Messianic prophecies of Isaiah and Micah, Jeremiah and Ezekiel, according to which the liberator would come out of Zion, would be a descendant of the house of David and would give laws to all the nations.[2] The rumour that the dominator of the world would come from Judaea had actually been circulating in Rome since Nero's time (Suetonius, *Nero*, 40. 2) and the 'mathematici' had warned the Emperor of his coming fall. They had also, however, promised 'the dominion of the East' and some, more explicitly, 'the rule of Jerusalem'. The prophecy became extremely topical at the time of the Jewish revolt and the Roman victory. Tacitus in his *Histories* (v. 13. 2), writing of the resistance of Jerusalem, says that 'most people were convinced that, in accordance with the ancient priestly scriptures, at that time the East

would become strong and men from Judaea would seize power'. He
adds 'these obscure words foretold the coming of Titus and Vespasian'; Suetonius confirms the existence of this rumour and its
interpretation in almost the same words: 'An ancient prophecy had
spread throughout the Western world, according to which at that
time, men from Judaea would have seized power. This had been
foretold of the Roman Emperor . . . but the Jews, interpreting the
prophecy as referring to themselves, rebelled . . .' The Roman
government knew that the great rebellion of 66 AD had been fed by
faith in the Messianic prophecies. Once they had succeeded in
putting down the rebellion, it was logical that they should try to
prevent a recurrence of the situation by arresting and keeping under
control the descendants of the house of David, to whom the
prophecies referred. We know from Hegesippus (see Eusebius,
Hist. eccl. III. 32. 3 ff.) that the search for the descendants of David
was also carried out under Trajan, and lead to the arrest and death
of Simeon of Clopas on the orders of the ex-Consul Atticus. What
strikes us in the account of the interrogation which Hegesippus
records as happening under Domitian is that it was, according to
him, the Emperor himself who questioned the prisoners, and that
he did so in Judaea. In fact, of course, Domitian never went to
Judaea. On this subject, various experts have expressed their views:
S. Giet[3] believes that the second episode is a duplication of the first
one, and should be attributed to Vespasian rather than Domitian;
E. M. Smallwood[4] believes that the first version also contains an
error and that we should read Titus for Vespasian because
Vespasian had, in fact, left Judaea before the fall of Jerusalem.
Titus would have taken this action before his return to Rome in
71 AD.

I, too, believe that a mistake had been made and I, too, have an
explanation to offer. In the first place, the mistake was made by
Hegesippus rather than Eusebius. It is quite certain that Hegesippus
spoke of Domitian and that Eusebius has quoted from him
verbatim. Two factors testify to this: first, the use of the wording
'Domitian Caesar' (Eusebius *Hist. eccl.* III. 20. 1) which is typical of
Hegesippus rather than Eusebius (see ibid. 32. 6 on Trajan); when
Eusebius mentions Vespasian in an indirect quotation in III. 12, he
does not use the word 'Caesar'. Second, Tertullian also used
Hegesippus as his source when he mistakenly attributed the
suspension of persecution to Domitian, in direct contrast to all other
sources.[5]

So Hegesippus was talking about Domitian. His source was the story as it had been handed down orally, probably from acquaintances of the two who had been arrested, who, as we have seen were still alive at the time of Trajan. When these witnesses were recounting the trial which took place under Trajan, they distinguished clearly between the part played in the proceedings by Trajan himself (who was far away at the time) and the part played by the ex-consul Atticus who condemned Simeon to death. When they are recounting the trial under Domitian, they are quite clear that the interrogation took place before the Emperor himself, to whom the prisoners were conducted by an 'evocatus'. The account they give is so detailed (the accusation, the *evocatus*, the economic situation of the accused, their status as manual workers testified to by their work-roughened hands) that we can exclude the hypothesis that the witnesses were mistaken on this point and that they were attributing to the Emperor a trial conducted by a mere governor. For the same reason, we can be quite sure that the prisoners had not been taken to Rome for their interrogation; the atmosphere is entirely Palestinian and nothing in the story suggests that they had been transferred to Rome for questioning. So, as we know that Domitian never went to Judaea, it follows that somewhere along the line a mistake was made, either by the witnesses themselves when telling their story, or by Hegesippus when recording it in his *Hypomnemata*. In my opinion, the mistake lies in the name given the emperor. Rather than Domitian, I believe it was probably Titus, Caesar, like his brother, in 69 AD, or else, perhaps, Vespasian himself. We need not be surprised to find a mistake of this kind. The story was, after all, handed down by word of mouth and recorded many years after the events had occurred, and it would have been natural that an allusion to the trial of some Christians by a Flavian emperor would have brought to mind the persecutions under Domitian. In fact, in Hegesippus' account, the release of the two prisoners (despised by 'Domitian' for being 'simple men') was followed by the issue of an edict putting a stop to the persecution of the Church.

Eusebius does mention 'persecution' and an 'edict'; but he was referring to the Jews. He quotes Hegesippus indirectly, and uses his account of Vespasian's order to 'search out the descendants of David' (*Hist. eccl.* III. 12). In this case 'Vespasian' may indeed mean Vespasian himself, in 69 AD, or alternatively Titus in 71. It therefore seems likely that Hegesippus divided what was actually one episode (the search, either under Vespasian or Titus, for the descendants of the house of David) into two separate ones: Vespasian, well known for his part in the Jewish war, would have been responsible for the persecution which 'menaced' the Jews, while Domitian, equally well known as the persecutor of the Christians in 95/6 AD, would have carried out the 'persecutions against the Church' and the interrogation of the two Christian members of the family of Jesus, who were likewise descendants of the house of David.

Moreau[6] used this same passage from Hegesippus as the foundation for his theory that there was no persecution of the Christians under Domitian. In reality, Hegesippus' information proves the opposite. The fact that he claims that the Christian descendants of David were sought out and interrogated in Palestine by Domitian (who never went there), on the basis of an edict issued by him against the church, can only mean that Hegesippus knew of the existence of an anti-Christian edict decreed by Domitian. Tertullian (*Apol.* v. 4), writing after Hegesippus, knew about Domitian's persecution from other sources (Melito in particular) and recognised it as being second in ferocity only to that of Nero. However, basing his account on Hegesippus, he was forced to attribute to Domitian the edict which suspended the persecution, an edict which all other sources, pagan and Christian alike, agree in attributing to Nerva. 'Domitian', Tertullian writes, 'who was a kind of half-Nero for cruelty, had also tried; but being also only half a man, he easily put a stop to what he had started, after having also called back those he had banished' (*Apol.* v. 4).

I shall come back to the question of Domitian's persecution later. In the meantime, we can safely attribute the search for the descendants of David and the interrogation of Judas' nephews to Vespasian or Titus, and not to Domitian. This brings us to conclude that the first contact the Flavian emperors had with the local Christian community, and with the story of Christ and his kingdom, certainly occurred during the time of the Jewish revolt, just as Sincellus reported. At that time, the Christian community had removed itself from Jerusalem to Pella, in order to avoid being involved in the uprising (Eusebius, *Hist. eccl.* iii. 5. 3) and this fact, together with the direct interrogation of Judas' nephews, must have convinced the Flavians that the Christians were not in any way politically dangerous to the empire.

It is important to bear this first-hand knowledge of the Christians in mind if we want to understand the tolerant (or at least not hostile) attitude the Flavian emperors adopted towards the Christians, including the Roman Christians, up to the last years of Domitian's reign.

J. Speigl[7] underlines the tolerant attitude of the Flavian emperors and claims that it provides an explanation for the words with which St Luke ends the Acts of the Apostles (written during this period, according to Speigl). It would also explain, he says, the lack of hostility with which Flavius Josephus, Hebrew historian and chronicler for the Flavians, refers to the Christians in his *Jewish Antiquities*, as well as the evident approval with which Clement of Rome speaks of the empire in his first letter to the church at Corinth.

Leaving open the question of the date of the Acts (which I personally believe pre-date the Flavians) and that of Clement's epistle (which I believe to have been written during the time of Nerva and Trajan's joint reign)', Flavius Josephus' attitude to the Christians is in any case significant enough. In his account of the violence committed by the Sadducees against the Christians of Jerusalem at the time of the death of James the Less, his tone is one of cautious disapproval, while he definitely approves of the 'moderate' Jews who went to the new governor to protest (*Jew. Ant.* xx. 9. 1 ff.). Evidently, he was here simply reflecting the attitude to the Christian question which he knew to have been adopted by the court.

The Christians under the Flavian Dynasty: the Question of Domitian's Persecution

In my opinion, the personal contact Titus and Vespasian had with the Christians in Judaea was not the only element to influence their attitude to the new religion (which must, after all, have seemed to them to be just another Hebrew sect). We must also bear in mind the direct contact the Flavians had with the Christians in Rome itself, and I am alluding to the presence of Christians among the members of the collateral branch of the family — that of Vespasian's brother Flavius Sabinus. News of them comes to us from pagan sources, Dio and Bruttius, writing on the subject of Domitian's persecution, and must therefore be examined in the context of the persecution itself. In 1960,[8] I attempted to prove that a persecution of the Christians did take place under Domitian and that some members of the Flavian dynasty were, indeed, Christians

(Flavius Clemens and the two Flaviae Domitillae), as were various members of the aristocracy (in particular Acilius Glabrio) who were condemned to death by Domitian in 95 AD.[9]

Since the publication of my studies, the question of Domitian's persecution has been the subject of renewed research on various sides. S. Rossi and J. Speigl continue to doubt that Domitian's persecution ever happened. Rossi[10] discounts the references made by Christian authors and maintains that Dio's account was dictated by his personal hatred for Domitian. Speigl[11] believes Dio combined Suetonius' passage (*Domitian*, 15) on the death of Flavius Clemens 'ex tenuissima suspicione', with a Christian source. W. H. C. Frend, E. M. Smallwood and A. M. Rabello[12] all interpret Dio's passage as evidence that the members of the Flavian family had been converted to the Hebrew faith. P. Keresztes[13] accepts that Christians were persecuted and believes that some members of the imperial family were Christians. He also gives Bruttius' information its due worth and agrees that Domitian's niece, Flavia Domitilla (deported to Pontia) was certainly a Christian. However, he maintains that Flavius Clemens, his wife and the other members of the aristocracy condemned to death were Hebrew converts rather than Christians. P. Pergola[14] has compared literary sources with the findings of excavations (particularly those he has conducted in Roman burial places) and has come to the conclusion that all the Flavian family members mentioned by Dio and Bruttius were Christians. However, bearing in mind what Suetonius had to say on the subject of Flavius Clemens and Acilius Glabrio, he interprets Domitian's persecution in political terms. Lastly, H. Bengston[15] has now accepted both the fact of a persecution under Domitian and that Flavius Clemens and Flavia Domitilla were converts to the Christian rather than the Hebrew faith.

From this brief résumé of the *status questionis*, it becomes clear that the focal point of all recent debate on the subject is the passage from Dio concerning the sentences passed in 95 AD. At this stage, I think we should re-examine the whole question, taking this passage as our point of departure. I must, however, make it clear from the start that I am only discussing the nature of the accusations brought against some members of the Flavian family and the aristocracy (that is, whether the charge was for conversion to Judaism or to Christianity), not the existence or otherwise of an anti-Christian persecution under Domitian. On this last question I have nothing to add to what I wrote on the subject in 1960; and in fact recent studies carried out by Keresztes, Pergola and Bengston have accepted my views on this question. The reality of a persecution was well known to all the Christian commentators, from the Shepherd of Hermas to Melito, from Hegesippus to Tertullian, and is confirmed not only by contemporary Christian sources, from Clement's First Epistle to the Revelation of St John, but also, as we have seen, by the pagan writers Pliny and Bruttius. In order to prove that the persecution never actually happened (and I do not personally believe this is possible), each reference would have to be explained away separately. The sudden calamities which befell the Christian community in Rome (Clement) would have nothing to do with persecution; the references in the Revelation would be either purely eschatological or else a recollection of Nero's persecution; the Shepherd of Hermas' references would also be eschatological; Melito would have accused Domitian of persecution to prove that bad emperors persecute the Christians; Tertullian would have based his account exclusively on Hegesippus' mistaken identification of the emperor who persecuted the Christians. But even if it were feasible to find a convincing explanation for each reference, I still maintain that the mere fact of there being so many individual reports of the persecutions having taken place, makes it unreasonable to harbour any serious doubts on the subject. Let us, therefore, go on to examine Dio's account of the trial of Flavius Clemens and the other 'Jewish sympathisers'.

Chapter 14 of Dio's Book 67 (in which we find the epitome of Xiphilinus and Zonaras included with Chapters 13 and 15) can easily be dated, thanks to the references to the consulate of Clemens, who was killed while still in office (14. 1), and the reference to the consulate of the succeeding year, 96 AD, that of Domitian's death (14. 5). The year in question was thus certainly 95 AD. The historical context of Dio's story is complex: Cecilius Rufinus had been expelled from the senate for dancing; more important, Arulenus Rusticus, Herennius Senecio and other Stoics had been condemned for keeping alive the memory of Thrasea; the philosophers of the opposition were suffering various kinds of repression because of their refusal to worship Domitian or to call him 'dominus et deus' (Chapter 13); and we find the first signs of the conspiracy which, with suspicions growing as to the real facts behind Clemens' death (14. 4), was to culminate in the assassination of Domitian himself (Chapter 15). Incidentally, it is interesting to note on the subject of the assassination plot that in giving the details (the

list of conspirators' names written on lime-tree leaves and delivered
to the Emperor's wife by an innocent child) Dio matches his account
with the stories of the death of Commodus which were circulating in
his times.[16]

The epitome seems to be reasonably faithful and complete and is
not only interested in recounting in detail the murders of important
people: Chapter 14, for example, begins with news of the paving of
the road between Sinuessa and Puteoli. Immediately after this, Dio
continues his chronicle:

> Domitian killed, along with many others, Flavius Clemens while
> he was consul, even though he was his cousin and married to one
> of his relations, Domitilla. Both were accused of atheism, on
> which charge many others who had turned towards Jewish
> customs were also condemned; of these only a few were put to
> death while others were deprived of their worldly goods.
> Domitilla was only banished to Pandataria. He then put to death
> Glabrio who had been consul with Trajan. Against him, other
> charges were brought besides those brought against the many,
> including that of having fought with wild beasts. Domitian,
> spurred on by envy, had conceived for him a profound rage,
> particularly after he had forced him, while he was consul, during
> the Juvenilia at Alba, to kill a great lion, and not only had he
> suffered no harm, but had also handled it with the greatest skill.

The accusations and convictions in Dio's account can be divided
into three groups: (1) the charge of atheism brought against Flavius
Clemens and Domitilla, and the respective sentences of death for
one and banishment for the other; (2) the accusation of atheism
brought against the 'many others who deviated towards Jewish
customs' with the respective sentences of death for some and confiscation of property for others; (3) the same charge as 'those brought
against the many' — that is atheism once again — of which Glabrio
is accused (along with that of having fought with wild beasts, an
episode which went back to the year 91), and for which he lost his
life.

The one accusation common to all three groups is that of atheism
(*impietas*), that is, of having refused to worship the gods of Rome
and, in particular, of course, Domitian himself. To be precise, this
second refusal (particularly serious in the case of an Emperor who
demanded to be called 'dominus et deus' (Dio, 67. 13. 4 and Suet.

Dom. 13. 2)) implied the accusation of *maiestas*, that is of *asebeia*,[17] and it is interesting to note on this point that Dio himself, in the epitome of Xiphilinus (68. 1. 2), telling of Nerva's decision to free those imprisoned under charges of *asebeia* and to repatriate the exiles, also reminds his readers that Nerva forbade the bringing of charges for *asebeia* and 'Jewish customs'.

It was this refusal to worship the gods of Rome and the Emperor himself which brought about the death of Flavius Clemens, Acilius Glabrio and 'many others', the deportation of Domitilla and the confiscation of property of others again. The question of 'deviation towards Jewish customs' was raised explicitly only for the second group, although it was implicitly directed at all of them as *a circumstance of common guilt* in the same way that the practice of Stoicism appears in the preceding chapter (Dio, 67. 13. 3) as the common factor in the death sentences passed on Herennius Senecio, Arulenus Rusticus and 'many others' and the exile of 'all the rest'. In fact, refusing the *adoratio*, these last were actually suspected of plotting against the Emperor, as becomes clear from what subsequently happened in the case of Juventius Celsus. Those who 'deviated towards Jewish customs' and were condemned in 95 AD were therefore condemned for atheism (*impietas*) and asebeia (*maiestas*) exactly as the Stoics in 93/4 AD had been condemned for impiety (*maiestas*); the charge was the same whether the fault was 'Jewish practices' or Stoicism. In fact, of course, from a legal point of view we know that the profession of Stoicism (the most widespread and 'traditional' of the philosophies of the Roman state) was not, and never would be, punishable by death. In the same way, those who adopted foreign customs, or at least customs which were alien to Roman tradition, could not be punished by death, although they could be punished in a variety of other ways: those who 'improfessi Iudaicam viverent vitam' had been subject to a fine since some years previously (Suet. *Dom.* 12. 2), senators could be expelled from the senate (as Dio tells us happened to Caecilius Rufinus for dancing and, perhaps, to Acilius Glabrio for fighting wild beasts), and in other cases economic sanctions could be applied and notes of infamy served (Suet. *Dom.* 7. 3). But the adoption of foreign ways did not, in itself, carry the death penalty.

There was in particular no question of condemning to death those who 'adopted the customs' of a religion like Judaism which was officially recognised by the Roman state, even if since the year 70 its followers had had to pay a tax — the so-called *fiscus Iudaicus* —

which, incidentally, Domitian had decided to increase.[18] From the time of Vespasian, the right to profess the Hebrew faith cost one didrachm, a sum which also bought exemption from official religious observances, including the worship of the emperor. The position of the aristocrats accused of conversion to the Hebrew faith would, therefore, have been perfectly regular if they had openly admitted their faith and paid their didrachm to the authorities. At that point, any charge of atheism or impiety would automatically have been dropped. Their behaviour would probably have been considered scandalous, at least as far as the men were concerned (it was considered quite normal for women, even women of the aristocracy), but their punishment would not have gone beyond moral sanctions and harassment of various kinds. They would certainly not have been condemned to death. However, we know that some time round the years 90 to 92 AD[19] (the period in which Domitian increased the Jewish tax), there had been an increase in the number of accusations brought before the tax officials of people who, *without declaring themselves to be Jews* (*improfessi*), were living a Jewish life, and of others again who 'dissimulata origine', were avoiding the tax (Suet. *Dom*. 12. 2). Suetonius' 'qui improfessi Iudaicam viverent vitam' and Dio's 'those who deviate towards Jewish customs' would seem to have a good deal in common and, in fact, we know that an intervention of Nerva's did much to improve the lot of both categories. He supressed the Jewish tax (not to be confused with the *fiscus Iudaicus* which still had to be paid regularly), celebrating the event by minting a coin inscribed 'fisci Iudaici calumnia sublata', and he also made it illegal to bring charges of asebeia and 'Jewish living' (Dio, 68. 1. 2).

Who were these *improfessi*? Smallwood (pp. 378 ff.) calls them a 'nebulous' category which could include converts to either Christianity or Judaism. It seems to me, however, that doubts about their identity only make sense if nothing more than the payment of a tax was involved. When, on the contrary, not to admit to professing the Hebrew faith meant exposing oneself to accusations of atheism and therefore the death penalty, when, that is, the question became penal rather than merely fiscal, it is difficult to imagine what would have prevented converts to Judaism from openly declaring their faith and thereby avoiding all the severer punishments, including the death penalty itself.

The victims of 95 AD did not do this, however. Despite having, apparently, adopted Jewish customs, these aristocrats did not claim the protection allowed to followers of a *religio licita*, and were executed for refusing to worship the gods of the empire and the emperor himself. The only logical explanation for this refusal (and incidentally Dio makes a clear distinction between the refusal of the Stoics and that of the Jewish converts) is that they were in fact converts to Christianity rather than to the Hebrew religion. As we know, it was normal for the Christian religion, known to be an off-shoot of Judaism, to be accused of atheism both in the minds of the general public and before the tribunals, and this situation continued throughout the second century and was certainly true at the time when Dio was writing. Independently from the account of Dio, we have an unequivocal report of the conviction for Christianity of another Flavia Domitilla (niece rather than wife of Flavius Clemens), which comes to us from the pagan chronicler Bruttius (writing before Eusebius, who refers to him anonymously in his *Hist. eccl.* III. 18) The passage which interests us (Peter, fragment 3 also familiar to Jerome and Sincellus) has been preserved by Malalas, together with two other fragments, one mythological and one on Alexander the Great. According to Bruttius, then, in the fifteenth year of Domitian's reign (95 AD) the Emperor 'condemned with many others' Flavia Domitilla, daughter of a sister of the consul Flavius Clemens, and banished her to the island of Pontia for having born witness for Christ. The same story is told by Jerome, by Malalas (x, p. 262 D) and by Sincellus (I, p. 650 D), who also speaks of Clemens's death 'for Christ'.

I have attempted to prove elsewhere[20] — and the most recent studies agree with me on this point[21] — that there is no connection between Bruttius and Dio and that the Flavia Domitilla of Bruttius' account, exiled to Pontia, is not the same Flavia Domitilla that Dio records as having been exiled to Pandataria. However, the two stories complement each other; for example, both talk of the 'many others' condemned together with the person or persons in whom the author is directly interested. What makes Bruttius particularly interesting and, indeed, made Eusebius and other Christian writers prefer him to Dio as a source, is that in his fragments we find the specific use of the term 'Christian' in place of the cautious circum-locution preferred by Dio.[22]

However, this does not mean, as Keresztes would have us believe,[23] that Bruttius' Flavia Domitilla was the only true Christian while the others were converts to the Hebrew faith. Both Bruttius and Dio record that she was convicted with 'many others' and among these we are bound to include Dio's Flavius Clemens and his wife (and, as Pergola reminds us, the study of ancient Christian cemeteries confirms this[24]) as well as Acilius Glabrio, who was condemned, as Dio says, 'for the same reasons'.

In fact, Acilius Glabrio can be seen as the link between the Stoics and the Christians. Dio tells us, as we have seen, that he was condemned for other crimes *as well as* 'those of the many'; Suetonius (*Dom.* 10. 2) tells us that he was executed together with other ex-consuls (Civica Cerealis and Salvidienus Orfitus) while already in exile and that all of them were condemned 'quasi molitores rerum novarum'. Far from contradicting Dio's account, Suetonius actually confirms it in two important points; we find the 'other crimes' — political in nature — which, together with the charge of atheism, were the reason for his being executed, and we also find confirmation of Glabrio's having been sent into exile some time before he was sentenced to death, probably as a result of the Alba incident recounted by Dio.[25] So, some time after 91 AD Glabrio was sent into exile as 'molitor rerum novarum', as a member of the political opposition, and not as a Christian. (The year of his exile may well have been 94, when Caecilius Rufinus was expelled from the senate for 'moral' reasons.) In 95 he was put to death as a Christian, together with Flavius Clemens and other members of the Christian aristocracy. What strikes us in this account is that Glabrio was condemned to death in 95 when he had already been in exile for at least a year. This leads me to believe that Domitian already knew him to be a Christian in 94 AD but that he had not yet decided to punish Christianity with death. Thus, the factor which changed exile into execution would seem to be not so much the discovery of Glabrio's religious tendencies as the Emperor's sudden decision to eliminate Christian converts from the ranks of the aristocracy. In other words, although tension had already existed for some time between the imperial government and the Christians in all walks of life (the increase in the Jewish tax at the expense of the *improfessi* had seen to that), it appears that it was only in the year 95 that Domitian took the decision officially to accuse the Christians as atheists and Christianity as atheism.[26]

According to Suetonius (*Dom.* 15. 1), Flavius Clemens was condemned in 95 AD 'repente ex tenuissima suspicione' and, in fact, the sentence was passed in the same year in which Domitian himself had honoured his cousin both by awarding him the honorary consulship and by nominating Flavius' sons as his heirs. The choice of the word 'repente' is thus far from fortuitous; it evidently refers to a very precise situation and it is interesting to note that, in his letter to the Corinthians, Clement of Rome uses the 'unexpected and sudden' nature of the 'disasters' which struck the Roman community as his excuse for not having intervened (I *Clementis* I. 1).

That the Christian Flavius Clemens should have been convicted 'suddenly and unexpectedly' at the same period in which the Christians in Rome were suffering 'sudden and unexpected troubles and misfortunes' seems to be extremely significant. I personally believe that Domitian's sudden break with his cousin sparked off his decision to incriminate all Christians for whom, up to that moment, the protection of an influential member of the imperial family had provided a certain measure of security. Suetonius, Dio Cassius and even Juvenal (if only indirectly and by implication) all agree that the death of Flavius Clemens marked the beginning of the dramatic crescendo of accusations and convictions which eventually brought about the fall of Domitian and his tyrannical reign. 'Quo maxime facto' says Suetonius (15. 1) immediately after his account of Clemens's death, 'maturavit sibi exitium. Continuis octo mensibus tot fulgura facta nuntiataque sunt ut exclamaverit: "Feriat iam quem volet . . . " ', and Dio recalls (67. 14. 4) that, after the conviction of Clemens and the others, Domitian 'suspected everyone'. Juvenal does not name Flavius Clemens, but laments the death of Acilius Glabrio and finishes his fourth satire by saying that, after having killed 'impune et vindice nullo claras inlustresque animas', Domitian himself was killed 'postquam cerdonibus esse timendus coeperat' (IV. 151 ff.). We know that Stephanus, procurator for Domitilla, together with Sigerius and Parthenius (Dio, 67. 15), was involved in the plot which succeeded in putting an end to Domitian's life in September 96 (Suet. *Dom.* 17. 1), and Philostratus adds that Stephanus' motive was to revenge Flavius Clemens' death (*Life of Apollonius of Tyana*, VIII. 25. 1). We have no reason to believe that Stephanus was a Christian, and there is no evidence to show that the Christians were implicated in the plot in any way. Indeed, Tertullian (*Apol.* XXXV. 44–5) mentions Sigerius and Parthenius when reminding his readers that the Christians had never plotted against an emperor and that all conspiracies, past and present, had been the work of pagans. This passage acquires an added interest when we remember how topical the subject of the assassination plot was at the time of Commodus. Under these circumstances, it is extremely unlikely that Tertullian would have used such a dangerous example, if the Christians had indeed played some part in Domitian's death.

Excluding, then, the possibility of an abortive Christian plot to seize power, centred round the figure of Flavius Clemens (Suetonius, in any case, speaks of 'ex tenuissima suspicione'), the question remains as to what kind of suspicions could have induced Domitian first to order the execution of the cousin whom he had until a few months previously trusted implicitly, and then to round up all his fellow Christians as well.

When we compare Dio Cassius' account with that of Suetonius, it becomes clear that the answer to this question is to be found in Domitian's religious attitude. Clemens and the other Christians, those belonging to the ruling classes as well as the nameless 'many others' without any social standing, were being accused of atheism, that is, of refusing to worship the gods of the empire. We can exclude the possibility that Domitian only discovered his cousin's sympathy with the Christian religion for the first time in 95 AD; it is far more probable that he had simply not realised until then that his cousin's faith obliged him to refuse to take part in the religious functions of the state. The problem could have come to a head during Clemens' term as consul in 95 when, according to Suetonius, he behaved with 'contemptissima inertia', showing, that is, a distinct tendency to retire from public life. In fact, it was precisely by abstaining from public functions that he had been able up to that moment to hide from the Emperor the extent to which his new faith was radically incompatible with the religious traditions of which Domitian himself was such a conscientious guardian.[27] If this hypothesis is correct, the connection between the sudden and unexpected arrest of Flavius Clemens and the sudden and unexpected persecution of the Christians becomes evident. The collection of the Jewish tax had, during the previous years, made it possible for the authorities to differentiate between the *improfessi* and the official members of the Hebrew community, who were protected by belonging to a *religio licita*. Once the *improfessi* had become identifiable, they could be accused of atheism.

To sum up the analysis we have undertaken in this chapter, we can say that the persecution carried out under Domitian had a far-reaching influence on the future development of the relationship between the Christian religion and the Roman empire, for three reasons:

1. The persecution helped to identify the Christians once and for

all. Up to that moment, except when an emperor had specifically decided to penalise them (as happened under Nero), the Christians had been protected by the legitimacy of the Jewish religion, even if only as *improfessi*. From then onwards, the refusal to worship the gods of the empire was no longer accepted as the exemption from state religion allowed to a *religio licita*. Lacking a precise colloca-tion, Christianity now came to be considered not only a *superstitio illicita* but also a form of atheism, of impiety. Under Domitian, Christianity is defined as an individual religious transgression, and from now onwards it takes on the legal shape by which it will be recognised both in the public mind and in the tribunals throughout the second century, up to the time of the edicts of Valerian.

2. Domitian's persecution affected not only Rome, but the whole Roman empire, as Epictetus' mention of Epirus and Pliny's of Bithynia reveal. However, the group to be hardest hit was undoub-tedly the Roman aristocracy. And it is here, in the behaviour of Flavius Clemens, that we see for the first time the *inertia*, the abstention from political activity ('contemptissima', Suetonius) which doubtless arose from motives of prudence but which caused a sense of outrage among the ruling class which had always consi-dered participation in public functions as one of its principal duties. Already under Domitian, then, we begin to see the first stirrings of what was to become, under Marcus Aurelius, one of the main bones of contention between the Christians and the Roman government.

3. Domitian's persecution also provides us with the names of some of the important families of Rome (the Flavians themselves and the Acilii Glabriones) who, together with those already known at the time of Claudius (the Sergii Pauli and the Pomponii Graecini), kept up secret relations with the church throughout the second century. It may well be that we owe to them the more or less explicitly pro-Christian attitude adopted by some emperors in periods when the senate and public opinion were increasingly hostile to the Christians. Indeed, from St Ignatius' letter to the Romans, it seems clear that the church of Rome was on occasion able to bring certain pressure to bear on the imperial court.

Notes

1. On Philostratus' story, see P. Desideri, *Dione di Prusa* (Florence, 1978), pp. 22 ff. p. 50 n. 31.
2. On the subject of the Messianic aspect of the revolt, to be attributed more to the

Sicarii than the Zealots, see G. Iossa. *Giudei, Pagani e Cristiani* (Naples, 1977), pp. 64 ff.

3. S. Giet, *L'apocalypse et l'histoire* (Paris, 1957), p. 93.

4. E. M. Smallwood, *The Jews under Roman Rule* (Leiden, 1976), pp. 351 ff.

5. J. Moreau is right in saying ('La Persecution du Christianisme dans l'Empire Romain' in *Coll. Mythes et Religions*, 32 (Paris, 1956)) that it was from Hegesippus that Tertullian took his information on Domitian's revocation of the persecution (see below).

6. Moreau, 'La persecution', pp. 37 ff.

7. J. Speigl, *Der römische Staat und die Chriesten* (Amsterdam, 1970), pp. 5 ff.

8. M. Sordi, 'La persecuzione di Domiziano', *Rivista di Storia della Chiesa in Italia*, 14 (1960), pp. 1 ff.

9. See M. Sordi, 'I Flavi e il cristianesimo' in *Atti del Congresso Internazionale di Studi Vespasiani* (Rieti, 1981), pp. 137 ff.

10. S. Rossi, 'La cosiddetta persecuzione di Domiziano', *Giornale Italiano di Filologia*, 15 (1962), pp. 303 ff.

11. Speigl, *Der römische*, pp. 20 ff.

12. W. H. C. Frend, *Martyrdom and Persecution in the Early Church: A Study of a Conflict from the Maccabees to Donatus* (Oxford, 1965), pp. 113 and 214–17; Smallwood, *The Jews*, pp. 376 ff.; A. M. Rabello, 'The Legal Condition of the Jews in the Roman Empire', *Aufstieg und Niedergang der römischen Welt* (*ANRW*) II, 30 (1980), p. 697.

13. P. Keresztes, 'The Jews, the Christians and the Emperor Domitian', *Vigiliae Christianae*, 27 (1973), pp. 1 ff., and in *ANRW* 23 (1979), p. 257 ff.

14. P. Pergola 'La condamnation des Flavies "chrétiens" sous Domitien', *Mélanges de l'École Française de Rome*, 90 (1978), pp. 497 ff.

15. H. Bengston, *Die Flavier* (Munich, 1979), pp. 235 ff.

16. It is pertinent to compare Dio (67. 15. 3) and Herodian (I. 17) on this point. On this question see F. Grosso, *La lotta politica al tempo di Commodo* (Turin, 1964), pp. 400–2.

17. Smallwood, *The Jews*, p. 379.

18. On this problem, see Smallwood, *The Jews*, pp. 345 ff. (and p. 371).

19. The date 90–2 has been worked out from references made by Martial — see Smallwood, *The Jews*, p. 377. 92 AD is also the year in which, Pliny tells us (*Ep.* x. 96. 6), some of the Christians of Bithynia abandoned their faith.

20. Sordi, 'La persecuzione di Domiziano', pp. 6 ff.

21. Keresztes, 'The Jews, the Christians', pp. 18 ff; Pergola, 'La condamnation', pp. 418 ff.

22. As I have already said elsewhere, I believe Dio's caution can be explained by the fact that the persons concerned were of senatorial rank.

23. Keresztes, 'The Jews, the Christians', pp. 26 ff.

24. Pergola, 'La condamnation', pp. 412 ff.

25. On this episode, see also Juvenal (*Sat.* IV. 95 ff.) and Fronto (*Letters to Marcus Aurelius Caesar* V. 23).

26. That Domitian was openly tolerant of the Christians in his own *domus* is confirmed by a recent interpretation of Pliny, *Panieggricus* 49. 8 (see A. Barzanò, 'Plinio il Giovane e i cristiani alla corte di Domiziano', *Rivista di Storia della Chiesa in Italia*, 36 (1982), pp. 408 ff.).

27. Suet. *Dom.* 8. 3 (on the restoration of the ancient penalty for incest among the Vestals) and 8. 5 ('ne qua religio deum impune contaminaretur').

4 Trajan's Rescript and the Volte-face of the Antonine Emperors

The arrival on the scene of Nerva and Trajan marks the beginning of the auspicious period known as the Antonine Empire.[1] Thanks to Trajan's conquests, it was a period of prosperity and, fundamentally, of peace, especially during the middle years under Hadrian and Antoninus Pius. Urban life was in full expansion and its vitality was an essential element of the life of the whole empire, which many saw as a confederation of free cities. Imperial ideology found its voice in the writings of the Greek rhetoricians and panegyrists from Dio Chrysostom to Aelius Aristides, and in the Latin, Pliny. All these extolled the enlightened and liberal character of the monarchy and the civil character of the Principate, which found its highest expression in the method of choosing the monarch's successors: not by dynastic succession, nor by violent military deliberation, but according to merit, with the emperor adopting the chosen candidate with the consent and approval of the senate.

The Stoic philosophy which since earliest times had inspired, almost *naturaliter*, the Roman soul and the mentality of the senate, had been persecuted by Nero and the Flavians (above all, Domitian) because of its opposition not only to the cult of the living emperor, but also to all forms of autocracy. Now, Stoicism and the ideals of the state were fused into one, ascending the throne in the person of Marcus Aurelius. Never before had philosophy and reason been given so much honour as when, during the reigns of the enlightened Antonines, the emperor himself was pleased to accept the title of Philosopher. And yet at the same time, never before had an age seen such a powerful resurgence of the irrational, such a spreading of oriental cults and magical practices, such a chasing after miracles and prodigious happenings, or such religious fanaticism among the masses. The writings of the intellectuals are pervaded by a religious piety still rooted in the ancient Greek and Roman traditions, but they are now also imbued with a new enthusiasm for Egyptian mysteries and Chaldean oracles. This intellectual climate did much to reinforce the conviction that the stability of the Empire was founded on the *pax deorum*, a conviction which had become somewhat obscured by the rationalism and scepticism which had dominated the last years of the Republic and the first century of the Empire.

The worship of the emperor is now officially discouraged, but the sacred nature of the Empire itself is taken for granted by everyone and the ruling classes are prepared to take part in various religious exercises which would have been considered incompatible with the Stoicism of the first century. A significant symptom of this change of outlook can be seen in the different attitudes shown by Curtius Rufus and Arrian in their respective accounts of Alexander the Great (the *imitatio* of whom had, incidentally, never been more ideologically central to Roman theories of power than during this period). Curtius Rufus, writing in the first century (under the Julio-Claudians according to some and the Flavians according to others), utterly condemns the Macedonian's claim to divine honours, seeing it as a sign of oriental corruption and tyrannical and sacrilegious pride. Arrian, on the other hand writing under the Antonines, finds no difficulty in justifying Alexander's claim, considering the honour he asked for as being no more than a sign of the sacred nature of power and its exercise. The Antonine emperors themselves do not ask to be worshipped, indeed, they discourage it, but the masses and even the intellectuals compete with each other in bestowing divine honours on the emperor and his family. The title 'dominus', which had so shocked the Romans when Domitian first assumed it, is now common currency, even when officially rejected. A silent revolution is taking place within the empire and the concept of *dominatio* is quietly growing up from the original concept of the *princeps*. This is fundamentally a cultural transformation, and even the emperors themselves are influenced by it. In the meantime, behind the façade of prosperity and security we begin to see the stirrings of the crisis which was to afflict the third century and which first came to the surface as early as the reign of Marcus Aurelius. City life, apparently so prosperous, begins to show the first signs of financial trouble and has to be helped out by the central government; the barbarians are on the move, frontiers are being breached and, for the first time since the days of Marius, bands of invaders penetrate Italy itself, reaching as far south as Aquileia; earthquakes, famine and pestilence devastate Asia and cause a kind of religious panic among the pagans who desperately search for a scapegoat; civil rule begins to reveal its military basis, including for the first time the title of proconsul among the official titles of the emperors, a title which from the time of Augustus had given the emperor, with *imperium maius et infinitum*, the command of all the armies; the practice of the adoption of heirs to the imperial throne reveals itself to be a transitory measure, destined to be put on one side by the first emperor to produce male children of his own.

By the time Marcus Aurelius comes to the throne, the transformation is complete and rule by a civilian *Princeps* has given way to rule by military dynasty, with stability guaranteed more by the approval of the troops than by that of the senate. Under Marcus Aurelius the empire is forced into military expansion once more and the emperor's wife for the first time officially takes the title 'Mater Castrorum'.

In this new cultural and religious climate the hostility which the pagans of the first century felt towards the Christians now begins to flourish once again. The Christians are seen as the culprits who are bringing divine retribution down on the empire with their rejection of traditional forms of religion and their atheism. The *pax deorum* has been undermined and the pagan masses demand some decisive action on the part of the state in order to restore it. Even the cultural leaders of the time reflect the general atmosphere of hostility towards the Christians: Tacitus, Pliny and Suetonius condemn the new religion as 'superstitio prava' and 'immodica', 'nova' and 'malefica', Marcus Cornelius Fronto brings out once more the old slanders on the subject of the *flagitia* and Aelius Aristides curses the impiety of the new 'atheists'. Only sceptics and rationalists, like Lucian and Galen, regard the Christians with mocking detachment or at most with a kind of tolerant respect and are prepared to ridicule their fideistic outlook, though not apparently feeling any preconceived antipathy towards them. Under the Antonine emperors, the state itself seems to have steered a middle course between the benevolent sympathy of some of the first-century emperors and the open persecution of others. With Trajan's rescript, the relationship between Christianity and the state is regulated in wording which, though ambiguous, does at least give some stability to the situation and which was destined to remain law until the time of Valerian. In fact, the state is anxious not to upset public opinion by vetoing the right to take the Christians to trial, but at the same time the imperial rulers are convinced that Christianity does not pose any kind of political threat and they have no intention

of allowing indiscriminate application of anti-Christian legislation
to go unchecked. They therefore decide to define Christianity as a
strictly personal and individual religious transgression and they
forbid official investigation of, or searches to be made for, its
adherents. Interpretations of Trajan's regulation were to oscillate
between the widest and most favourable (that of Hadrian) and the
narrowest and most rigorous (that of Antoninus Pius), until Marcus
Aurelius, after an initial stiffening of the persecution, went on to
make a compromise which eventually evolved into the atmosphere
of tolerance so characteristic of the Severan era.

During the course of the second century, the conflict between
Christianity and the mentality and culture of the times became
steadily more evident, manifesting itself in the ideological battles
between the Christian apologists (from Justin to Melito,
Athenagoras to Tertullian) and the first pagan polemicists (from
Fronto to Celsus). Despite the growing debate, the ruling powers
kept on neutral ground during this period, refusing to commit
themselves to finding a political solution to the controversy and
firmly adhering to their decision to take action against the Christians only on the basis of private accusations being brought against
them.

But let us consider individually the attitudes of each of the
Antonine emperors.

Nerva

In the year 96, after the fall of Domitian, Nerva demonstrated for
the last time his firm decision not to take action against the Christians. He recalled those who had been banished[2] and forbade the
bringing of actions for atheism or practicing of Jewish customs (Dio,
68. 1. 1–3). The fact that he chose to issue a coin to mark this act of
clemency[3] shows how seriously he meant this measure to be taken
and it leads us to wonder how much Nerva himself was under
pressure from influential pro-Christian elements in his entourage.
This need not surprise us; after all, families such as that of Acilius
Glabrio, disgraced during Domitian's persecution, were now back
in positions of power and influence after the fall of the 'tyrant'. The
fact remains, however, that when Fronto as suffect consul (from 1
September 96 (Dio, ibid.)) made his protest against Nerva's
measures, he was only showing the first indications of a mentality

which was by now dominant in the senate and giving voice to the general feeling of hostility to which this kind of act of clemency gave rise. Indeed, Trajan — adopted as joint ruler by Nerva in 97 — did not repeat his adoptive father's veto when he took over as sole emperor in 98. In fact, while accusations of practising Jewish customs gradually disappear from the scene during the second century, charges of atheism acquire ever greater importance. As we shall see from his rescript to Pliny, Trajan considered atheism to be the only transgression implicit in Christianity, and he considered it worthy of the death penalty.

Trajan's Rescript to Pliny

Trajan's rescript (Pliny, *Ep*. x. 97), is the acid test to which all questions concerning the legal basis of the persecution of the Christians must be put. In fact, as we have already mentioned, the rescript was to regulate the whole question of the persecutions right up to the times of Decius and Valerian. Today, as in the past, historians are divided on the subject of the rescript: some believe it was a special measure, others (though fewer than in the past) see it in terms of the application of *coercitio*, while others again believe the Christians were to be punished according to the normal legal code and, in particular, according to the laws which had applied to religious crimes since before the advent of Christianity.[4]

Nobody denies the authenticity of the rescript itself, or of the letter from Pliny which gave rise to it (x. 96). Likewise, no one seriously suggests any longer that the rescript contains later interpolations.[5] The rescript is, without any doubt, the oldest existing official document on the subject of relations between Christians and the state.

The actual location of the trials which caused Pliny to write to Trajan can be identified on the basis of the position of the letter itself in the correspondence; it must have been either Amisus (referred to in letter 92) or Amastris (letter 98), both on the East coast of the Black Sea. The date, once again from the correspondence, must be some time between 18 September and 3 January of the second year of Pliny the Younger's governorship in Bithynia, but opinions differ as to when his governorship took place. Some put it between 109 and 111 AD while others opt for the years between 111 and 113. The trials and the correspondence to which they gave rise would thus belong to the autumn and winter of 110/11 or 112/13.[6]

Pliny begins his letter by saying that he has never been present in person at any of the trials of the Christians ('Cognitionibus de Christianis interfui nunquam'). This means that in Pliny's time, about fifteen years after Trajan came to the throne, trials of Christians by provincial governors were evidently not new or unknown, but a common occurrence. Pliny's self-confessed ignorance ('ideo nescio, quid et quatenus aut puniri soleat aut quaeri'), comes from a lack of personal experience in the field; evidently he had not previously had the occasion to be present at one of these trials, either as governor or as a member of the *consilium principis*. The question he poses, however, has nothing to do with doubts about the punishability of professing the Christian faith, but with the legal procedures normally followed at these trials. Although he had obviously received no previous instructions from Trajan and despite his lack of experience in the field, he never seems to have doubted that Christianity was a crime and he had, as he himself recounts, sentenced self-confessed Christians to death (ibid. 96. 3 — 'perseverantes duci iussi').

Pliny, therefore, knew that confessed Christians were guilty before the law. We can guess at the contents of the law, or at least Pliny's version of it, from the tests he set for those who denied the charges of Christianity brought against them (ibid. 96. 5). They were to sacrifice to the gods, offer prayers with libations of wine and incense before an image of the Emperor and speak ill of Christ. As far as Pliny was concerned, the crimes implicit in Christianity were thus obviously *impietas* (atheism), *superstitio illicita* and lack of reverence to the emperor. In other words, they were religious crimes which, because of the refusal to worship the emperor, took on political implications (though Trajan had, in fact, neither imposed nor asked for worship).

Pliny does not believe that Christianity constitutes a political threat to the state or that, beyond their refusal to worship the gods and the emperor, the Christians were guilty of atrocities or obscene acts (the famous *flagitia*) or, indeed, of any kind of action prejudicial to the morality or security of the state. In his letter to Trajan, Pliny writes at length on the results of the interrogation under torture of two women, probably deaconesses, which he had undertaken in order to find out what went on during the Christians' gatherings. He concludes: 'I found nothing more than a malignant and immoderate superstition' (ibid. 96. 8). This part of the letter is important, comprising as it does the first pagan account of early Christian liturgical meetings and the eucharistic feast.[7] It also, I believe, provides us with the key to the significance of the whole letter. Pliny knows of Trajan's profound mistrust of any kind of assembly taking place in Bithynia and his fear of secret societies (*hetaeriae*) and he is trying to put the Emperor's mind at ease on this point.[8] He goes about this by describing Christian meetings with the terminology usually used in connection with the *coniurationes* (ibid. 96. 7 — with the mention of pre-dawn gatherings and the *sacramentum*), but he then goes on to explain that the aims of the Christians are exactly opposite — the Christian 'sacrament' did not bind its followers 'to the performance of some kind of crime, but to keep their word not to commit theft, rapine or adultery and not to refuse to repay a loan'. Indeed, he underlines the Christians' commitment to a morally and legally blameless life. In writing in these terms I believe Pliny reveals the true *animus* of the rescript: he no longer justifies the suspension of the trials ('ideo dilata cognitione') and his appeal to the Emperor in terms of his own inexperience ('ad consulendum te decucurri . . . res digna consultatione'), but, as he makes clear himself, in the hope of being able to avoid a useless massacre ('propter periclitantium numerum' (ibid. 9)). The outcome of the interrogation is an indirect defence of the Christians against accusations of the famous *flagitia* and against the suspicion of constituting a danger to the state. It is this position which leads him at the end of the letter to put forward, indirectly, the three questions in which he was originally interested:

If discrimination should be practised with regard to age, if children, being of a tender age, are to be taken as no different from those of maturer years, if pardon may be granted to penitents, or if having once been a Christian, no longer being one makes no difference; if the *nomen* in itself — that is, simply being a follower — in the absence of shameful acts should be punished, or whether punishment should be the consequence of the transgressions caused by being a follower (ibid. 2).

He ends up (ibid. 9–10) by cautiously suggesting a policy of clemency.

I do not agree with those who, even recently, have claimed that Pliny's only problem was what to do with apostates, even if this is certainly the only one of his three questions to which Trajan gave a reasonably explicit answer. In reality, the central question to which Pliny wanted an answer was, what is to be considered punishable, the *nomen* in itself or the *flagitia cohaerentia nomini*? And the possibility of granting *venia* for the *paenitentia* of the apostates lies, Pliny feels, in the answer to this question. Pliny's question, then — and here I agree with Wlosok and Keresztes — is whether Christianity is a penal offence or a mental aberration, a *culpa* or an *error*. Put in these terms, we see that the problem was characteristic of Roman law, which did not pardon 'penitents' who were guilty of crimes against the physical person of others or against the state (except where — as happened in the famous trial of the Bacchanals in 186 BC — the accused collaborated with the authorities in bringing their accomplices to trial) but which differentiated between sentences for crimes of deed and crimes of thought or word. The case put forward by Ulpian, (VII. 1. 'De officio proconsulis') for the *mathematici* and *vaticinatores* posed the question of whether their punishment was for *scientia* or for *exercitium* and *professio*;[9] a question very similar to the one Pliny asked concerning Christians. The fact that they had doubts on the subject, despite legislation having existed on this point since the days of the republic, can be explained by the complexity of the situations they had to face. Should the Christians or the *mathematici* be punished simply for adhering to the Christian faith (*nomen*) or knowing about astrology (*scientia*), or should they be punished for the crimes which Christianity or a knowledge of magic would lead them into committing? As we can see, the analogy is close, even if not entirely appropriate. The practice of a religious faith is one thing and a knowledge of the stars is another, and the effects which the two are likely to have on the everyday life of their followers will be widely different. Pliny himself, in fact, goes on to make a further distinction between the religious practices of the Christians and their moral code, and concludes that in both cases he could find no traces of the *flagitia* attributed to the Christians by the public.

It is precisely the fact that he finds no trace of *flagitia* among the Christians, who are therefore guilty of a purely religious error ('I found nothing else . . .'), which gives rise to Pliny's perplexity as to what kind of punishment should be inflicted on them if their crime is only a crime of the *nomen* they bear. This is why he appeals to the Emperor, in the hope of obtaining a less strict ruling, one which would at least take into account the age and sex of the accused and allow the 'penitents' to be pardoned.

The question of being convicted for the *nomen* (a question which was to play such an important part in the Acts of the Martyrs and the Christian *apologiae*) is not, therefore, a Christian invention originating in the traditional importance of the Name in the Hebrew tradition. It is, on the contrary, very much a question of Roman law. But to be condemned for the *nomen* means to be condemned for being a Christian; not for atheism or for *superstitio*, which were both to some extent transgressions 'cohaerentia nomini', but for Christianity itself. This points to the existence of a special law, in which the *nomen*, the fact of being a Christian, is in itself forbidden: 'non licet esse Christianos.'[10]

Thus, by analysing Pliny's letter, we come back to the existence of a special law which, however vague in its outlines, evidently forbade the Christians the right to exist. Nero was the first to put this law into practice, but, as it was not anulled with the *abolitio* of his other laws, we have good reason to believe it dates back even further than Nero's reign. Apart from Nero, the, the only other news we have of a law of this kind is the account Tertullian gives us of the *senatus consultum* of the year 35.

To return to Pliny's letter, it must be said that, if Pliny was hoping to obtain a clear answer from Trajan, an answer that would give him the chance to exercise a certain cautious mercy in the shelter of some precise guidelines, he must have been very disappointed with the answer he actually received. Trajan's reply is a masterpiece of ambiguity. He avoids giving a single straight answer to the three questions put to him by his governor and friend, and, despite the belief to the contrary of most experts, not even the question of apostasy is adequately addressed. Trajan allows apostates to be pardoned, not because they have denied their faith, but simply as 'suspecti in prateritum'. He allows the suspicion to remain suspicion, suggesting to Pliny that he should limit himself to asking the accused if they are *Christians now* rather than *if they have ever been Christians*. By suggesting this course of action, Trajan destroys all the psychological effect that a declaration of apostasy should have, an effect on which Pliny was counting to bring many deviants back to the religion of their fathers. In other words, Trajan makes it clear that he is not particularly interested in 'correcting' the Christians. Moreover, after having congratulated Pliny on his excellent conduct of the trials, he goes on to suggest, between the lines, that in future his approach should be different: not only should he avoid asking any questions concerning the prisoner's past, he should also limit the number of 'tests' to which the apostates were put to prove the sincerity of their renunciation. From now onwards, prayers before the emperor's image and the anathema of Christ could be dropped, leaving only the sacrifice to the gods.

On two points Trajan is categorical and absolutely clear: there must be no official searches and investigations ('conquirendi non sunt') and Christians can only be persecuted on the receipt of a personal, not anonymous, accusation. The second point, the refusal to accept anonymous denunciations, is in fact in line with the policy of Trajan's whole reign and not a question of special treatment for the Christians. The first point is certainly the more interesting, especially when taken in conjunction with the fact that Trajan makes no comment on Pliny's information about the associative aspects of the Christian religion. This silence is most unexpected in Trajan, given his fears for Bithynia. On another occasion, Pliny had asked permission from the Emperor to form a fire brigade in Nicomedia. It was to comprise fewer than 150 men and would help to cope with the frequent and disastrous fires in the area (*Ep*. x. 33). Despite the fact that Pliny himself was to direct the proceedings, Trajan refused his permission on the grounds that in Bithynia any excuse for association immediately became an excuse for forming an *hetaeria* that is, a subversive political group, and was to be prevented at all costs. Even the forming of *eranoi*, mutual help organisations, was only tolerated among the inhabitants of Amisus on the basis of previously established agreements and laws, but were forbidden to everyone else 'so as not to create disorders and unlawful reunions' (ibid. 93). In the name of public order, Trajan even forbade the ritual distribution of baskets containing provisions or money on the occasion of weddings and other festivities (ibid. 117). Under these circumstances, I can only see as extremely eloquent the Emperor's silence on the question of the Christians' right to assemble and his advice to Pliny not to intervene in any way as far as Christian gatherings were concerned, thus accepting Christianity as a purely personal religious transgression to be punished only on the receipt of information from private individuals. Evidently, even before receiving Pliny's report, Trajan was so convinced of the political harmlessness of the Christians that he was prepared to make some sort of exception for them when it came to applying the rigid laws forbidding the right to associate in Bithynia and to advise his governor to take no notice of Christian reunions or assemblies. Implicit in his wording is also the recommendation to the Christians themselves to be prudent enough not to lay themselves open to charges of illicit behaviour. Trajan could not repeat Nerva's veto, which was by now unpopular with the general public and, to a certain extent, with the senate too. For the same reason, he could not grant Christianity official recognition. He thus chose deliberately to speak in generalised terms, avoiding the sort of detailed precision which could be used to strengthen the existing anti-Christian law and leave him no room for maneouvre, and limiting as far as he could the number of occasions on which the law could be applied. The intention embodied by the rescript seems to be confirmed by what we know of the trials of Ignatius at Antioch and Simeon at Jerusalem.[11]

Tertullian was right, in my opinion, when he called Trajan's rescript a 'sententiam necessitate confusam' (*Apol.* II. 7) — and it is worth noting the 'necessitate', showing as it does how well the apologist understood the 'confusion'. Equally, I would agree with him when he says that the rescript constituted an attempt on the part of the Emperor to circumvent the existing anti-Christian laws: 'Quales leges istas . . . quas Traianus ex parte frustratus est . . . (ibid. v. 7)). In reality, Trajan's rescript was a compromise which both factions, the Christians and the intransigent pagans, tried to turn to their own advantage: the Christian apologists from the time of Hadrian, and , later, Justin (at the time of Antoninus Pius), put forward Pliny's plea for a distinction between *nomen* and *flagitia*, while the pagans tried to urge the state to allow the Christians to be searched out as members of an 'irreligious' sect whose existence endangered the *pax deorum*. Like all compromises, Trajan's rescript did, in fact, allow some room for maneouvre, and it also created a certain balance which it would have been dangerous to upset. For this reason, and despite the different interpretations given by each individual emperor, the rescript remained officially in force right up to the time of Valerian. Even Decius, in his drive for religious restoration, considered he was faithfully and conscientiously applying Trajan's rescript, rather than introducing innovations of his own. Only with Valerian, in 275, was a break made with Trajan's formulation, when he decided that the church itself constituted an unlawful community and that this, as well as the individual religious fault of practising the Christian faith, was to be persecuted.

Hadrian's Rescript to Minicius Fundanus

A first attempt to give a pro-Christian interpretation to Trajan's rescript was given by Hadrian in his rescript to the proconsul of Asia of the year 124/5, Minicius (or Minucius) Fundanus. The text is preserved in its Greek version and with very few variants as a footnote to Justin's first *Apologia* (I *Apol.* 68) and by Eusebius (*Hist. eccl.* IV. 9). Rufinus' Latin text is only a translation from Eusebius and does not derive from the original. Hadrian was forced to intervene when the Asian provincials sent him a petition via Fundanus' predecessor Licinius (or Serenius) Granianus. From the rescript itself (and it is our only source for the whole episode) it would appear that the petitioners wanted the state to take more drastic steps against the Christians. Hadrian refuses to do so, and confirms Trajan's policy of only allowing the Christians to be charged through normal legal channels. In line with the rest of his legislative policies,[12] he also establishes that the onus of producing evidence lies with the accusers rather than with the accused and that the governor is to punish perpetrators of false accusations. The *animus* inspiring this document is clearly one of opposition to the fanaticism of the masses, from whom Hadrian would evidently like to save the Christians; but the text is ambiguous when it comes to the question of what kind of evidence must be brought against the Christians if the accusers are to prove, as the rescript stipulates, that 'they are doing something against the laws'.

This wording has given rise to a good deal of debate, both in ancient times and in the present day. It certainly adds to the general atmosphere of uncertainty which surrounds the whole question of Hadrian's rescript.[13] Some maintain that, as Christianity was in any case illegal, all the accusers had to do was to prove that the accused practised the Christian faith — a situation not much different from that of Trajan's times, with the single difference that evidence now had to be produced by the prosecution rather than the defence. Others interpret the formula as automatically including Pliny's distinction between *nomen* and *flagitia*, in which case it would not have been enough to prove that the accused was a Christian; there would also have to be proof of other crimes having been committed. Because of the rider to the rescript (on the basis of which, in this case, the governor would have to punish 'according to the severity of the crime'), the second interpretation is preferable to the first. Indeed, if the only punishable crime were, as in Trajan's time, that of practising the Christian faith, the crime and punishment would have been the same for everyone.

This interpretation, which was, after all, the one offered by Christian apologists throughout the second century,[14] is confirmed by several indications.

1. There was, in fact, a period of Hadrian's reign during which a self-confessed Christian could be pardoned and anti-Christian trials included investigations into common crimes.[15]

2. Hadrian's attitude towards the Christians seems to have been, even according to pagan sources, apparently marked with a certain interest in and sympathy with the Christian faith. In the *Historia Augusta* we are told that, before Alexander Severus' time, Hadrian had already thought of giving Christianity official recognition and had had temples prepared without statues, ready to be consecrated to Christ.[16] Phlegon of Tralles, freedman and literary spokesman for Hadrian, wrote about Christ and St Peter in his works and recounted various miracles and prophecies which had come about.[17] It is likely that the prophecy mentioned by Phlegon and erroneously attributed by him to St Peter, was in fact Christ's prophecy of the fall of Jerusalem and the destruction of the temple. A prophecy of this kind would naturally be of great interest to the court of Hadrian, who was involved in a difficult war in Judaea between 132 and 135 AD. Hadrian's rescript to Fundanus actually pre-dates the Jewish rebellion by about ten years and certainly had nothing to do with it, but I would not discount the possibility that the fact that the Judaean Christians dissociated themselves from the anti-Roman rebellion on that occasion (as they had in 70 AD) further reinforced Hadrian's disinclination for taking action against them. If Malalas' account of the martyrdom of Simeon in Jerusalem is accurate, and if this episode occurred in 115/16 AD,[18] it would also look as if Trajan in his last years followed a similar course. He would, that is, have ordered an end to the trials of the Christians even when the charges brought against them were perfectly legal and the Christians were self-confessed; and this, just at the time when anti-Roman uprisings were proliferating throughout the Jewish communities during the period of the Parthian War in Egypt, Mesopotamia, Cyrenaica and Cyprus as well as in Palestine itself. It would thus look as if Hadrian's policy was actually anticipated by Trajan.

Antoninus Pius and the Rescript against 'New Religions'

We know from Melito, who wrote his apology under Marcus Aurelius, that Antoninus Pius was against making any changes in the anti-Christian laws. In various rescripts to the Thessalonians, the Athenians and all the Greeks, he gave instructions 'not to make any innovations on the Christian question' (see Eusebius, *His. eccl.* IV. 26. 10). We also know, however, that, from the first year of his reign, the Christians were being condemned for their faith once again, not only in the provinces, but in Rome itself. Pope Telesphorus was martyred in the first year of Antoninus Pius' reign and Ptolemy and Lucius were both tried under the Prefect of Rome, Lollius Urbicus, as Justin recounts in his First *Apologia* (Chapter 2).

Urbicus firmly rejected Lucius' attempt to appeal to Hadrian's rescript, with its stipulation that punishment was to be inflicted for 'acts against the law' rather than for professing the Christian faith. As far as Urbicus was concerned, the crime was precisely that of being a Christian; and, in fact, as we have already seen, the wording of the rescript could legitimately be interpreted to mean this.

With the coming to power of Antoninus Pius, then, Hadrian's rescript was not rejected, but it began to be interpreted in its most restrictive sense, as a mere confirmation of the regulations laid down by Trajan, with the only difference being that the burden of proving the guilt of the accused lay with the accuser (as the cautious approach of Ptolemy's prosecutor demonstrates), rather than the accused.

In reality, the whole spiritual and cultural climate of the court had undergone a profound change with the coming to power of this conservative emperor whose loyalties were with the traditionalist elements of the senatorial class (Marcus Aurelius, *Meditations*, I. 16). If we compare a text of Ulpian's with that of his fellow-jurist, Paul, it appears that Antoninus Pius addressed a rescript to Pacatus, legate of Gallia Lugdunensis, which formulated a new set of regulations for the punishment of those who introduced 'new sects and religions unknown to reason'. The penalties were to be deportation for the *honestiores* and death for the *humiliores*.[19]

The rescript did not mention the Christians and was probably not aimed at them at all, the intention being to put a stop to the spread of magic and astrology. There is no doubt, however, that this regulation could be — and indeed was — used against the Christians too. In the writing of Aelius Aristides and in public opinion as quoted by Lucian,[20] we do in fact find charges of novelty and irrationality being brought against the Christians during this period, as we also find the Christian apologists beginning to refute them. Far from being 'new', they insist, the Christian religion is based on the books of the Old Testament, considerably older than Greek knowledge, and, far from being 'irrational', the Christian religion is much more reasonable than the fairy-tales accepted by the pagans.

We have said that, despite the changes in the general mood, Antoninus Pius had more than once recommended that his provincial governors conform to the regulations established by his predecessors and not set in motion official investigations of, or searches for, the Christians. However, we know of at least one occasion on which this recommendation was certainly flouted, and that is the trial of Polycarp, which took place in Smyrna some time round the year 155. Local functionaries, who were at that time still responsible for searching out *latrones* (*Dig.* 48. 3. 6), chased and caught Polycarp who had fled from Smyrna to avoid arrest. Once captured, they took him before the governor, Statius Quadratus, proconsul of Asia, who interrogated him before a mob which howled abuse against atheists and Christians. The trial ended with Polycarp's conviction as a Christian.[21] It is quite clear from the account that the Roman judge is aware of the irregularity of trying a Christian who has been the victim of an illegal search. He shows considerable embarrassment in his interrogation, avoiding any hint of an accusation of Christianity and even pretending to be ignorant of Polycarp's religious beliefs, in the hope that the defendant himself will be tricked into confessing to being a Christian.

Did the Emperor react in any way to the abuse committed at Smyrna? Christian tradition has preserved two copies of a rescript of Antoninus Pius to the *koinon* of Asia: one reported by Eusebius in the *Historia ecclesiastica* (IV. 13) and the other in a Parisian codex to Justin's Second *Apologia*. Eusebius attributes the rescript to Antoninus Pius, but with the titulature of Marcus Aurelius in the first year of his reign (161 AD); the Parisian codex quotes it with the title (corrupted) Antoninus Pius, in the year 157. When the two versions are compared, it becomes clear that the original document, authentic or not, must be attributed to Antoninus Pius.[22] When we take out what must be Christian interpolations to the text[23] and clear up the doubts which arise from such an explicit and unambiguous exoneration of those who confessed to being Christians (which, incidentally, would tie up with the legend, denied by Tertullian, that

Marcus Aurelius would have abolished the conviction of Christians for the *nomen*), this rescript is still clearly a reprimand. The *koinon*, that is the indigenous community organisation and the local functionaries, is rebuked for stirring up trouble for those it accuses of atheism, ignoring the fact that the gods are certainly able to take care of such people without any help. Its members are also accused of losing their heads over the earthquakes which have struck their region,[24] and of allowing official searches to be carried out for Christians,[25] contrary to the regulations issued by the Emperor's father (Hadrian) and by the present Emperor himself on more than one occasion. Brought back to its original form in this way, the rescript could well be authentic and, given the content and the date, might well be the Roman government's answer to the abuse of power perpetrated by the local authorities of the province of Asia on the occasion of Polycarp's trial.

To sum up: the cultural climate has changed and the reactionary attitude of Antoninus Pius is certainly not favourable to the Christians. In the provinces, especially in the East, the fanatical mob brings pressure to bear on the authorities to take action against the Christians who, they say, have brought down the wrath of the gods in the form of earthquakes and other natural disasters. But despite this generally antagonistic mood, the Roman government under Antoninus Pius continues to uphold the policy of limiting the number of occasions on which the Christians can be actively persecuted.

Marcus Aurelius and Commodus: the Beginnings of a New Relationship Between the State and the Christians

The reigns of Marcus Aurelius and Commodus (who ruled with his father as Augustus from 176/7 AD and succeeded him in 180), mark both a turning-point in the history of the empire — Gibbons dates the decline of the empire from this period — and a complete change in imperial policy towards the Christians. We can see signs of this change in the Anti-Christian trials of the period, in the increase in polemic and apologetic activity, and in the new legislation, which was a prelude to the settlement finally reached under the Severans.

The trials of the Christians under Marcus Aurelius point to the existence of three distinct phases in imperial policy. The first corresponds to the period between 161 and 169 AD, when Verus was co-ruler with Marcus Aurelius. Our basic source for this period is the account of Justin's trial, from which it is clear that legal procedure had not changed since Antoninus Pius' days. Some Christian sources (the later Acts of Justin, the Life of St Abericius, Orosius, VII, 15. 4) link the intensification of anti-Christian activity with the issue of an edict on sacrifices, a *prostagma*, which they connect with that issued later by Decius, but which in reality belongs as part of the general measures taken throughout the empire between 166 and 168 AD (they are also mentioned in the *Historia Augusta: Life of Marcus*. 13). These measures were taken in answer to the problems the empire was facing at that time: the plague had followed on the heels of the Parthian war, and, for the first time since the days of Marius, the Germanic invaders were pressing on the borders and had even, alarmingly, made incursions on to Italian soil, Anti-Christian trials at this time were still conducted according to Trajan's regulations: charges must be brought by private individuals and official investigation and search were not allowed. The trials ended with convictions for personal religious transgression. However, in the interrogation of Justin undertaken by Junius Rusticus, prefect of Rome (162–7) and friend of Marcus Aurelius, we begin to see the emergence of a new interest in the communal life of the Christians and in their meeting-places, an interest which could mark the first step towards a change in legislation.

The second phase concerns the period around the year 177 when Marcus Aurelius was about to adopt, or had just adopted, his son Commodus as his co-ruler. During this period the persecution was intensified. From Melito we know this was particularly true in Asia, Athenagoras tells us the same for Greece and, as we know from the famous trial at Lyons in 177, even Gaul was involved in this escalation.

On the occasion of its eighteenth centenary, this trial has recently been examined thoroughly and carefully from every point of view, and I refer readers to the results of this research for an analysis of the religious, political and cultural situation in Lyons and its Christian community at the time of the trial.[26] On the aspect which interests us, that is the relationship between Christianity and the Empire, I myself have referred elsewhere to the new features brought to light by these studies,[27] which we can summarise as follows: (1) the right of the governor, the legate of Tres Galliae, to subject Christians to official search and investigation; (2) the fact that, in the eyes of the governor, apostasy was not sufficient to prevent conviction; (3) the attitude of Marcus Aurelius who, when asked for advice by the governor, went back to the traditional ruling on apostates laid down by Trajan and ordered them to be pardoned, but did not interfere in any way with the right to carry out official searches.

Having put into perspective the problem of the apostates (whom the governor, convinced of the existence of *flagitia*, had kept in custody but whom Marcus Aurelius wants pardoned), the real innovation of this trial is the Emperor's consent on the matter of official search and investigation, a consent which neither Trajan nor any of his successors had ever given. When we consider that the Christians were being subjected to the same treatment in various parts of the empire during the same period, it seems clear that Marcus Aurelius had decided to intervene more actively against the Christians than had his predecessors, for whom Christianity had not been considered to be a danger to the state. News of this state of affairs comes to us through Melito (Eusebius, *Hist. eccl.* IV. 26. 5) who talks of 'new decrees' — *kainà dogmata* — for the province of Asia, and Athenagoras (*Presbeia*, I. 3), while Celsus (VIII. 69, Bader) would seem to confirm what they say.

The Roman government had begun to regard the Christian communities as politically suspect, and the reason for this was the spread of Montanism, with its rigidly intransigent attitude to the state, its identification with the anti-Roman spirit of the Jewish revolts, its openly provocative behaviour, its charismatic and prophetic claims and its thirst for martyrdom. When Montanism first appeared on the scene, it must have been difficult for pagan observers to distinguish clearly between it and mainstream Christianity, as we can see from the writings of Celsus:[28] although he knew the details of a good many Christian heresies, he never mentions Montanism, attributing to the Christian religion in general many characteristics which were exclusively Montanist. We find the same confusion in Marcus Aurelius' *Meditations*.[29] Writing on the subject of the Christian martyrs, he records with care the spirit and behaviour typical of the Montanist attitude to martyrdom. In fact, of course, before becoming a separate doctrine, Montanism had been a kind of religious revival movement, striving for renewal within the church and advocating a complete withdrawal from the affairs of the world in view of the imminent *parusia*. Because of the sincerity of its religious commitment, the movement did in fact gain the respect of many Christians, even when they could not agree with its fanaticism or the extravagance of its 'prophecies'. For this reason it became extremely difficult to draw any kind of clear demarcation line between the two.[30] It is, therefore, hardly surprising if the pagans misunderstood the situation and included all the Christians in the suspicion and perplexity which should have been reserved for the Montanists alone. After all, Christianity was a fast-growing movement with a strong community organisation and, clandestine as it was, there was no way of keeping it under control. Given this state of confusion, the Christians must have appeared not only to offend the religious feelings and traditions of the masses, but also to be a genuine danger to the state, if Montanism was going to encourage its followers to refuse public office and military service at precisely the moment the Empire most needed the co-operation of all its citizens. And, with barbarian pressure building up, the solidarity of all citizens of the Empire had never been more necessary.

Without openly revoking Trajan's prohibition of the *conquirere* of Christians, Marcus Aurelius went round it by extending the right to search and investigate to include new categories, adding the *sacrilegi* to the original *latrones*.[31] Without having to rely on private denunciations, governors could now *conquirere* the Christians whenever state security seemed to call for it, on the grounds that public opinion had accused them of sacrilege.[32] It was on the basis of this measure that the governor of Tres Galliae could, in 177, proceed against the Christians in Lyons and Viennes, without being accused of abuse of power by the Emperor when his advice was sought.[33] In those years, it must have seemed to Marcus Aurelius, as it did to Celsus (VIII. 68, Bader) that the persecution of the Christians was a necessary act of legitimate self-defence on the part of a state faced with the threat of a subversive minority. In reality, of course, it was a tragic misunderstanding; neither the Great Church nor the majority of the Christians actually shared the anti-Roman, anti-state ideals of the followers of the new prophecy, and the Montanists' charismatic claims and often exhibitionistic and provocative search for martyrdom had been condemned by church leaders from the start, especially in the East where the movement first began.[34] Between 176 and 177, Athenagoras of Athens, Melito of Sardis, Apollinaris of Hierapolis and Miltiades all addressed *apologiae* directly to Marcus Aurelius himself, attempting both to clear up the misunderstanding and to stress the Christians' loyalty to the Roman empire.[35] It may be that, when Celsus wrote his *True*

Word, he was answering the Christians' *apologiae* on behalf of the Emperor. If so, despite the violent tone natural to polemics, whether religious or politcal, it could be read as a cautious proposal of peace, an attempt to find a *modus vivendi* that would allow the Christians to come out of hiding and offer their services to the empire as ordinary citizens. In fact, Celsus does invite the Christians to 'collaborate with the Emperor with all your strength in everything right, to fight for him, to participate in his military campaigns . . . to command his troups with him . . . to accept public office when necessary(VIII. 73 and 75, Bader).

Thus we come to the third phase of Marcus Aurelius' policy towards the Christians. If we are to accept Tertullian's report regarding the liability to punishment of those who brought charges against the Christians regardless of the guilt of the accused,[36] it would seem that a new relationship between church and state began to emerge now, at the end of Marcus Aurelius' reign. Certainly under Commodus we find the church emerging from hiding and beginning to be recognised openly, if not officially, by the state. Hippolytus, a contemporary, refers in his *Philosophumena* (IX. 12. 10) to the episode in which Commodus' mistress Marcia intervened with the Emperor on behalf of Victor, Bishop of Rome, to ask him to pardon the Christians who had been exiled to Sardinia, even though the Emperor himself had compiled the list of those who were to be deported. This is not simply an edifying anecdote, quoted as evidence of pro-Christian sentiments in a woman who was Empress in everything but name (Herodian, I. 16. 4); rather it is a sign of the changing attitude of the state towards the church. The Empire now acknowledges the existence of Christianity as an established ecclesiastic organisation and is prepared to live with it peaceably. This is still a *de facto* rather than a *de jure* situation, and Christianity can still be punished in individuals and persecuted as a *religio illicita* according to the old laws (as long as regular charges are brought), but at the same time the Church becomes the legitimate proprietor of places of worship and burial, thanks to the regulations in force for cultural and funereal *collegia*.[37] With a few brief periods of local persecution, this state of affairs was to last throughout the period of the Severan emperors and their successors, right up to the time of Valerian.

The state, then, acknowledges the hierarchy of the church and often has friendly dealings with it, while at the same time denying its existence on a formal level. At the root of this new attitude, we find

Marcus Aurelius' desire (heard through the voice of Celsus) to integrate the strong Christian minority into the life of the state. Celsus had exhorted the Christians to participate in military campaigns and to accept public office and, in exchange for their co-operation, the emperor is prepared to offer religious toleration. In fact, after Marcus Aurelius, the Christians do seem to have dropped the cautious reluctance to accept public office which had, indeed, characterised their behaviour throughout the Antonine period. Contemporary sources begin to speak openly of Christian senators and knights, and Christian *formulae* appear for the first time in public inscriptions.[38] The moment Christianity is able to emerge from the shadows, we find its members taking full part in the life of the times. At the same time, the official pagan hierarchy is working towards syncretism, collecting all the various and different forms of worship into that of the *summus deus* of the many names, the *deus invictus* of the solar religion. These tendencies help to diminish the mistrust that had been felt in many circles for the followers of the *unus Deus*; in fact, religious syncretism and religious tolerance go hand in hand throughout the period of the Serveran emperors.

Notes

1. The first of the Antonine emperors was actually Antoninus Pius, from whom Marcus Aurelius took his name (Imperator Caesar Marcus Aurelius Antoninus Augustus). Septimius Severus took the name from Marcus Aurelius and his son Commodus, and passed it to his sons by means of a fictitious adoption. Alexander Severus eventually dropped the name after it had been discredited by Elagabalus and his excesses.

2. According to church tradition, St John was among these (Eusebius, *Hist. eccl.* III. 23. 1). Tertullian, who was certainly mistaken, says that Domitian himself was responsible for the restitution of the exiles: ('restitutis quos relegaverat' (*Apol.* v. 4)).

3. Cf. H. Mattingly and E. A. Sydenham in *Roman Imperial Coinage* (*RIC*), II, p. 227 no. 53 (the legend 'Fisci Iudaici calumnia sublata' surrounds a date-palm, emblem of Judaea). The minting of the coin did not denote an end to the collection of the Jewish tax, but did put a stop to the irregularities and abuses of which the *improfessi* had been victims. See W. H. C. Frend, *Martyrdom and Persecution in the Early Church: a Study of a Conflict from the Maccabees to Donatus* (Oxford, 1965); P. Keresztes, 'Rome and the Christian Church, I' in *ANRW* II. 23. 1 (1979), p. 260.

4. For bibliography, I refer readers to my article in *Rivista di Storia della Chiesa in Italia*, 14 (1960), pp. 344 ff.; see also J. Speigl, *Der römische Staat und die Christen*, (Amsterdam 1970), pp. 45 ff.; J. Molthagen, 'Der römische Staat und die Christen in zweiten und dritten Jahrhundert' (Göttingen, 1970), pp. 24 ff.; A. Wlosok, *Rom und die Christen* (Stuttgart; 1970), pp. 27 ff.; P. Keresztes, 'Rome and the Christian Church', pp. 273 ff. A. N. Sherwin-White provides an analysis in *The Letters of Pliny* (Oxford, 1966), Appendix V, pp. 772 ff, as does R. Freudenberger, *Das Verhalten*

der römischen Behoerden gegen die Christen (Munich 1969). An up-dated *status quaestionis* can be found in P. Cova's 'Plinio il giovane e il problema delle persecuzioni', *Bollettino di Studi Latini*, 5 (1975), pp. 293 ff.

5. On the doubts raised by L. Hermann in 'Hierius et Domitius', *Latomus* 13 (1954), pp. 343 ff., see Keresztes, 'Rome and the Christian Church', pp. 274 ff. (with notes).

6. Sherwin-White dates Pliny's governorship in Bithynia between 109 and 111 AD; Freudenberger between 111 and 113.

7. Cf. M. Sordi, 'Sacramentum in Plinio *Ep.* x. 96. 7', *Vigiliae Christianae*, 19 (1982), pp. 97 ff.

8. On Trajan's fears of associative life in Bithynia, see Pliny, *Ep.* x. 34; 93; 117.

9. Cf. *Mosaicarum et Romanaruno Legum Collatio* xv. 11. 2: 'sed fuit quaesitum utrum scientia huiusmodi hominum puniatur an exercitium et professio.'

10. Unlike Sherwin-White (*Letters of Pliny*, p. 783) I would discount the possibility of 'pertinacia' having any technical value here or that it can alone, without any special legislation, justify the death penalty for contempt of court.

11. On the martyrdoms of Ignatius and Simeon (Eusebius, *Hist. eccl.* III. 32 ff.) see M. Sordi, *Il cristianesimo e Roma* (Bologna, 1965), pp. 132 and 146 ff.

12. *Dig.* XXII. 5. 3 (the jurist Callistratus records a series of rescripts, five of which were Hadrian's to provincial governors — nos. 1, 2, 3, 4, 6 — dealing with the question of how to hear witnesses and evaluate their evidence. No. 3 is particularly interesting for its severity towards prosecutors who are unable to prove the truth of their accusations. For the case of a certain Alexander, see *Dig.* XLVIII. 2. 7.)

13. For bibliography on this subject, see Sordi in *Rivista di Storia della Chiesa in Italia* 14, (1960) pp. 344 ff. and P. Keresztes, 'The Jews, the Christians and the Emperor Domitian', *Virgiliae Christianne*, 27 (1973) and in *ANRW* 23 (1979), pp. 287 ff.

14. This is the line taken by Justin in his First *Apologia* and by the Roman martyr Lucius to whom Justin refers at the beginning of his Second *Apologia*. It is interesting to see that Christian *apologiae* first started appearing under Hadrian, with the works of Aristides and Quadratus (of which only some fragments have survived). The fact that Antoninus Pius interpreted the rescript in its most restrictive sense does not mean that Hadrian did the same; and of course the ambiguous wording of the rescript allowed for very different interpretations.

15. Justin, I *Apol.* 7; Lucius, *De Morte Peregrini*, 16.

16. *SHA Vita Alex.* 43, 6–7. Whether or not this information is historically reliable, it is still significant that a pagan source like the *Historia Augusta* should record Hadrian's favourable attitude to the Christians' faith.

17. Cf. Jacoby's *Die Fragmente d. griechischen Historiker*, 16, no. 257.

18. Malalas XI. 273, 5 (p. 44 in Schenk von Stauffenberg); cf. Sordi, *Il cristianesimo*, pp. 146–7.

19. On the subject of the rescript to Pacatus (C. Prastina Pacatus Messalinus, legate of Gallia Lugdunensis) and its contents, see M. Sordi, 'I nuovi decreti di Marco Aurelio contro i cristiani', *Studi Romani* 9 (1961), pp. 372 ff. and also in *Annales Valaisannes* (Société d'Histoire du Valais Romand), *Marc Aure*, ed. R. Klein (Darmstadt, 1979), pp. 184 ff.

20. Lucianus, *De Morte Peregrini*, 11, records that Christ was killed in Palestine because he had introduced this 'new cult' into the world. Aelius Aristides, *Orationes* XLVI (Dindorf 402), speaks of the Christians as the 'wicked ones in Palestine' who were leading the people away from Greek customs and no longer honouring the gods.

21. For the date of Polycarp's death, see M. Sordi, 'La data del martirio di Policarpo e di Pionio', *Rivista di Storia della Chiesa in Italia*, 15 (1961), pp. 277 ff.

22. On the questions raised by this rescript, see Sordi 'La data', pp. 281 ff. and *Il*

cristianesimo, pp. 167 ff. and 427. See also Keresztes, 'The Jews, the Christians', pp. 294 ff.

23. I would opt for interpolations rather than forgeries. A characteristic example is the first sentence of the rescript in which the Emperor says that it is 'up to the gods to keep watch so that these men do not escape punishment, because it is they, far more than you, who should punish those who do not wish to worship them' (Eusebius, *Hist. eccl.* IV. 13. 2). This statement, modelled of course on Tiberius' famous 'deorum iniurias, dis curae' (Tac.*Ann.* I. 73. 6), is typical in Roman political tradition. In the Paris codex at the foot of Justin's *Apologia*, after the mention of the punishment the gods will inflict, we find the addition 'if they could'.

24. Mention of the various earthquakes (Eusebius, *Hist. eccl.* IV. 13. 4) have come to us from pagan sources (*SHA Vita Antonini* 9; Dio, LXX. 4) and have been dated on the basis of Aristides, to the years 142/3, 147/8 and 151/2; cf. W. H. Waddington, *Mémoire sur la chronologie de la vie du rheteur Aelius Aristides* (Paris, 1867), pp. 40 ff.; cf. Keresztes, 'The Jews, the Christians', p. 293.

25. The text (Eusebius, *Hist. eccl.* IV. 13. 6) says 'elaunete kai diokete', using the technical terminology of the official right to search.

26. *Les martyres de Lyon (177)* (Paris, 1978). The source for the trial is the letter sent to the churches of Asia by the church of Lyons and Viennes, and quoted by Eusebius (*Hist. eccl.* V. 1. 2 ff.).

27. M. Sordi, 'La ricerca d'ufficio nel processo del 177' in *Les martyrs de Lyon* (see note 26), p. 177.

28. On the question of Celsus and his possible role as mouthpiece for Marcus Aurelius, see M. Sordi, 'Le polemiche intorno al cristianesimo nel II secolo e la loro influenza sugli sviluppi della politica imperiale verso la Chiesa', *Rivista di Storia della Chiesa in italia*, 16 (1962), pp. 17 ff. (with bibliography), and *Il cristianesimo*, pp. 179 ff. E. R. Dodds also emphasises the political aspects of the 'true doctrine' of Celsus in his *Pagans and Christians in an age of Anxiety: Some Aspects of Religious Experience from Marcus Aurelius to Constantine* (Wiles Lectures, 1964, pub. Cambridge, 1965). Dodds believes Celsus' work was aimed at encouraging the Christians to be better citizens.

29. *Meditations*, XI. 3; see Sordi, 'Le polemiche', pp.6 ff. G. Iossa, however, gives a different view in his *Giudei, pagani e cristiani*, (Naples, 1977), pp. 109 ff.

30. On the religious attitudes of the Christians during the second century and on the influence exerted by the Hebrew conception of martyrdom, see Frend, *Martyrdom and Persecution* pp. 18 ff.; on Montanism, its origins and its chronology, see also note 11 in Sordi's *Il cristianesimo*, pp. 467 ff. (with bibliography). On the social and revolutionary aspects of Montanism, see M. Mazza, *Lotte sociali e restaurazione autoritaria nel III secolo* (Facoltà di Lettere e Filosofia, University of Catania, 1970), pp. 535 ff. M. D. H. Kraft dedicated a paper to the problem of Montanism at Lyons, published in *Les martyrs de Lyon*, pp. 233 ff.

31. For a discussion of the extension of the right to search to include the *sacrilegi* (*Dig.* I. 18. 13 and XLVIII. 13. 4. 2) and the similarity between this report and that given by Melito (via Eusebius, *Hist. eccl.* IV. 26. 6) on the 'new decrees' which gave governors under Marcus Aurelius the right to search out Christians, see Sordi, 'I nuovi decreti', and *Il cristianesimo*, pp. 176 ff. and now in *Les martyrs de Lyon*, p. 179 and *Marc Aurel*, p. 176. On this question see also A. Wlosok in *Gymnasium* 82 (1975), pp. 117 ff. (D. Berwig, 'Mark Aurel und die Christen', (Diss. Munich,1970)).

32. Tertullian, *Apol.* II. 4; cf. Sordi, *Il cristianesimo*, p. 429.

33. See above.

34. Already in the epistle of the Church of Smyrna on the martyrdom of Polycarp, we see a critical attitude developing towards Montanism, or at least towards the tendencies which were to lead to Montanism. The same can be said of the controversy underlying the episode of Quintus Phrygius.

35. Of the four apologists who addressed Marcus Aurelius in these years, two, Apollinaris and Miltiades, are well known for their anti-Montanist position. For a discussion of the positions taken by the apologists on the various controversial points (loyalty to the empire, military service), see Sordi, 'Le polemiche', pp. 12 ff. and *Il cristianesimo*, pp. 185. ff. See also, especially for Melito's attitude, Speigl, *Der römische Staat*, pp. 170 ff.

36. Tertullian, *Apol.* v. 6. On this provision, see Sordi, *Il cristianesimo*, pp. 193 ff.

37. *Dig.* XLVII. 22. 1. gives us an account of the dispositions which made the *collegia tenuiorum* and those *religionis causa ipso facto* legitimate, and of the advantages granted to these *collegia* under the Severi. For a discussion of how the church made use of these dispositions, see Sordi, *Il cristianesimo*, pp. 468 ff. (with bibliography) and below.

38. For the possibility that the senator Apollonius (who died under Commodus) was a Christian, see M. Sordi, 'Un senatore cristiano dell'età di Commodo', *Epigraphica* 17 (1955), pp. 104 ff. E. Gabba disagrees ('Il processo di Apollonio' in *Mélanges . . . offerts à J. Carpocino* (Paris, 1966), pp. 397 ff.) but I do not find his arguments convincing. For Christian senators during the reign of Septimius Severus, see Tertullian, *Ad Scap.* IV. 6 (on the 'clarissimae feminae' and the 'clarissimi viri huius sectae'). A Christian formula, 'receptus ad Deum', appears in the funeral inscription of M. Aurelius Prosenes, *cubicularius* of Caracalla (*Inscriptiones Latinae Selectae (ILS)*. 1738 = *CIL* VI. 8498).

5   The *De Facto* Tolerance of the Severan Age

There seems to be some discrepancy between what we know of the general climate of tolerance under the Severi, and the account of anti-Christian persecution under Septimius Severus which we find both in the *Historia Augusta* and in later Christian sources.

The Supposed Edict of Septimius Severus against Christian Proselytism

Eusebius (*Hist. eccl.* VI. 1 ff.) speaks of a persecution of the churches under Septimius Severus and describes the results this persecution had in Egypt during the prefecture of Q. Maecius Laetus (201/2 AD) and that of his successor Subatianus Aquila (206–10; not, in fact Laetus' immediate successor, as Eusebius seems to think). A report of this persecution also comes to us from Sulpicius Severus (*Chronicles*, II. 32. 1–2), Orosius (VIII. 17. 4–5) and Jerome (*Chron. Hieron* (Helm) p. 212). In the *Historia Augusta* (*Vita Sev.* 17. 1), we find that Septimius Severus, during his visit to Palestine,[1] 'Palaestinis plurima iura fundavit. Iudaeas fieri sub gravi poena vetuit. Idem de Christianis sanxit.' The information in the *Historia Augusta* concerns converts to both Christianity and the Jewish faith; Eusebius' account of the persecution in Egypt centres on the catechism school of Alexandria, telling the story of Perpetua and Felicitas who, together with fellow *catechumeni*, died for the faith under the procurator Hilarianus, substitute for the governor Minucius Timinianus who had died during his term as proconsul, in 202 or 203. Putting together these two versions, historians have all agreed until recently that Septimius Severus' persecution was aimed essentially at putting a stop to Christian proselytism and propaganda first by preventing new conversions and then, above all, by attacking the new converts[2] ('Christianos fieri sub gravi poena vetuit'). This, then, would have been the content of Septimius Severus' edict. Breaking with the practice of inter-vention-by-rescript characteristic of the Antonine emperors, Septimius Severus would have made use of an edict to introduce the new policy which, clearly and openly hostile to the Christians, was to re-emerge in full force during the second half of the third century, after an interval of tolerance under his immediate successors.

In recent years, however, many historians[3] have contested this version of the events and now doubt whether a general persecution under Septimius Severus ever actually took place. The fact that the majority of the martyrs of this period were *catechumeni* is not necessarily a consequence of conscious decision on the part of the Emperor to strike at new converts rather than at established Christians; it simply means that in this period the role of catechumen was beginning to be part of the organisation of the church. And in fact it is not even true that the older Christians were not persecuted — Leonidas, Origen's father, also lost his life at this time, despite having been a Christian for many years. Neither is it true that the persecution was carried out systematically or without interruption as would be expected if an imperial edict were being enforced. In reality, it occurred sporadically and on a local level, as we can see from the events in Egypt, which did not happen at all as Eusebius would have us believe, with Subatianus Aquila as immediate successor to Maecius Laetus. In fact, the interval of persecution under Laetus was followed by a period of tolerance during the prefecture of his real successor, Claudius Julianus, under whom the Christians in Egypt were left in peace to reopen their school and Origen could once again hold his doctrine classes. Only when Aquila came to power some years later did persecution start again.[4]

To these arguments, we must add the fact that no contemporary writer, either pagan (Dio Cassius and Herodian) or Christian (Clement of Alexandria, Hippolytus and Tertullian), makes any mention of a general persecution under Septimius Severus. Nor is it simply a matter of an *argumentum e silentio* because the reports of both Tertullian and Hippolytus confirm that there were, indeed, local outbreaks of persecution, sometimes extremely violent, during the first part of Septimius Severus' reign. But their evidence contradicts the hypothesis of there having been an imperial edict on the subject. They themselves attribute the outbreaks to the usual problems of mass prejudice fomented by pagan or Jewish agitators, or by the personal religious zeal of a particular provincial governor. They exonerate the Emperor himself of any responsibility, and, indeed, they paint a picture of him as being by no means hostile to the Christians and even on occasion friendly towards them (Tertullian, *Ad Scapulam*, IV. 5–6).

When we remember the notorious severity and hostility of Hippolytus' attitude to the state, we must recognise that his evidence is particularly significant on this point. In his commentary on the Book of Daniel,[5] written some time around 202 when the persecution was particularly violent, he compares the Emperor to Darius who, fond of Daniel and hoping to save him, is forced by the satraps to throw Daniel to the lions in accordance with the law which forbade a subject to worship any god other than the king. When Daniel is miraculously saved, Darius rejoices (III. 31. 2 ff.). According to Hippolytus, then, Septimius Severus was, like Darius, not personally responsible for the persecutions of the time; responsibility was divided between, on the one hand, various governors and magistrates (the 'satraps' of the Bible, always ready to slander the faithful), and, on the other, the pagan and Jewish masses who were constantly spying on the Christians, making unexpected incursions into prayer meetings, and dragging the faithful before the tribunals, accusing them of being enemies to Caesar (ibid. I. 15 and 20). In his *Ad nationes*, and in the the later *Apologeticum* (written at the time of the Emperor's *vota decennalia* in the spring or summer of 202 AD[6]) and in his *Ad Scapulam* (written shortly after Septimius Severus' death), Tertullian paints a similar picture, in the *Ad nationes* (VII. 19) he reports on the assaults made against the Christians 'in ipsis arcanis congregationibus'; in the *Apologeticum* (XXXVII. 2) and the *Ad Scapulam* (III. 1) he writes of the popular uprisings organised against the Christians with the intention of forcing the magistrates to take more effective action against them; again in the *Ad Scapulam* (IV. 6), he mentions Septimius Severus' open opposition to one of these uprisings. He also quarrels with those who accuse the Christians of being enemies of the Emperor while they are in reality, he insists, the Emperor's most loyal subjects (*Apol.* XXXV). Responsibility for the trials and convictions of the Christians must be attributed, he says, solely to the magistrates.[7]

It is also Tertullian in his *De corona* (written in 211) who recounts how worried the African Christians were that an imprudent act by a Christian soldier might have repercussions on the 'tam bonam et tam longam pacem' (I. 5). In the year 202/3 Perpetua and Felicitas had been martyred in Africa and the same year saw the death of the Christians of Alexandria in Egypt (Eusebius is our source); and yet, in 211, even those who had personally witnessed the events called Septimius Severus' reign a period of stability and peace for the church. In the same way, Commodus' reign had also been judged stable and peaceful, according to the anonymous anti-Montanist writer quoted by Eusebius (*Hist. eccl.* v. 16. 19), despite the persecutions of Arrius Antoninus in Asia and Vigellius Saturninus in Africa. Evidently, for those who were there at the time, the serious troubles of 202 and 203 were taken as purely local events and not as indictions of a general persecution, desired by the Emperor and ordered by an imperial edict.

In fact, the whole question of this edict (which only the *Historia Augusta* mentions) is full of pitfalls. For example, what sense would there be in issuing an edict threatening grave penalties for Christian converts when Christianity had in any case been punishable by death since the first century, even for those merely born of Christian parents? Furthermore, by placing the prohibitions *Judaeos fieri* and *Christianos fieri* on the same terms, the 'edict' of the *Historia Augusta* presupposes a historically and juridically impossible identification of Christianity, *superstitio illicita*, with Judaism, a *religio licita* since the times of Caesar and Augustus. And, indeed, on the basis of this comparison we can go on to prove the inaccuracy of the whole of this report. The regulation which forbade the Jews to make converts was issued, not by Septimius Severus, but by Antoninus Pius (*Dig.* xLVIII. 8. 11; see Paul, *Sententiae*, v. 22. 3–4) as part of his policy of returning to the Jews the right to worship according to their own traditions, a right which Hadrian had proscribed. During Septimius Severus' reign this regulation had fallen into disuse, so much so, in fact, that, during the so-called 'persecutions' of Severus, Donninus converted to the Jewish faith to avoid being convicted as a Christian (Eus. *Hist. eccl.* vi. 12. 1). Septimius Severus and his successors erected monuments in Galilee in honour of the Jewish communities; the *Digest* (xxvii. 1. 15.66 and L. 2. 3. 3) tells of the exemption from pagan religious functions of Jews employed in the public sector. Both these facts confirm the tolerant and even favourable attitude shown by the Emperor towards the followers of the Hebrew faith and remove any residual doubts on the subject left by the report in the *Historia Augusta*. We can thus conclude that Septimius Severus did not issue an edict against either Jews or Christians. The question which remains to be asked is why later pagan and Christian sources should have reported persecution during this period.

From the point of view of the Christian writers (Eusebius and those writing after him), the events which occurred in Africa and

Egypt and under Septimius Severus suffice to explain how a few local episodes of persecution could be transformed into evidence of a general persecution throughout the empire. News of the martyrdom of Perpetua and Felicitas and the tragic events at the school of Alexandria, both occurring in 202 AD and both extremely violent, spread throughout the Christian world and even led some to believe that the Anti-Christ was about to appear.[8] We should also bear in mind another significant fact: in my opinion, the 'sollemnia Caesarum', the 'vota et gaudia Caesarum' of which Tertullian speaks in his *Apologia*, are the *vota decennalia* of the year 202, which, in their turn, coincided with the return of Septimius Severus to Rome, the marriage of Caracalla, the *natalis* of Geta and the third *liberalitas*.[9] Nothing would be more natural than that there should be an increase in anti-Christian feeling under these circumstances. During the imperial festivities and their religious ceremonies, the abstention of the Christians would be more than usually apparent and would appear more than usually scandalous to the pagans. This would be particularly true in Africa, Septimius Severus' home province, where a sense of local patriotism gave the cult of the emperor an added importance. Here, the Christians' abstention provoked the masses to a furor of persecutory zeal and the authorities were importuned to take decisive action against them. Crowd psychology naturally fused religious and political crimes into one, with the result that the Christians were called, Tertullian tells us, 'hostes publici'. The most fanatically anti-Christian and zealous of the magistrates were only too pleased to take advantage of the wider powers they had been given by Marcus Aurelius, and 'partim animis propriis partim legibus obsequentes' (Tertullian, *Apol.* xxxvii. 2), but above all in response to public feeling [10] they proceeded to search out, try and convict the Christians. It is interesting to note, however, that even here the sentences were carried out according to the old laws (Tertullian explicitly mentions that Trajan's rescript was still valid), and not in obedience to some new edict, or on the express desire of the Emperor himself. Indeed, the Emperor had shown his basic goodwill towards the Christians on more than one occasion and was evidently convinced that there was no political threat coming from that quarter.[11]

As far as the erroneous report in the *Historia Augusta* is concerned, it probably has a different origin. We have already seen that it is characterised by a mistaken assimilation of the Christians and the Jews in its account of the Severan legislation. It is interesting to note that we find a similar situation — but this time with the Emperor's blessing and with a detailed knowledge of the differences between the two religions — in four of the six mentions of Christianity to be found in the *Vita Serveri Alexandri*[12] in the same *Historia Augusta*, as well as in the *Life of Elagabalus* (3. 4) on the subject of his decision to unite in his temple the religions of the Jews, the Samaritans and the Christians. Thus it seems likely that we are dealing with a fixed pattern of interpretation which tends to see all the Severan emperors' dealings with the Christians and Jews in one light. In the *Vitae* of Elagabalus and Alexander Severus, the tendency is towards tolerance, however, while only with Septimius Severus do we find the insistence — certainly mistaken as far as the Jews were concerned — that the Emperor's attitude was hostile. Perhaps we might add something more on the characteristics of the source from which the *Historia Augusta* took its information. The reports of severe punishments for Jews and Christians (*Vita Sev.* 17. 1) are linked, as we have seen, with a journey to Palestine undertaken by Septimius Severus, a journey whose date was erroneously changed from 199 (when it actually took place) to 201/2 AD. Its purpose was, apparently, to provide new legislation for the local populations. This account, however, seems to be a duplicate of another episode reported in the same *Vita Severi* (14. 6), which gives a far more favourable interpretation of the Emperor's behaviour towards the inhabitants of Palestine.[13]

The author of the *Vita* in fact probably obtained his information from two different sources, one of which saw the new regulations as restrictive and the other as lenient. From inscriptions it would seem that these regulations had to do with the military and administrative reorganisation of the province of Syria–Palestine, and their aim would have been to avoid a recurrence of the kind of revolt which had taken place under Pescennius Niger.[14]

It would thus appear that our author took his information on the Christians from a source which tended to show Septimius Severus' policies in Palestine in a very severe light. Only a few pages earlier (ibid. 16. 7) our author gives a report of a Jewish triumph by the same emperor which, as has been proved,[15] is entirely without foundation and has to be taken as the product of a forger's imagination. The same hand is certainly responsible for the report on the anti-Christian, anti-Jewish edict, which looks like a clumsy copy of the accounts, similar if opposing in content, to be found in the *Lives* of the other Severi.

De Facto Toleration from Septimius Severus to Elagabalus

Having dealt with the question of a possible general persecution, we can see that Septimius Severus' reign was, on the whole, a period of religious tolerance of a 'bona et longa pax' in the relationship between the Christian religion and the Roman state. There were, undoubtedly, brief intervals of local persecution, and some of these were violent, but, as in the second century, these were provoked by the hostility of the masses and were only allowed where the local governor wanted to prove his zeal by attacking a category which public opinion accused of being enemies of the emperor because of their refusal to worship him. At the time of Septimius Severus, the chief pretext for taking action against the Christians was certainly this question of the cult of the emperor. It was, however, a pretext rather than a genuine reason; the Emperor himself had clearly shown that he did not consider a refusal to worship him a particularly grave fault in the Christians, and, indeed, had personally defended from the fury of the crowds various Christian men and women of the senatorial class, knowing as he did how politically loyal they were.[16] Neither was this question taken as the formal motivation for bringing charges against the Christians, who continued to be accused and convicted on the basis of ancient anti-Christian laws and Trajan's rescript. The Christians themselves, however, realised how serious the consequences would be if their absence from public festivities were to be interpreted as reflecting their attitude to the state, and after the episodes of 202/3 they did their best to clear up all misunderstandings on this point. From now onwards, they took part in any and all public ceremonies which were not in direct conflict with their principles. Tertullian himself, by now a Montanist, tells us with indignation (*De idololatria*, xv. 1 ff.) that on the occasion of the *gaudia publica* of 211 or 212 — perhaps in honour of the accession of Caracalla and Septimus Geta, or for the general amnesty declared by Caracalla after Geta's death — the Christians of Carthage were the first to decorate their houses with lanterns and bay boughs. In answer to their more severely orthodox critics, the Christians said they were only giving to Caesar what was Caesar's. In the *De corona* already quoted above, written while Geta was still ruling with his brother in 211, Tertullian also notes with disgust that the Carthaginian Christians disapproved of the soldier who, in the camp of the Third Augustan legion, had in an excess of scruple refused to place the crown on his head and had broken a military rule because 'de habitu interrogatus nomini' (by all the Christians) 'negotium fecerit', thereby endangering 'tam bonam et longam pacem' (ɪ. 4–5).

As we have already seen, the Christians had been tolerated since Marcus Aurelius' time in direct proportion to the extent to which they were prepared to participate in the public life of the empire without allowing their prejudices to interfere. It is for this reason that the ideological battles fought by Tertullian during these years in the *De corona*, the *De idololatria* and the *De fuga* cannot be seen merely in terms of a confrontation between strictness and laxity. The real battle was between the Montanists' desire to enclose Christianity in a state of sectarian isolation, and the Church's intention of taking part in the political and social life of the empire (as long as this did not actually entail a betrayal of principle), in a conciliatory spirit which said much for their prudent and responsible sense of reality. This line of conduct, a kind of tacit concordat between church and state, allowed the Christians to live their community life freely and to organise their increasingly numerous 'assemblies' (Tertullian speaks of *turbae* (*De fuga*, 14. 1)) as and when they wanted. Indeed, somewhere between 200 and 220, possibly in 216, a council of 71 bishops could meet in Africa under the presidency of Agrippinus. Some time before 115, during Caracalla's reign, the legate of Arabia could send to the Prefect of Egypt and the Bishop of Alexandria to ask for Origen to be sent to him as he wanted to hear him preach. The civil and religious authorities are approached each in the language appropriate to their functions, a state of affairs that would be inconceivable in a state dedicated to persecution, and which can be taken as truly symbolic of the atmosphere of the times (Eusebius, *Hist. eccl.* vɪ. 19. 15). The Legate of Arabia was able to act through official channels because his interest in Christian theology was by now shared by many members of the court itself. It was during this period that Bardesanes dedicated his dialogue on destiny and free will to Caracalla, or perhaps Elagabalus,[17] in the same way that Hippolytus was later to dedicate a *Protecticus* to Severina (probably Aquilia Severa, the vestal married by Elagabalus) and a tract on the resurrection to the Empress Julia Mamaea, mother of Alexander Severus. The school of Alexandria which so interested the Legate of Arabia was, at this time, attended by many cultivated and learned pagans (Origen, see Eusebius, vɪ. 19. 12); and indeed not many years later it was not just a provincial governor but the Empress Julia Mamaea herself who summoned the

celebrated Origen to Antioch, where she was stationed with the
army in preparation for the war in the East.

The example of tolerance given by the Severan dynasty did not,
however, put a stop to local episodes of persecution, even under
Caracalla. Tertullian refers to one such episode in his *Ad Scapulam*,
addressed to P. Julius Scapula Tertullus, the proconsul governing
Africa from 211 to 213 AD. In this work (IV. 8) we also find references to acts of persecution carried out by the commander of the
Third Augustan legion and the governor of Mauritania. It may well
be that the episode of the crown mentioned above influenced
Scapula to a certain extent; but it does not seem to have had repercussions in other parts of the empire. Most historians now agree
that, even when Roman citizenship was extended to all the subjects
of the empire in 212 (the famous *Constitutio Antoniniana*), this was
not taken as an excuse for a general increase in persecution, as was
thought in the past.[18]

When the dynasty came back into power after the brief reign of
Macrinus, this climate of tolerance bordering on favour increased
rather than diminished, first under Elagabalus and then under
Alexander Severus, with their grandmother Julia Maesa and their
respective mothers Julia Soaemias and Julia Mamaea. Elagabalus
honoured the sun god above all others and subordinated all the
other gods of the empire and all other forms of worship to his
supreme deity. At the same time, the young Emperor's immature
personality and oriental upbringing (he came from a priestly family
of Emesa) led him into various forms of deviant behaviour and
excess. Paradoxically, the state of affairs actually favoured the
development of the religious policies originally elaborated by Julia
Domna's circle and adopted by Caracalla (who called himself
'philoserapis' and worshipped Serapis as 'Zeus, Serapis, Helios,
invincible lord of the world'). According to this policy, syncretism
and a process of subordination were to transform Roman
polytheism into the worship of one supreme deity, the *summus deus*
of which all other gods were no more than manifestations or single
aspects.[19] It was natural that in Elagabalus' new religion a place
should be found for the Hebrew religion and Christianity together
with the ancient gods of the empire, and that symbols of all these
were to be transferred to the temple he erected to his god on the
Palatine (*Historia Augusta*: *Vita Heliogabali* 3. 4).

In the year of the assassination of Elagabalus, that is 222 AD, Pope
Callistus and the priests Calepodius and Asclepiades were also

killed during a popular uprising in Rome. In the Acts of their martyrdom, written later but not without some credible details, we are told that the bodies of the two priests were dragged round the city before being thrown into the Tiber, and that Callistus, having been thrown out of the window of his house into a well (on the site of the present-day Santa Maria in Trastevere), was then stoned there. Given the similarity between the date and manner of death of the head of the church and those of the Emperor and his mother (dragged through the streets of Rome by the soldiers and the crowd before being thrown into the Tiber) it is tempting to see something more than a coincidental resemblance between the riot in which Callistus and the two priests lost their lives and the assassination of Elagabalus and Soaemias. In the eyes of the mob the Christians, who had been favoured by Elagabalus in the past, may well have seemed to be the Emperor's accomplices. Be that as it may, however, popular feeling had no effect on the attitude of the state towards the Christians. As we have already seen, Elagabalus and his mother had followed the best traditions of the dynasty towards the Christians, a line which was to be developed systematically and consistently by Alexander Severus and Julia Mamaea.

Alexander Severus' Policy Towards the Christians

I have already mentioned that the *Historia Augusta* gives several accounts of Alexander's pro-Christian, pro-Jewish outlook. According to the author of the *Vita Alexandri*, the Emperor was tolerant towards both Jews and Christians and himself included Christ and Abraham among his household gods, together with Orpheus, Apollonius of Tyana and the greatest among his predecessors. As Hadrian had done before him, he even wanted to erect a temple to Christ and to include him among the gods of Rome. So great was his respect for the Jewish and Christian ecclesiastical organisations that he took some of their practices as examples to be followed when choosing provincial governors and magistrates (for example, the practice of the *probatio* for priests). When a dispute arose between the Roman Christians and the *popinarii* as to who should occupy a public building, Alexander Severus intervened with a rescript in favour of the Christians, saying it was better for the premises to be given to them than to the 'popinarii ut quemadmodum illic deus colatur'. He also knew of the golden rule of the

Christians — do not do unto others what you do not want done unto
you — and adopted it as his favourite motto, having it inscribed on
the walls of his palace and on public buildings and having it
proclaimed in the tribunal.[20]

Quite apart from any possible moral scheme or personal interest
the author of the *Historia Augusta* may have been following when
he emphasised the tolerance of the pagan Alexander's attitude to
the Christians,[21] the fact remains that this late compiler of the *Vita
Alexandri* does no more than repeat what the Christian writers
themselves explicitly state and what all sorts of evidence go to
confirm. We have already seen that Hippolytus dedicated a tract on
the resurrection to Julia Mamaea, a woman who, according to
Eusebius, was deeply interested in Origen's teaching (*Hist. eccl.* VI.
21. 3–4), as well as being extremely pious (VI. 21. 3) and whom
Orosius goes so far as to call a Christian (VII. 18. 7). It is worth
adding that, during this period, the erudite Christian, Sextus Julius
Africanus, dedicated his *Kestoi* to Alexander and founded the
Pantheon library in Rome on the Emperor's request. This fact
confirms what both Eusebius (ibid. VI. 28) and Orosius (VII. 19. 2)
had to say on the progressive christianisation of the court of the last
of the Severi. By now, the Christian religion was being practised
openly throughout the empire. It appears that the chapel of Dura
Europus, the first real 'Christian church' of which we have news,
dates from the period of Alexander Severus and was, perhaps, built
for the Christian soldiers of the Roman army stationed in that
area.[22] The unequivocally Christian inscriptions of Phrygia and Asia
Minor, with the so-called Eumeneia formula, also date from this
period. In this general climate, the sympathy and even admiration
which the *Historia Augusta* attributes to Alexander's dealings with
the Christians come into focus and can be seen as reflecting a precise
historical situation. This last of the Severan emperors meticulously
restored the traditions of Roman worship after the deviations of
Elagabalus, but at the same time he imitated his predecessor in his
protection of the Jews and Christians. He combined a sincere
feeling for the Divine with a lively moral sense and we can say that,
under him, the religious policy of the Severi reached its most refined
and subtle expression. He was deeply convinced of the essential
one-ness of the deity or at least convinced of the existence of one
God, predominant over all the various attributes and manifestations of godhead. With this *summus deus* of the many names, he
hoped to offer the empire the possibility of finding a new spiritual

unity to which everyone, pagans, Christians and Jews alike, could see themselves as belonging, 'ut quemadmodum deus colatur'. Here, the Severan ideal of syncretism is seen at its highest and, perhaps, most conscious stage of development.

This movement towards syncretism, with its ideals of religious tolerance, was seen by the most perspicacious Christians as actually constituting a danger to their faith. At the same time, the more traditional and orthodox of the pagans saw it as a danger to the empire. In the year of Alexander's death, 235 AD, Origen reaffirmed in his *Exhortation to Martyrdom* (Chapter 46) the profound difference that existed between the One True God of the Christians and the vague supreme deity of the pagans. Only a few years previously, while Alexander was still alive, the pagan historian Dio Cassius, in his famous speech to Augustus (LII. 36. 1–2), had Maecenas give the advice that the gods should be worshipped 'according to native custom', that others should be forced to do likewise and that those who worshipped according to foreign customs should be hated and punished: 'and this not only for the sake of the gods but because people who introduce new gods and persuade many to adopt foreign customs are a danger to the monarchy.' Using Maecenas as his mouthpiece, it was perhaps Dio Cassius himself, senator and consul, who was covertly suggesting to the tolerant Alexander the need for intolerance towards foreign religious practices, and it is not impossible that the foreign cult against which Alexander was being warned was, in fact, Christianity.[23] From the passage of the *Historia Augusta* already cited (*Vita Alex.* 43. 7) it appears that Alexander, like Hadrian before him, wanted to go a step further than merely tolerating the Christians and hoped to give them official recognition, removing once and for all any legal grounds for persecution. However, he was prevented from doing this 'ab his qui consulentes sacra reppererant omnes Christianos futuros si id fecisset et reliqua templa deseranda'. As I have suggested more fully elsewhere, this passage may echo the same preoccupations as those brought forward by Dio; and the young Alexander would have been hindered from abrogating the old anti-Christian laws[24] by his desire not to upset the senatorial class, made up for the most part of the old school of conservative pagans.

But even without an abrogation of the old laws or an act of formal recognition for their religion, the Christians were by now becoming well integrated into the life of the empire at all levels, including that of the ruling class. Not much more than 20 years after Alexander's death, in 258 AD, Valerian listed with great precision the *senatores*, the *egregii viri* and the *equites Romani* among the Christians he intended to punish: this leads us to believe that there must have been a fairly high proportion of Christians among the ruling classes of the empire at that time. Because of the lack of contemporary evidence, these Christians must remain nameless and faceless, but, along with the descendants of the senatorial families that had embraced Christianity in the first century, we catch glimpses of members of the new ruling class, made up of equestrian families of eastern extraction. The rise of this class had been encouraged by the Severi (and, indeed, by the last of the Antonines), and we know that it was the East which had produced the greatest number of Christian sympathisers and converts between the end of the second and the middle of the third centuries. Domitius Philippus, a native of Lycia, prefect of the guards and acting prefect of Egypt under Gordian III, was a Christian;[25] so was M. Julius Philippus, an Arab from Bosra and praetorian prefect under the same emperor.[26] They are typical of the new equestrian class, less tied to traditional customs and beliefs than the senators and closer than these to the seat of imperial power which, thanks to the changes taking place at all levels of political life, was assuming ever greater significance and weight during this period. Both these men were, as we have seen, connected with the East and it was in the East that Christianity had, since the first century, made the most converts. From the East came, at the time of Commodus, the senator Apollonius (perhaps one of the Claudii Apollonii of Smyrna); from the East came, at the time of Alexander Severus, the Emperor's friend and counsellor Sextus Julius Africanus who was Palestinian; from the East came, some years later under Valerian, the senator Asturius, either governor of Arabia himself or son of the governor of Arabia Bassaeus Astur.

During the first half of the third century, then, christianisation and orientalisation of the empire go hand in hand.

The Anti-Christian Reaction of Maximinus of Thrace

A first and still uncoordinated and clumsy reaction to the steadily increasing influence of Christianity at all levels of the state and the court occurred under Maximinus the Thracian, the Emperor elected at Magonza in 235 by the same troops who had assassinated

Alexander and Mamaea. According to one hypothesis, based on a statement of Eusebius (*Hist. eccl.* vi. 28), Maximinus issued an edict against the Christian clergy in which he 'ordered to be put to death' only those church leaders who were responsible for making the gospel known. This version, however, differs from that of a contemporary bishop, Phirmilian of Caesarea, who, writing 22 years after 235 AD, describes the persecution in Cappadocia under Maximinus as having been a purely local affair (Cyprian, *Epistles*, 75. 10). In fact in the present day few historians continue to sustain the hypothesis of an imperial edict.[27] On the other hand, the first part of Eusebius' account would seem to be much more interesting as well as being easier to verify. According to Eusebius, Maximinus' persecution sprang from his 'resentment of the House of Alexander, made up for the most part of Christians'. This is confirmed by two other sources: Herodian (vii, 1. 3–4) says that Maximinus 'immediately' eliminated all Alexander's friends, senators and servants alike (and here, his mention of the *therapeia pasa* corresponds with Eusebius' mention of the *oikos* of Alexander, made up for the most part of Christians); the *Historia Augusta* (*Vita Maximini*, 9. 7–8) speaks of the suppression of 'omnes Alexandri ministros' and of the suspicion under which all Alexander's friends fell.

We can probably also include in this 'purge' the deportation of the Bishop of Rome, Pontianus, and his rival Hippolytus, who were sent to Sardinia on 28 September 235. (Once there, the two made peace and Hippolytus urged his followers to heal the schism which had divided the church in Rome since the days of Callistus.) It is known that Hippolytus was on good terms with Julia Mamaea, a fact which would explain why he was arrested, and his arrest together with that of Pontianus was in all probability what gave rise to Eusebius' theory of an imperial edict issued directly against the leaders of the Church.

Originating in personal and political motives rather than religious ones, Maximinus' actions against the Christians cannot be seen in terms of a real persecution and, in any case, his action did not last long. With the accession of Gordian III, the tolerance of the Severi was once again established, a tolerance that was destined to last throughout his reign, from 238 to 244 AD.

Notes

1. In the *Historia Augusta*, this journey follows immediately on Caracalla's assumption of the *toga virilis* in Antioch in 201 and his nomination as consul on 1 January 202. In fact, the visit to Antioch took place on Septimius Severus' return journey from Egypt rather than on his way there. He reached Egypt on December of the year 199 and left by sea towards the end of the 200. Therefore, his visit to Palestine must have taken place at the end of 199, not in 201 or 202.

2. For a general résumé of modern opinion on Septimius Severus' attitude to the Christians, see K. H. Schwarte, 'Das angebliche Christengesetz des Septimius Severus', *Historia*, 12 (1963), pp. 185 ff. For the traditional opinion which attributes a persecutory edict to Septimius Severus, see K. Baus, 'Von der Urgemeinder zur frühchristlichen Grosskirche' and in the *Handbook of Church History*, trans. and ed. by H. Jedin and J. Dolan (Freiburg 1965); W. H. C. Frend, *Martyrdom and Persecution in the Early Church: a Study of a Conflict from the Maccabees to Donatus* (Oxford 1965) pp. 319 ff., and 'A Severian Persecution' in *Studi in Onore di M. Pellegrino* (Turin, 1975), pp. 470 ff.; P. Kawerau, *Geschichte der Alten Kirche* (Marburg, 1967), p. 86; P. Keresztes, 'The Emperor Septimius Severus: A Precursor of Decius', *Historia*, 19 (1970), pp. 565 ff.

3. Schwarte, 'Das angebliche', pp. 185 ff.; M. Sordi, *Il cristianesimo e Roma* (Bologna, 1965), pp. 217 ff.; J. Molthagen, 'Der römische Staat und die Christen im weiten und dritten Jahrhundert', *Hypomnemata*, 28 (Göttingen, 1970), pp. 38 ff.; J. Speigl, 'Die Christenpolitik des Septimius Severus', *Munch. Theol. Zeitschr.*, 20 (1969), pp. 181 ff.

4. Cf. Molthagen, 'Der römische Staat', pp. 40 ff. On the chronological succession of the Prefects of Egypt in these years, see F. Grosso, 'Claudio Giuliano, prefetto d'Egitto dal 203 al 205/206', *Rendiconti dell'Accademia Nazionale dei Lincei*, 22 (1967), pp. 55 ff.

5. On the question of the identity of Hippolytus, a collection of papers by various authors has now been published under the title *Ricerche su Ippolito, Studia Ephemeridis Augustinianum* 13 (Rome, 1977). It is particularly important to distinguish in this context between Hippolytus, the author of the *Philosophumena* and the work *On the Resurrection*, and Hippolytus the author of the *Comment on Daniel* and on *The Anti-Christ* – see V. Loi in *Ricerche su Ippolito*, p. 72. The first certainly lived in Rome between the pontificate of Zephyrinus and the reign of Alexander Severus, and he wrote nothing after the year 235 (see p. 84). According to Loi he was certainly the Roman presbyter referred to in the works listed on the statue (ibid. p. 86). The author of the works belonging to 'Block B' to which the *Comment on Daniel* belongs was, Loi believes, a bishop of the Christian East who lived in the first half of the third century AD and was a contemporary of the Roman presbyter. Simonetti (ibid. p. 125) reaches the same conclusion, studying the *Contra Noetum*. The fact that the author of the *Comment on Daniel* came from the East does not in any way diminish the significance of his writing, in the context of this work. In any case, according to the evidence he was a contemporary of the Hippolytus of Rome.

6. See Sordi, *Il cristianesimo*, p. 474 (note 13) and p. 226 ff. for the reasons for choosing the year 202 in preference to 197.

7. Tertullian, *Apol.* I. 1 'Romani imperii antistites'; *Ad Scap.* (P. Julius Scapula Tertullus, proconsul of Africa from 211 to 213).

8. A Christian chronographer, Judas, mentioned by Eusebius (*Hist. eccl.* VI 7), ended his chronicle at the tenth year of Septimius Severus' reign (201/2), so certain was he that the Anti-Christ was about to appear.

9. Tertullian, *Apol.* XXXV, 5, on the 'Sollemnia Caesarum'; ibid. XXXV., 4, the 'vota et gaudia Caesarum'; cf. Sordi, *Il cristianesimo*, pp.475–6.

10. Tertullian, *Apol.* III. 2: 'Quod odio publico necessarium est.'

11. Even more significant than the episode of Torpacius Proculus or the fact of Caracalla's Christian wet-nurse (Tert. *Ad Scap.* IV. 5) is, to my mind, Septimius Severus' attitude to the Christian senators when these were attacked by the crowd: 'Sed et clarissimas feminas et clarissimos viros Severus sciens huius sectae esse non modo non laesit verum et testimonio exornavit et populo furenti in nos palam restitit' (*Ad Scap.* IV. 6.). We do not know precisely when this event took place, but it could well be that it belongs to the period of Septimius Severus' journey to Africa in 203/4 which followed the outbreak of persecution in 202/3. We certainly know that after 203 the persecution lost its impetus and this fact might be explained by the Emperor's intervention.

12. *Vita Severi Alexandri* 22. 4; 29. 2; 45. 6; 51. 7.

13. *Vita Sev.* 14. 6: 'Palaestinis poenam remisit quam ob causam Nigri meruerant.'

14. On the action taken by Septimius Severus in Palestine, see M. Sordi, 'Giudea, Siria, Palestina all'epoca di Settimio Severo', *Bollettino di Studi Latini*, 1 (1971), pp. 251 ff. Recently the subject has also been studied by A. Rabello, 'The Legal Condition of Jews in the Roman Empire', *ANRW* II. 30 (1980), p. 698, where the author underlines the parallels between the *Vita Severi* 17. 1 and the *Vita Alex.* 22. 4.

15. J. Hasebroeck, *Untersuchungen zur Geschichte des Kaisers Septimius Severus* (Heidelburg, 1921).

16. See above. For Christian loyalty to the emperor, see Tertullian, *Apol.* XXXIII. 1 ('noster est magis Caesar a nostro Deo constitutus'); cf also ibid. 35.

17. In his 'La democratizzazione della cultura nel "Basso Impero"' (*XIth Congrès International des Sciences Historiques*, *Rapports* II (Stockholm and Uppsala, 1960), p. 37), S. Mazzarino suggests that it was Caracalla to whom Bardesanes' dialogue was dedicated (possibly the same as the 'Book of the Laws of Countries'). Eusebius (*Hist. eccl.* IV. 30. 2) and Jerome (*De viris illustribus*, 33) mistakenly thought the dialogue was dedicated to Marcus Aurelius, and date Bardesanes accordingly. In fact, Bardesanes was a contemporary of Caracalla and Elagabalus. It may be that the dialogue was actually supposed to have Elagabalus as its interlocutor (his name was Varius Avitus before his accession to the throne); cf. Sordi, *Il cristianesimo*, pp. 434–5. On Bardesanes, see also M. Mazza 'Lotte sociali', *restaurazione autoritaria nel III secolo* pp. 552 ff.

18. In E. Perrot's 'Sur l'Edit de Caracalla de 212 et les persécutions contre les Chrétiens' (*Revue Histoire de Droit Francais et Etranger*, 4th series, 3 (1924), p. 367 ff.), the author claims that the *Constitutio Antoniniana* opened the way to a general persecution of the Christians. H. Grégoire, P. Orgels, J. Moreau, A. Maricq in 'Les Persécutions dans l'empire Romain' (*Mem. de la Cl. des Lettres de l'Acad. de Belgique* (Brussels, 1951)), refute this theory, pp. 119 ff., n. 35, pp. 121 ff., n. 37.

19. On the subject of solar religion, see L. De Giovanni, *Constantino e il mondo pagano* (Naples, 1977), pp. 110 ff.

20. *Vita Sev. Alex.* 22. 4; 29. 2; 43. 6; 45. 6; 49. 6; 51. 7. On the question of the inscription of Salona, which I believe belongs to the time of Alexander Severus, see M. Sordi, 'A proposito di un'iscrizione di Salona', *Rivista di Filologia e Istr. Class.* (1961), pp. 301 ff. See also O. Montevecchi 'Nomen Christianum' in *Paradoxos politeia, studi patristici in onore di G. Lazzati* (Milan, 1970) p. 490.

21. On this question see S. Settis, 'Severo Alessandro e i suoi lari', *Athenaeum*, 50 (1972), pp. 237 ff.

22. On the chapel at Dura Europus see A. Quacquarelli, 'Note sugli edifici di culto prima di Constantino', *Vetera Christianorum*, 14 (1977), pp. 243–4. He believes it could have been a synagogue transformed into a Christian church.

23. For the significance in the third century of the speech of Maecenas in Dio, see Sordi, *Il cristianesimo*, pp. 244 ff.; Molthagen, 'Der römische Staat', pp. 76 ff.

24. It was during these years that Ulpian, praetorian prefect and imperial counsellor until 228, collected these laws in the VII book of the *De officio proconsulis*

(*apud* Lactantius, *De divin. inst.* v. 2).

25. On the question of Cn. Domitius Philippus' faith, see M. Sordi, 'Un martire romano della persecuzione di Valeriano' *Rivista di storia della chiesa in Italia*, 33 (1979), pp. 40 ff.

26. On the question of the religion of M. Julius Philippus, the future Emperor Philip the Arab, see below.

27. That Maximinus' persecution consisted of a simple purge of Alexander's friends is maintained by: G. M. Bersanetti, *Studi sull'imperatore Masimino de Trace* (Rome, 1940), p. 96; Grégoire p. 40, and Moreau, p. 89 in 'La persécution du christianisme dans l'Empire Romain' in *Coll. Mythes et Religions* 32 (Paris), 1956. That it consisted of a few localised incidents of persecution is claimed by: L. De Regibus, *La crisi del III secolo* (Genoa, 1945), p. 23 and *Politica e religione da Augusto a Constantino* (Genoa, 1953), p. 104. For more recent ideas on the subject, see: A. Bellezza, 'Massimino il Trace', *Istit. di Storia Antica dell'Università di Genova*, 5 (1964), pp. 122 ff. (with bibliography); Sordi, *Il cristianesimo*, pp. 247 ff.; A. Lippold, 'Maximinus Thrax und die Christen', *Historia*, 24. (1975), pp. 479 ff.

6   Philip the Arab and Decius: The First Christian Emperor and the 'Pagan Restoration'

At the end of the second century, Marcus Aurelius and Celsus had accused the Christians of keeping themselves apart from public life and had asked them to collaborate in it more fully. Now, in the new atmosphere of tolerance which lasted from Commodus to the Gordians (with the exception of Maximinus' brief reign), the situation was reversed. Seeing the enthusiasm with which the emperors and empresses viewed Christianity, the more conservative elements of society began to fear that, far from retiring from public life, the Christians were in fact becoming all too active in ever greater numbers and at all levels of the life of the empire. As the *Historia Augusta* relates on the subject of those who tried to prevent Alexander's accession, the fear was that everyone, including the Emperor and the state itself, would become converted to Christianity and that the old religion would be abandoned completely.

Philip the Arab and Christianity

When the *consulentes sacra* (probably the haruspices) warned the young Alexander that the empire would shortly become Christian, the coming to the throne of the first Christian emperor was, in fact, not far off. Thirteen years after the death of the last of the Severi, in the year 244, the Christian M. Julius Philippus, successor to and former praetorian prefect of Gordian, came to the throne. He was an Arab, a native of Bosra, which already in the first decades of the third century was the seat of a flourishing church under the bishopric of Beryllus, and of a school of theology. Because of the deviations of this school both in matters of Christology and on the immortality of the soul, a synod had been convened and Origen himself had intervened to correct their errors. Both Philip and his wife Otacilia Severa corresponded with the great theologian.[1]

Rumour had it that Philip had been responsible for the military uprising which had led to the death of his predecessor Gordian III during his campaign in Persia. It is interesting to see that in Eusebius' account (*Hist. eccl.* vi. 34), the news of Philip's having been a Christian is linked with the news (doubted, incidentally, by Eusebius himself) of the first public penitence to be inflicted on an emperor by a bishop. It is understandable that Eusebius, in his capacity as ecclesiastical adviser to Constantine, should have had some doubts on the subject — it may well be that Constantine himself put off his baptism until the eve of his death to avoid just this kind of situation. But Eusebius' doubts were probably unfounded as we also hear of Philip's penance from another source. John Chrysostom (*De Sancto Babyla in Julian.* 6), quotes the Antiochan tradition according to which Philip made his penance in that city, and attributes the initiative for it to the Bishop Babyla, a contemporary of Philip's who died under Decius. We cannot, moreover, take the *logos* of this information as being an early version of Theodosius' famous penance, because, as Eusebius' account makes clear, the story of Philip's was in circulation at least half a century earlier.[2] I personally believe the story to be true and that Philip did penance in the spring of 244 AD when, after eliminating Gordian, the new Emperor might well have found himself in Antioch.[3] If this episode did take place, it shows that the steady growth of Christianity throughout the empire was creating new problems for the church. Evidently, the idea that, as far as faith and morals were concerned, the Emperor was 'intra Ecclesiam non supra Ecclesiam',[4] was not a discovery made by St Ambrose after the empire had been Christian for a good 70 years; it was a problem which had already presented itself to the church from the moment when, in a predominantly pagan world, a Christian emperor first ascended the throne of the Caesars. As in the case of Theodosius, the Bishop's decision to impose penance on Philip was provoked by a public crime rather than a personal one (in the case of Theodosius, the massacre of Thessalonica; in the case of Philip, the direct or indirect responsibility for the death of Gordian). Again, as in the case of Theodosius, the Bishop's decision to impose penance on Philip was not the consequence of a general, public denunciation, but was a pastoral measure, born of the Emperor's desire to enter the church as one of the faithful and of the Bishop's awareness of his responsibility as pastor with the obligation of *parresia* which his office imposed on him.

The cases differ, however, inasmuch as Theodosius' penance was imposed in Milan, one of the principal cities of an already Christian empire, whereas Philip's took place in Antioch and news of it probably spread only among the local Christian communities. The Emperor was never asked to make a public confession of his responsibility for Gordian's death, which continued to be officially attributed to sickness and which was not followed by the *damnatio memoriae*.[5] The Emperor's participation in Christian penitential rites did not, in any case, compromise his prestige or detract from the support given him by the troops who had elevated him and who kept him in power for five years, from 244 to 249 — a relatively long period in those tormented and difficult years of military anarchy.

It is precisely the length of his reign which leads us to take another look at least at the military and political merits of this Emperor, despised as an incompetent coward by later pagan writers and never rehabilitated by the Christians after the conflict between Constantine and Licinius (who, perhaps precisely in order to gain the support of the Christians, had claimed to be descended from Philip).[6] Recent studies have shown that contemporary writers, both the pagan Dexippus and the Christian author of the thirteenth Sibylline Book, tell of a very different Philip, a courteous and courageous general treacherously killed by Decius' emissaries at Beroa in Thrace, on his return journey from a victorious campaign against the Scythians.[7] From the study of some papyri it has also come to light that Philip tried to introduce an important tax reform in Egypt (and I see no reason why it should not have been intended for the rest of the empire as well), in which the burden of the taxes levied for liturgical expenses, by now intolerably high, would be lifted from the shoulders of the city dwellers and spread more evenly among the whole population.[8] The fact that the huge quantity of coins minted for the formal celebrations marking Rome's thousandth anniversary bore the inscription 'Roma aeterna', points to Philip's intention of replacing the various deities of the empire with the political concept of Rome itself. The first Christian emperor was evidently attempting to work towards some kind of common ground on which the political ideal of Rome and the sacredness of its mission, guaranteed by *aeternitas*, would overcome all religious differences and be acceptable to the Christians as well (and in fact the Christians at that time believed the Roman empire protected the world form the coming of the Anti-Christ and would therefore last until the end of the world[9]). Later, this was to be the line chosen by the Christian empire for its own religious policy.

I believe the blackening of Philip's name, which went hand in hand with praise for Decius, was part of the historical manipulation carried out under Diocletian and is, in fact, directly connected with the anti-Christian policies of the last great persecution. During this period, the figures of Philip and Decius, the first Christian emperor and the 'restorer of paganism' ('restitutor sacrorum' is the entirely new title given to Decius in an inscription at Cosa — see below) became both topical and emblematic. Certainly, not only the later Orosius, but also the contemporary Bishop of Alexandria, Dionysius, and the anonymous Christian author of the thirteenth Book of the Sibyllines, all saw Decius' persecution as a direct consequence of and reaction to the open and obvious favour shown to the Christians by Philip.

This favour manifested itself in different ways. Permission was granted to the Christians to bring the remains of Pope Pontianus back to Rome from Sardinia, with solemn rites. After 70 years of forced silence on the subject, Origen was now allowed publicly to refute Celsus' accusations against the Christian religion. Without actually breaking with official state religion, of which he remained *pontifex maximus*, Philip was obviously cool in his relations with it, as can be seen from the coins minted in celebration of the thousandth anniversary of the founding of Rome, in 248 AD and from the nature of the celebrations themselves.[10] Already during Philip's lifetime, this bias in favour of the Christians had caused protest among the more uncompromising elements of the pagan establishment.[11] It had also unleashed the fanaticism of the masses which, out of hatred for the Emperor, fiercely persecuted the Christians of Alexandria during the last months of 248 and the first of 249.[12] Contrary to what the later re-elaborated accounts of the battle of Verona had to say, the deposition and execution of Philip and the young son he had co-opted as ruler were not prepared and carried out by the army, but were the result of the joint action of two other forces: on the one side, the senate of Rome, where the post of prefect was filled by Decius, an Illyrian related to ancient Etruscan families and close to the more traditional pagan circles,[13] on the other, the religious fanaticism of the masses, among whom the ancient dread of retribution for the impiety of the Christians was combined with a more recent and relatively widespread dissatisfaction with Philip's tax reforms.

Decius' Persecution and the 'Pagan Restoration'

In my opinion, Dionysius' account of the massacre of 249 is essential to our understanding of Decius' persecution, because, as well as giving us an account of the events, it also describes the atmosphere in which they took place. At a time when prolonged religious tolerance must have made persecution seem a thing of the past, it is significant that the Christians knew perfectly well that the fall of Philip was the signal for persecution to start once again. Evidently, in the struggle between Philip and Decius, the religious question had been explicitly raised and Philip's adversary had managed to make it known that he was not only opposing Philip himself, but also his religious policy. About a year previously, in 248, Origen had written that the cause of the present troubles was that in the eyes of their enemies there were far too many Christians and that 'the government no longer persecutes them as in the past' (*Contra Celsum*, III. 15, see note 11). Like Dionysius, Origen was writing in Alexandria and the reactions of this city, one of the largest in the empire, could be taken as symptomatic. Whoever set himself up in opposition to Philip and his religious policy could be sure of the support of a large percentage of public opinion. Orosius, writing later (VII. 21. 2), sees the murder of Philip and his son as part of the struggle against the Christians, and, while his affirmation has been judged as anachronistic in the past, the recent discovery of the inscription at Cosa[14] — with the epithet 'restitutor sacrorum' since then used only by Julian — shows precisely how important the question of religious restoration was in Decius' political propaganda. Indeed, the atmosphere in Alexandria described by Dionysius on the eve of Decius' coming to power is that of a holy war, and the same anti-Christian tensions must have been felt in many other cities besides Alexandria, particularly the cities of the Hellenic East. This kind of popular feeling would certainly have been encouraged by the conservative elements of the ruling classes and, above all, by the senate which, as we have understood from Dio's allusions, was worried by the Emperor's tolerant attitude to the Christians. This general state of affairs must be born clearly in mind if we wish to locate Decius' edict in its precise historical context.

While some Christian sources are undoubtedly accurate and well informed (in particular the epistles of the contemporary bishops of Carthage and Alexandria, Cyprian and Dionysius), if we attempt to rely only on their information, we tend to come to the conclusion that Decius' edict was aimed directly and exclusively at the Christians. Failure to appear before the appropriate commission before the prescribed date would, according to them, amount to an explicit confession of being a Christian (thus, Cyprian, *De lapsis*, 3; see also Dionysius in Eusebius, *Hist. eccl.* VI. 40. 2; 41. 10). This was not so. From the wording of the *libelli* which have come down to us from Egypt, the Christians do not appear to have been explicitly mentioned in the edict, neither does it seem to have been only Christians or suspected Christians who had to present themselves before the commission (one of the *libelli*, from Arsinoe, concerns a priestess of the goddess Petesuchos, who can hardly have been suspected of being a Christian). Equally it appears that there was no need to testify to not being a Christian. In fact, when we consider that to obtain the *libellus* it was necessary not only to make a libation, but also to sacrifice and to taste the flesh of the sacrificed victim in front of the commission, and then to testify to having always sacrificed to the gods and worshipped them religiously,[15] it would certainly seem that, at least from a formal point of view, Decius' edict was aimed at all the citizens of the empire and that a confession of Christianity was not even contemplated.

This does not mean, however, that the edict did not have any intention of striking a blow at the Christians, or, as has been suggested recently,[16] that it was simply supposed to bring the Christians back to traditional forms of worship without forcing them to renounce their religious beliefs. From Trajan's rescript onwards, sacrificing to the gods had always been the trial to which suspected Christians had been put, precisely because it was known that it was impossible to force those 'qui sunt revera Christiani' (Pliny, *Ep.* X. 96) to do so. The offering of sacrifice thus meant a denial of Christian faith not only in the eyes of the Christians themselves but also in the eyes of the general public, as the scenes described by Dionysius make clear (see Eusebius *Hist. eccl.* VI. 41. 11). By imposing on all the citizens of the empire the proof of loyalty which Trajan had required only from the Christians, Decius in effect put the entire empire on trial, and with the pretext of saving Roman tradition he actually subjected it to one of the most trying acts of oppression of its whole history. When Decius took the *cognomen* 'Traianus' on becoming Emperor, the line he was intending to follow was immediately clear: to restore to the letter Trajan's rescript after the long interval of religious tolerance. But in reality he wholly perverted the spirit of the rescript.[17] The policy of religious restoration, probably used by him during his campaign against Philip, was intended to gain Decius the favour of that part of public opinion and the senate which had disapproved of the religious policy of Philip (and indeed of all the Severan period) and had bitterly criticised the attitude the Emperor had adopted towards the Christians for the past half century.

The fact that Decius' persecution was 'propagandistic' and demagogical in nature explains, in my opinion, both why it took so long to put the edict into practice and why it was eventually implemented in such different ways in different regions of the empire, according to the degree of popularity or unpopularity with which the edict was received by the local population. From contemporary documents it appears that the first anti-Christian action taken in Rome dates from when Decius arrived in the city, in the autumn of 249 AD. Some members of the clergy were arrested and kept in confinement for at least a year. In January, Pope Fabianus was killed. Later, shortly before Easter (that is about March or April of the year 250), the edict requiring everyone to sacrifice to the gods was published. In Rome, the edict made a few martyrs and a limited number of apostates: the martyrs were some *insignes personae* who were too well known to go unobserved, and the apostates did not number many more and were simply those who gave way to fear and rushed to the Capitol to offer sacrifice. Those who did not panic, or who, half-way up the hill to the Capitol, listened to the exhortations of the priests of the Roman church and turned back, were mostly able to avoid both sacrifice and apostasy without incurring reprisals. By the autumn of 250, Rome had become a refuge for the Christians of the provinces, who were escaping from the rigours of a far fiercer persecution, and when, in the spring, Decius left the capital, the sense of freedom and safety was such that a large gathering of bishops and the faithful met to elect a successor to Fabianus, without bothering to take any kind of precautions.[18]

The situation was very different in those provinces where anti-Christian feeling ran high. In Africa, as in Rome, persecution took place in two distinct phases. The first action happened in January 250 (not long after the arrest of the clergy in Rome and about the time of Fabianus' death) and was orchestrated by the masses rather than the authorities. Having seen which way the Emperor's policies were tending, the people organised riots in order to incite the authorities to convict the Christians in general, and Cyprian in particular. Arrests were made, but, at least to begin with, sentences were mild, being limited to deportation rather than death. Cyprian himself chose to leave home in order not to cause any kind of provocation. Then, perhaps in the late spring, the edict itself arrived in Africa and persecution became more violent, with Christian prisoners being tortured and put to death.[19] Thus, the mild sentences of January and February were not, as has been maintained,[20] the result of the edict at all, for the simple reason that the edict had not yet arrived in Africa at that date. When it did make its appearance, death sentences and torture began to be the order of the day, but they were the result of the edict and were not punishments inflicted for crimes committed by the Christians in the interim period.[21]

The situation in Egypt fully confirms this version of events. According to Dionysius, popular persecution of the Christians had begun a full year before the issue of the edict; indeed, it had even begun during the last period of Philip's reign. In another letter (see Eusebius *Hist. eccl.* vi. 40. 2), Dionysius states that the action taken by Sabinus, whose prefecture began in September 249, started *before the arrival of the edict* with the arrest of Christians and an official search made for the Bishop himself. Dionysius only escaped arrest by staying in his own house, where no one thought of looking for him.

This phase of the persecution in Egypt corresponds exactly with what happened in Rome in the autumn and winter of the year 249/50, and in Africa in the January of 250. Then — says Dionysius (ibid. 41. 10) — the edict arrived, after which various Christians, particularly those in public positions (like the *insignes personae* of Rome), presented themselves before the authorities, some spontaneously, others called by name, and declared they had never been Christians. Some people fled, others were arrested.

All 43 of the *libelli* which have come down to us from Egypt are dated between June and July 250 AD.[22] Now, we know from Cyprian (*De lapsis*, 3) that a day had been established within which an appearance had to be made before the authorities; so, if the first *libellus* is dated 12 June, the edict cannot have arrived in Egypt much before the beginning of that month. In Egypt, as in Africa, persecution as a consequence of the edict had therefore begun only in the late spring. Where they have not been proved to be later interpolations, the dates recorded in the Acts of the Martyrs also confirm this.[23]

To sum up: from a chronological point of view, Decius' persecution was divided into two distinct phases throughout the empire.
The first phase, which started with Decius arresting the priests in
Rome, consisted of popular demonstrations (particularly in the
provinces where the Christians were more numerous) and these
demonstrations were aimed at forcing the authorities to take more
active steps against the Christians. These riots usually ended up with
arrests and deportations. Later, but only when he was certain of
public support, in March or April of the year 250, Decius published
his famous edict, which was then enforced in different ways
according to the reactions of the local populations.

In Alexandria, Carthage and Smyrna the local populations had
already in the past shown their disapproval of tolerance on the part
of the emperors and now collaborated actively with the authorities
by searching out the Christians, by encouraging them to apostasy,
by inciting the magistrates to greater severity and, above all, by
turning out *en masse* to offer sacrifice, which, of course, had the
effect of isolating the Christians from the rest of the population. In
Rome, on the other hand, (and perhaps in other parts of the
empire), the population appears to have taken very little active
notice of the edict and its consequences. If the clergy of Rome could
with impunity hold back some of the frightened Christians on their
way to the Capitol, it was probably because many people, including
the pagans themselves, refused to respond to Decius' appeal. After
all, it was a most unusual course of action to force on an empire in
which, by tradition, religion had always been a collective affair and
individuals had never been obliged to perform private acts of
worship. In any case, the result of the edict in Rome was to make it
impossible to isolate the Christians from the rest of the population.
The enormous religious census which Decius had conceived with
the typical logic of totalitarianism actually failed in the capital city
itself, where the deep-rooted traditions of religious and racial tolerance[24] made persecution distasteful, even to the pagans. Even
Decius himself, when he took a personal part in the interrogation of
the Christians, avoided passing the heaviest sentences.[25]

In reality, the Romans had never liked Decius; and when he left
the city in the spring of 251, on his way to fight the barbarians,
'cupientissimo vulgo', they set up another emperor in his place
(Aurelius Victor, *de Caesaribus*, 29; Cyprian, *Epistles*, 55. 9), and
after his death were quick to condemn his memory.

Enforced unevenly and according to the mood of the fickle

public, opposed and boycotted at the political and ideological heart of the empire, Decius' edict with its pretensions of eliminating Christianity with 'certificates of good conduct' only managed to obtain a few superficial and cheap defections. False certificates proliferated, sold by corrupt officials and bought by frightened Christians who were not, however, prepared to go so far as to make a public renunciation of their faith. The dignity of the state was severely undermined by such practices and by the numerous *sacrificati*, *thurificati* and *libellatici* who, as soon as they had obtained a certificate, petitioned for readmittance to the church. The painful question of the *lapsi* which so perturbed the Christian communities in the years following the persecution, was in fact a dramatic, if paradoxical, confirmation of the vitality of the Christian religion and of the irresistible hold it had over the human spirit. The persecution was more humiliating than bloody, even if there were undoubtedly more martyrs than some modern historians like to admit, and to Cyprian (*De lapsis*, 5), writing immediately after its end, it seemed like a brusque but providential reawakening of the faithful, enfeebled by the long period of peace.

The persecution made the enemies of Christianity realise that, if they wanted to combat this religion effectively, the old laws according to which it was only a personal religious transgression were simply not enough. Equally it was no longer feasible officially to ignore the fact that Christianity was by now a community organisation. At this stage, it was necessary not only to recognise the existence of the Christian community, but to recognise it on a legal level and to persecute it as an institution. This Valerian did for the first time.

Notes

1. Eusebius, *Hist. eccl.* VI. 20 and 33 on Beryllus; VI. 37 on the errors of the Arabs. On the correspondence between Origen and Philip, and Origen and Severa (Otacilia Severa, wife of Philip), see ibid. 36. 3.

2. Eusebius doubted Philip's penitence, not his religious faith. That Philip was a Christian is also attested to by his contemporary, Dionysius, Bishop of Alexandria, albeit anonymously. On this question, see M. Sordi, *Il cristianesimo e Roma*, Bologna, 1965, pp. 253 ff. On the question of Philip's Christianity see also M. Jork, 'The Image of Philip', *Historia*, 21 (1972), pp. 320 ff. and Febronia Elia, 'Ancora sul cristianesimo di Filippo', *Quaderni Catanesi*, I (1979), pp. 267 ff.; L. De Blois, 'The Reign of the Emperor Philip the Arabian', *Talanta*, 10 (1975), pp. 11 ff., doubts that the Emperor was a Christian, but he ignores Dionysius of Alexandria and bases his

106   Philip the Arab and Decius

theory only on later sources. H. A. Pohlsander, in 'Philip the Arab and Christianity', *Historia*, 29 (1980), pp. 463–73, believes that Philip was not a Christian.

3. A useful reconstruction of Philip's actions in the East in 244 is to be found in L. Stefanini, 'L'ascesa al trono di Filippo l'Arabo', thesis, Università Cattolica di Milano, 1979/80.

4. Ambrose, *Sermo contra Auxentium*, 36 (marginal note to epistle 21, *Maur.* = 75, Faller), of the year 386 AD.

5. *SHA Vita Gordiani*. 31. 2 and 7

6. Ibid. 34. 5–6. This information appears in the last chapter of the *Vita* along with the dedication to Constantine. The detail is significant, quite apart from doubts about the dating of the *Historia Augusta*.

7. In his 'The End of the Philippi' (*Chiron*, 6 (1967), p. 427), S. Dušanic has come to the conclusion from the study of a fragment of John of Antioch (going back to Philip) that there never was a battle at Verona and that Philip was treacherously murdered at Beroa on his way back from a victorious expedition. A mention of treachery is also to be found in another contemporary work, the *Sibylline Oracles* (XIII. 79–80). The confusion between the names 'Verona' and 'Beroa' and, above all, the reversing of the positions of Philip and Decius, make it highly likely that we have here a case of historical manipulation. The version of the story of the two Emperors as we know it was being told at the end of the third and beginning of the fourth centuries, when Diocletian's persecution against the Christians was in full swing. In an attempt to verify the real course of events, the Institute of Ancient History of the Catholic University of Milan has recently carried out considerable research into the reigns of Philip and Decius, and I hope to be able to publish the results in the near future. In the meantime, I call readers' attention to A. Bianchi's 'La politica di Filippo L'Arabo' and U. Marelli's 'L'impero di Decio', both theses, Universita Cattolica di Milano, 1981/2, (U.C. Milan, 1981/82) as well as to the work of Stefanini quoted above (see note 3).

8. A Bianchi, published in *Aegyptus* (1983).

9. Contemporary Christian thinking interpreted 2 Thessalonians 2: 6–7 to mean that the Roman Empire was the only thing that stood in the way of the coming of the Anti-Christ, and would therefore last until the end of the world (Tertullian, *Apol.* XXXII. 1), see below.

10. Sordi, *Il cristianesimo*, pp. 253 ff. and also 'Il cristianesimo e l'impero dai Severi a Gallieno', *ANRW* II. 23. 1 (1979), p. 358 n. 39.

11. In *Contra Celsum* III. 15 (written in 248), Origen records the protests of the pagans against a government which no longer persecuted the Christians. Likewise, Dionysius of Alexandria (see Eusebius, *Hist. eccl.* VI. 41. 9) records the concern of the Christians of the Egyptian capital at the thought of what would happen at the end of the reign of Philip, who had been 'too benevolent towards us' (and the use of the Greek comparative seems particularly significant).

12. Eusebius, *Hist. eccl.* VI. 41. 1 ff.

13. Decius' wife was Herennia Etruscilla and their sons took their names from their mother (Herennius Etruscus and Hostilianus)

14. *L'Année epigraphique* (1973), no. 235. The inscription is at present set in the wall at the entrance to the museum at Cosa. There is no doubt about the word 'Decius' which, despite its shallow chiselling, can be unmistakably deciphered by touch.

15. On the significance of the word 'always' ('I have *always* sacrificed to the gods and practised acts of piety' in P. Meyer, 'Die Libelli aus der decianischen Verfolgung', *Akademie der Wissenschaften der DDR*—formerly *Abhandlungen der Königliche Akademie and Aphandlungen der Preussische Akademie* (Berlin, 1910), no. 6, pp. 7 ff.), see now Sordi, *Il cristianesimo*, p. 275 and J. Molthagen, 'Der römische Staat und die Christen im zweiten und dritten Jahrhundert' *Hypomnemata* 28

(Göttingen, 1970), p. 63. In any case, the edict concerned the gods of the empire, not the cult of the Emperor himself.

16. Molthagen, 'Der römische Staat', pp. 70 ff.

17. Cf. Sordi, *Il cristianesimo*, pp. 277 ff. and also 'La data dell'editto di Decio', *Revista di Storia della Chiesa in Italia*, 34 (1980), p. 453. While attempting to revive the ancient religion, Decius in fact changed its very essence, making individual what had always been collectively national and imposing religious obligations which had been unknown before his time. On the conflict between Roman traditions and Decius' edict, see O. Fracassini, *L'impero e il cristianesimo* (Perugia, 1913), p. 247. On Decius' taking the name 'Trajanus' on his accession, see M. G. Arrigoni Bertini, 'Tentativi dinastici etc.', *Rivista di Storia dell'Antichità*, 10 (1980), pp. 200–1. (He attributes the *cognomen* to the outcome of a victorious campaign on the Dacian frontier but the historical manipulation of the whole of the history of Decius leads me to doubt that this campaign ever took place: see above, note 7.)

18. For the chronology of the Roman measures recorded in Cyprian's epistles, I refer readers to my *Il cristianesimo*, pp. 256–9 and also to 'La data dell'editto', p. 451 ff. A new study of the subject has recently been offered by L. Duquenne in his 'Chronologie des lettres de St Cyprien. Le dossier de la persécution de Dèce', *Subsidia Hagiographica*, 54 (1972), Brussels (in particular the table on pp. 159 ff.); this study does not, however, offer variations to the date here espoused.

19. For the chronology of the persecutions in Africa, see Sordi *Il cristianesimo*, pp. 269–71 and 'La data dell'editto', pp. 451 ff. The existence of two separate phases of persecution, independent of their relationship to the edict, is now confirmed in the reconstruction of the period in Duquenne's 'Chronologie des lettres', pp. 102 ff.

20. C. Saumagne, 'La persécution de Dèce en Afrique d'après la correspondance de St Cyprien', *Byzantion*, 32 (1962) pp. 1 ff.

21. Opposed to Saumagne, for different reasons, is C. W. Clarke, 'Double Trials', *Historia*, 22 (1973), p. 662.

22. For the *libelli* which are still extant and their relative dates, see Samonati under 'Libellus' in De Ruggiero's *Dizionario Epigrafico*, vi, 1 (Rome, 1924), pp. 813 ff. Also on the libelli, see P. Keresztes, 'The Decian Libelli', *Latomus*, 23 (1975), p.761 ff.

23. For the information to be gained from the Acts of the Martyrs, and in particular that of Maximus (Ephesus) and Pionius (Smyrna), see Sordi, *Il cristianesimo*, p. 273 and also 'La data dell'editto.', p. 455.

24. The city of Rome never saw popular anti-Christian uprisings. Even during Nero's massacre the population showed pity for the victims, as Tacitus himself tells us. In the same way, the anti-Jewish pogroms so frequent in Asia Minor and Alexandria never took place in Rome. The only apparent exception is the death of Pope Callistus, but this seems to have been a case of political rather than religious fanaticism (see above).

25. As was the case with Celerinus, a young African Christian who was tried in Rome in the presence of Decius himself and was subsequently released, despite his courageous confession of faith (see Cyprian's epistolary, in particular *Epistles*, 22. 1, from Lucianus to Celerinus).

7 Valerian and Gallienus: From Persecution to Recognition of the Church

Valerian's Persecution and the Revision of Anti-Christian Legislation

Valerian's persecution can be seen as a turning-point in the relationship between the Roman state and the Christian religion. After the long and contradictory compromise between the *de jure* right to convict Christians and the *de facto* tolerance of their existence, Valerian's persecution opens a new era, the era of official recognition which will culminate in the so-called 'edict of Milan'. Valerian decided that the old anti-Christian laws should be completely revised and in two detailed edicts known to us through the epistles of the contemporaries, Dionysius of Alexandria and Cyprian of Carthage, set about penalising Christianity as a church, as a hierarchy and as an organisational structure. Paradoxically, this negative recognition of the church on the part of Valerian actually served to untie the knots in the legal situation and prepare the way for Gallienus to make the first positive act of recognition of Christianity.

In order to understand Valerian's persecution (and the anti-Christian demonstrations which preceded it under Trebonianus Gallus[1]), we must remember the fears and superstitions which, fed by the plague and the natural and military disasters which rained on the empire in those terrible years, had reawoken in the masses. Cyprian's *Ad Demetrianum* and Dionysius's letter to Hermammon are living witnesses to this period of crisis, when the idea of an imminent end to everything, the empire and the world, was felt in different ways but with the same intensity among Christians and pagans alike. Along the Danube and to the East, the Goths and Persians were massing on the frontiers and overcoming the Roman legions (Decius was the first emperor to die fighting the barbarians, Valerian the first to be captured by them); the plague reaped its victims in city and country alike; famine threatened and it seemed the earth was no longer capable of bringing forth fruit. Cyprian, echoing Lucretius, attributes the troubles to the age of a world now close to death. The superstitious populace cried out against the Christians who, by renouncing the old gods, had brought all these calamities down on the empire. While the Christians believed the hour of the apocalypse had come,[2] the Romans regressed to a terrified belief in the ancient prophecies of the triumph of East over West.

In this nightmare atmosphere, reason gave way to panic[3] and religious persecution, finding the ideal climate in which to flourish, took the shape of an irrational attempt to placate the hostile forces with sacrificial blood, to send away the mysterious malediction by eliminating whatever seemed alien. As in the Middle Ages and in more modern times when the hunt was on for witches and plague-spreaders, so now, during the years of crisis of the Roman Empire, superstitious fear suggested the persecution of the Christians as the answer to all the calamities which had befallen the state. Political expediency had no part in this decision, even when the fears of the masses reached the ears of the Emperor and he took over the persecution himself with an unexpected and dramatic gesture.

Valerian came from Etruria, and like Decius was connected with the Etruscan world and with traditional paganism. His persecution of the Christians was thus not only sparked off by the superstitious fear of the wrath of the gods, but also by another fear, this time a terrestrial rather than a supernatural one. It was a fear we have already seen operating in the opposition of the senate to the tolerant attitude of the Severi and in the reaction to Philip the Arab and his policies: the fear of the 'christianisation' of the empire through its ruling classes, the fear that the empire itself might become Christian. If we examine this fear closely, we will see that, although it appears to be political, it is in fact religious. The reason for this is that, as in archaic times, its source was to be found in the identification of the state with fidelity to the gods of the state and to the state's religious traditions. Now, after the 'secularisation' of the first century, politics and religion are once more fused into one.

Valerian's decision to attack the Christians was not taken immediately, at the beginning of his reign. Contemporary sources, Dionysius of Alexandria as well as Commodianus,[4] agree that during the first years of his reign Valerian was extremely benevolent towards the Christians and 'that his whole household was full of Christians and was a church of God',[5] I myself believe that it was during this first period of Valerian's reign, a period which lasted from 253 to about half-way through 257,[6] that the centurion Marinus was martyred. Eusebius tells us this event occurred in a period of 'general peace' for the church and he mistakenly dates it after the edict of Gallienus (*Hist. eccl.* VII. 15. 1). As we know, it was not unusual for Eusebius to make this kind of mistake[7] and in this case the error comes to light from some significant details in his own account. Marinus, in a military camp at Caesarea in Palestine, was about to be promoted centurion when an envious colleague declared that 'according to the ancient laws' this could not be allowed because Marinus was a Christian and did not sacrifice 'to the emperors'. Marinus immediately admitted to being a Christian on being interrogated by the judge, Acheus, and confirmed his faith with added conviction after his meeting with Theotechnus, Bishop of Caesarea. He was then decapitated and his body was buried with many honours by Asturius, a Roman senator, a Christian and a 'friend of the Augusti' (Eusebius, ibid. 16. 1), who happened to be there at the time.[8]

Now, in telling the story of Marinus, Eusebius consistently speaks of the 'Emperors' and the 'Augusti' in the plural, while we know that after Valerian's capture and Saloninus' death Gallienus ruled alone. Clearly, therefore, Eusebius was mistaken in placing Marinus' death under Gallienus.[9] The fact that we are given the name of Theotechnus as Bishop of Caesarea also suggests that Marinus' death belongs some time after 254, because we know from Dionysius of Alexandria's letter to Pope Stephen (see Eusebius, *Hist. eccl.* VII. 5. 1) that in that year Theoctistus was still the bishop. Theotechnus only became bishop after the brief bishopric of Domnus, the immediate successor to Theoctistus (Eusebius, ibid. VII. 14. 1). The two daughters of Asturius, Rufina and Secunda, were martyred in the summer of 257 (Junius Donatus is named as urban prefect in the account of their passion, which would otherwise appear to be legendary), that is, at the beginning of July, according to the Hieronyman martyrology. Rufinus and the martyrology (*Acta* of the Martyrs, I pp. 222 ff.) tell us that Marinus' death was followed immediately by that of Asturius. If we put together all these elements, it seems probable that Marinus was martyred in the last months of 256 or the first of 257, that is, on the eve of the publication of the first edict, which appeared, as we know, in the summer of AD 257.

In my opinion, the dates of the deaths of Marinus and Asturius are important for two reasons. First, they help us to understand the nature of Gallienus' edict, which has often been misunderstood because of Eusebius' chronological error; second, because they suggest what may have been the pretext and the occasion which led Valerian, in a moment of general tension, to make such a sudden change in his policy towards the Christians.

In his letter to Hermammon (see Eusebius, *Hist. eccl.* VII. 10. 4 ff.), Dionysius of Alexandria more than once accuses the 'Minister of Finance',[10] Macrianus, of having encouraged Valerian to persecute the Christians. Many historians have accepted Dionysius' affirmation, even if with some reservations, explaining the persecution in terms of needing to fill the coffers of the state with the goods confiscated from the Christians.[11] However, the speed with which Gallienus restored all confiscated property on becoming Emperor makes me doubt this explanation. It also seems rather suspect to me that the whole responsibility for the persecution should be put at Macrianus' door in a letter written in 262, that is after Macrianus' death and during the reign of Gallienus, who was known to have been Macrianus' enemy. I would not go so far as to accuse the Bishop of Alexandria of a deliberate misrepresentation of the truth — on the contrary he shows himself to be an honest and well-informed witness to the events he relates. Macrianus probably was hostile to the Christians and may well have been one of the instigators of the persecution,[12] but I would exclude the possibility that the persecution and Valerian's abrupt change of policy were both exclusively his work, or that the motive behind the persecution was purely financial.

On the subject of the motives behind the persecution, there is a detail in Valerian's second edict which seems to me particularly revealing: Christian senators and knights were to be deprived of their positions and property in any case; then, if they continued to practise their faith they would be put to death (Cyprian, *Epistles* 80. 2).[13] For the first time in the history of the relationship between Christianity and the empire, apostasy was not enough to guarantee immunity from punishment. And equally for the first time, the intention was now clearly that of removing the Christians from positions of power, whether or not they decided to continue to practise their faith. In Rome and Alexandria under Decius, whether they were genuinely Christians or were only suspects, the *insignes personae*, the *demosienontes*, the senators, knights, Caesarians and local magistrates had been the first to appear voluntarily before the commissions to ask for the declaration which would make them safe from reprisals. Decius had not been interested in the sincerity of the apostates; he was only interested in the propaganda value of the great religious demonstration he had organised. And indeed, once the danger was past, many of the defectors returned to the church. For Valerian, on the contrary, the apostasy of Christian senators, knights and Caesarians was not enough. He wanted to purge the senate, the equestrian class and the court once and for all of all Christians and all those suspected of being Christian. In reality, he saw the situation from a completely different point of view from that of his predecessors, from Marcus Aurelius onwards. They had wanted the Christians to take part in the life of the empire at all levels; Valerian seems, on the contrary, to have had a real fear that the Christians were taking over the key positions in the empire and that the state was, indeed, becoming 'christianised'. This was, of course, the same fear that had animated the conservative members of the ruling classes around the first half of the third century, the danger against which Dio and the *haruspices* had warned Alexander Severus. It was the same threat that the pagans had seen in Philip the Arab. And it was the fear that was to emerge again under Diocletian and Galerius after the long period of peace following Gallienus' edict.

Valerian's sudden awareness of this 'danger' is all the more worthy of attention precisely because it was so unexpected. During the first part of his reign he had allowed his house to become filled with Christians to the extent that it became 'a church of God', according to Dionysius (see Eusebius, *Hist. eccl.* vii. 10.4). This expression may allude to Cornelia Salonina, Gallienus' wife, who was said to be a Christian,[14] but she was certainly not the only one. We have already heard from Eusebius that the Christian Asturius was a 'friend of the Augusti', a friend, that is, of Valerian and Gallienus during the period of their joint rule. We can take it that Asturius was probably closer to Gallienus than to Valerian, as it seems that Gallienus was the pole of attraction for the Christians at court, both before and after Valerian's capture.[15] At this point the figure of Asturius becomes extremely interesting. His death followed immediately on that of Marinus and must have taken place either before or at the same time as that of his daughters, at the beginning of Valerian's persecution in the spring or summer of 257. Now we know from Eusebius, always well informed on Palestinian matters, that Asturius had been involved in an incident at Caesarea

Philippi and in this case he states that his information came from people who had actually known Asturius and could still remember him.[16] The incident, which caused something of a scandal, took place near the source of the river Jordan and involved a false 'miracle' which occurred from time to time to the amazement and awe of the pagans. During a feast in honour of Pan, Asturius unmasked the workings behind the miracle, which from that time onwards never repeated itself.

The importance of this episode comes from the fact that both Commodianus[17] and Dionysius[18] refer to it as the spark which triggered off Valerian's persecution. It is true that the references they make are circumspect and somewhat obscure, but, comparing the two texts carefully, there can be no doubt that this was their meaning. Commodianus' reference in particular seems to indicate that the charge of sacrilege brought against Asturius by the citizens of Caesarea was actually addressed to the senate.[19] Given his exalted position as friend of the Augusti and governor of Arabia (if not he himself, then his father), the trial of this Christian senator was bound to cause a sensation, and it was easy for it to become a trial of Christianity in general. The accusations made by the devotees of the sanctuary would have been given a ready hearing by the pagan aristocracy, many of whom (like the unknown Demetrianus to whom Cyprian was writing at this time) were already convinced that the Christians were to blame for the wrath of the gods which was manifesting itself in the military and natural catastrophes of the period, the famine, the plague and so on. Like Dio at the time of Alexander Severus, other aristocrats believed that, by undermining faith in the gods, the Christians were attacking the principle of authority itself and were thus preparing fertile ground for the growth and proliferation of subversive underground organisations. The fact that in this case the attack on the gods had been made by a senator and 'friend of the Augusti' must have seemed particularly serious to these aristocrats. This time, when the populace pressed for drastic action to be taken against the Christians, their voice would have been joined by that of the senate.[20] The 'scandal' of Caesarea Philippi was taken as the consequence of the long period of imperial tolerance towards the Christians: to avoid a repetition of the same kind of ugly situation it was essential to take decisive action against the Christians once and for all. The church organisation must be uprooted, its influence over the ruling classes eradicated by means of a 'purge' of the senate, the equestrian class and the court. Gallienus was absent from the scene, fighting the barbarians in the West, and Valerian gave way. The two edicts authorising persecution, published respectively in 257 and 258,[21] satisfied all the points mentioned above and, learning from Decius' experience, they attempted to gain in effectiveness what they lost in range. Valerian did not try to isolate the Christians by putting the entire empire on trial. He went straight for Christianity as an institution and, modifying the old laws, attacked it as such for the first time. From 257 onwards, churches were closed, burial grounds and meeting-places were confiscated, bishops, priests and deacons were sent into supervised exile. Whoever violated these laws by organising or participating in meetings of the forbidden cult was threatened with death. Then, in 258 the order suddenly went out that, without need for further evidence beyond a simple act of identification, all the Christian ecclesiastics arrested previously, together with all Christian senators and knights, were to be put to death after having been deprived of their property and their positions. The matrons were to be sent into exile and the Caesarians were to be condemned to forced labour.

Apostasy, as I have already mentioned, could save the accused from death but not from the confiscation of property or from the loss of position. The fact that the edicts only refer explicitly to members of the ecclesiastical hierarchy and the lay members of the ruling classes does not mean that Valerian intended to leave the simple Christian unpunished or that, having abolished Christianity as a public institution, he was prepared to allow it to continue to exist in private (condemnation of the Christian religion and compulsory worship of the gods were clearly stated in the first edict). Undoubtedly, however, the Christians of the ruling classes were the ones Valerian intended to suppress immediately and completely, giving no one a chance to escape. The detailed and *ad personam* measures taken in 257 and 258 in the cases of Cyprian of Carthage and Dionysius of Alexandria (and doubtless of many other bishops too) show precisely how clear an idea the state had of church organisation and to what extent it was considered essential to dismember it.

As I have suggested from the start, it is precisely in this intention that we find the novelty of Valerian's persecution. He attacks the Christians of the ruling classes because, unlike his predecessors, he does not want the Christians to become integrated into the political life of the empire. Indeed, his fear is that the empire is falling too much under the Christian influence. He attacks the members of the ecclesiastical hierarchy because he understands that, if he wants to suppress Christianity, he must treat it as a church, that is as an institution. With Valerian, the Roman state recognises for the first time the existence of this institution, this ecclesiastical organisation, and for the first time it declares it to be illegal. Up until this moment, even if Christianity was punishable on an individual basis, the organisation, the church itself, had been allowed to exist, not by right of any special official recognition, but simply in merit of the existing laws on the right to associate.[22] Now, however, the church itself is declared illegal equally with the profession of the Christian religion. In this declaration of illegality, the state put into use all the knowledge of the ecclesiastic organisation that it had acquired throughout the long years of tolerance; it did not have to limit itself to making a generalised declaration because by now it was able to identify, and therefore strike directly at, each separate level of the hierarchy (bishops, priests and deacons) and to single out the ecclesiastic property to be confiscated (churches and cemeteries). The fact that the edicts could be so precise is, in my opinion, extremely important because it indicates a kind of official recognition of the existence of the church as institution. For the moment this recognition is only in operation as an instrument of prohibition and punishment, but it nevertheless constitutes the first step towards a more positive form of recognition: it lays the foundations for the church's future right to exist. Unlike all previous persecutions, including that of Decius, Valerian's persecution will not be able to end simply with the ceasing of hostilities and the restoration of the *status quo ante*. Anti-Christian legislation — which up to the time of Valerian had retained the imprecise contours of the general condemnation of the first century — was now substantially modified both in its juridical status and in its practical application, with every last detail clearly specified. By now, the persecution could only come to an end if and when the edicts themselves were revoked. Moreover, the abrogation of the edicts would automatically imply the acceptance of the church as such, no longer within the general framework of the laws on the right to associate, but as an existing and separate institution with its own hierarchy and its own legal status.

The Edict of Gallienus and the First Official Recognition of the Church

In view of what we have stated above, Gallienus' edict of tolerance cannot be seen as no more than a return to the situation as it had been before Valerian's persecution, despite what some historians claim to the contrary.[23] By abrogating his father's edicts and returning confiscated property to the bishops, Gallienus' first edict gave Christianity the legal right to exist. The old anti-Christian laws were *ipso facto* repealed and from now onwards could no longer be used either by the state or by private individuals to incriminate the Christians, as the trial of Maximilian in 295 demonstrates in the clearest possible way.[24] From then onwards, if the Christians were to be persecuted, new laws would have to be made, and this is precisely what happened when Diocletian's edicts set under way a whole new wave of persecution. And when, in his turn, Galerius decided in 311 to put a stop to this persecution, he had only to refer back to a previous juridical situation: 'ut denuo sint christiani et conventicula sua componant.'[25]

Gallienus' edict has not come down to us directly. The document preserved for us by Eusebius (*Hist. eccl.* VII. 13) is the rescript which the Emperor addressed to Dionysius of Alexandria and the other bishops of Egypt when in the first months of 262, having overcome the usurpation of the Macriani and Aemiliani, he could re-establish his power in the region. In this rescript, Gallienus simply extends to the regions previously in the hands of the usurpers the benefits he had already granted 'a long time ago' to the rest of the empire. The chief among these was the order that the local authorities should restore to the bishops their previously confiscated places of worship. In a different rescript sent to other bishops (known to Eusebius but not quoted verbatim) Gallienus deals with the subject of the cemeteries. It would be very interesting to know the precise legal formulae used by Gallienus and what official justification was given for the edict, but unfortunately it is lost to us. On the other hand we do have the equally precious rescript preserved by Eusebius. Particularly significant, in my opinion, is the fact that the Emperor did not limit himself to informing the local magistrates of his decisions and then leaving them to implement them; he himself took the trouble to inform the bishops personally, sending each of them a copy of his decisions 'so that they could make use of them and no one should make difficulties for them'.

With this rescript, the Christian communities acquired legal rights and the bishops were authorised, indeed invited, to exercise these rights before the law. Gallienus seems to have been perfectly aware of having created these rights and he wanted them to be implemented. By turning directly to the bishops as such, he was automatically recognising them as the authorities on ecclesiastical matters, and when, later, Aurelian had to arbitrate on the question of the church at Antioch, his legal standpoint was based on Gallienus' edict.[26]

The official recognition which the opponents of Christianity had so effectively blocked under various openly pro-Christian emperors (the mild Alexander, the Christian Philip) now became the logical consequence of the new legal situation created by Valerian's persecutory edicts. It was also made possible by Gallienus' undisguised opposition to the senate.

It is not, perhaps, a coincidence that Gallienus' change of policy towards the senate went hand in hand with the official recognition of the Christian religion which the senate had forbidden for the previous two centuries. Gallienus broke completely with the pro-senate policy of the preceding emperors, he forbade the senators military command and he cut them off from all the sources of real power. It was this break with the senate, this decision on the part of Gallienus to do without its consent, that made it possible for the Emperor to grant to the Christians the recognition which was so necessary for the well-being of the empire, but which the traditionalist thinking of the senate had always feared so much. It was certainly of no help to the unity of the empire to keep up a religious feud with a strong minority group which was more than willing to co-operate loyally with the state. Valerian's persecution had been a mistake made in the name of tradition and religion; Gallienus' official recognition of Christianity was a move made from motives of political discretion.

In his letter to Hermammon, Dionysius of Alexandria writes of the victory of Gallienus, 'the Emperor who is old and at the same time new', as a symbol of the rebirth which, after the apocalyptic crisis of the previous years, was to renew the earth with peace and justice. Having cast off its age and its wickedness, the empire is now flourishing again, and while the evil men who had called themselves kings are now left without a name, Gallienus 'accepted by and dear to God' had outlasted the fatal seven years prophesied in the Revelation of St John and had now entered the ninth year of his reign (Dionysius, see Eusebius, *Hist. eccl.* vii. 23. 4). The end of the world, expected by Christians and pagans alike, has not happened after all, and life goes on. The enthusiastic language with which the Bishop of Alexandria greets Gallienus' new era of religious peace blends naturally and harmoniously with the official propaganda heralding the return of the golden age.[27] The Alemanni have been beaten south of Milan, Sapore's Persians have been pushed back by Odenatus of Palmyra, the uprisings of the Macriani and Aemiliani have been quelled. Peace, albeit in the midst of many sacrifices and compromises, has been established once more. These 40 years which separate Gallienus' edict from the beginning of Diocletian's persecution are, in fact, unique in the history of the relations between church and state. This is a period of truly peaceful coexistence, *de jure* rather than merely *de facto*, during which the Christian religion is, like the Hebrew religion before it, allowed to exist as a *religio licita* within an officially pagan state. During this period, the faithful can, and do, offer the state their loyal cooperation without reservations, filling official positions and taking on responsibilities as fully accepted members of the community.[28] The state bases its attitude to the church on respect for its legal rights, avoiding the temptation to take over ecclesiastical power and not interfering in doctrinal questions. Solar syncretism, developing along the lines laid down during the Severan age, uses the *summus deus* of the many names to foster religious unity in a pluralistic empire; ideological confrontation and the exchange of ideas, no longer confined to the political arena, now develop and flourish in a climate of free cultural debate.[29]

Notes

1. These demonstrations took place during the sacrifices ordered by the Emperor to combat the plague (Cyprian, *Epistles*, 59. 6). Despite the demonstrations and the exile of Pope Cornelius to Centumcellae (ibid. 61. 3. 1), it would be inaccurate to speak of a real anti-Christian persecution under Trebonianus Gallus. On this subject, see M. Sordi, *Il cristianesimo e Roma* Bologna, 1965, pp. 283 ff.; see also J. Molthagen, 'Der römische Staat und die Christen in zweiten und dritten Jahrhundert' *Hypomnemata* 28 (Göttingen, 1970), p. 85.

2. The Christians' expectation of the apocalypse is clearly seen from the writings of Dionysius of Alexandria and Commodianus, as well as in the various millenarian movements which Dionysius did his best to combat: see J. Gagé, 'Commodien et le mouvement millénariste du III siècle', *Revue d'histoire et de littérature religieuses*, 41 (1961), pp. 355 ff.; M. Sordi, 'Dionigi di Alessandria, Commodiano ed alcuni

problemi della storia del III secolo', *Rendiconti della Pontificia Accademia di Archeologia*, 35 (1962/3), pp. 123 ff. and also Commodianus, *Carmen apologeticum* 892 ff., *Augustinianum*, 22 (1982), pp. 204 ff. I refer readers to the same articles for a discussion of the date of Commodianus' writings, around 260, which some historians still place during the fifth century. On the subject of milleniarism, see M. Simonetti, 'Il millenarismo in oriente da Origene a Metodio', *Corona gratiarum, Miscellanea patristica historica et liturgica*, E. Dekkers oblata I (Bruges, 1975), pp. 37 ff.

3. E. R. Dodds, in his *Pagans and Christians in an Age of Anxiety: Some Aspects of Religious Experience from Marcus Aurelius to Constantine* (Wiles Lectures, 1964, pub. Cambridge, 1965), gives an exposition of this period with its attitudes common to Christians and pagans alike: a hatred of the world and the human condition, the importance given to the supernatural, both divine and demoniacal, the attention paid to dreams and prophecies, the mystical longing for union with the deity.

4. Dionysius of Alexandria (*apud* Eusebius, *Hist. eccl.* vii. 10. 3); Commodianus, *Carmen Apologeticum*, 826 ff. Here we find mention of three and a half years, half of the fatal seven years. On the subject of the 'seventh year' of Valerian, the year — 259/60 — in which the Emperor was captured while persecution was at its height (as is now known from a papyrus), see M. Sordi, 'Dionigi di Alessandria e le vicende della persecuzione di Valeriano in Egitto' *Paradoxos Politeia* (Milan, 1979), pp. 292 ff.

5. Dionysius of Alexandria, see above (note 4), in the letter to Hermammon.

6. This is the famous three-and-a-half year period, agreed on by both Dionysius and Commodianus.

7. See, for example, the difficulties raised by the date Eusebius gives for the death of Origen (Hist. eccl. vii. 1) with the observations of Bardy: ibid. vii. 5. 3, the succession of Pope Sixtus to Pope Stephen. G. Bardy, comments: 'La chronologie d'Eusebe en ce qui concerne les papes devient de plus en plus fantasiste.' Other inconsistencies have recently been pointed out by C. Andresen in his 'Siegreiche Kirche etc.', *ANRW* ii. 233. 1 (1978), pp. 87 ff.

8. Asturius might perhaps be identified with M. Bassaeus Astur, son of Bassaeus Astur, praeside of Arabia and co-ruler with him or after him (*L'Année epigraphique* (1920), 73 from Bosra). For further information on this character, see G. Barbieri, 'L'albo senatorio da Settimio Severo a Carino (193–285 AD)', *Studi pubblicati dall' Istituto Italiano per la storia antica*, 6 (Rome, 1952), p. 260 n. 1486, see above.

9. Compare with E. Manni, *L'impero di Gallieno* (Rome, 1949), p. 67 (who was thinking of the time of the Macriani). For the proposed dating under Valerian and Gallienus, see Sordi, *Il cristianesimo*, pp. 287 ff. Some historians take the episode of Marinus as evidence that Gallienus' edict did not, in fact, grant legal recognition to the church. However, this is due to a widespread ignorance of the arguments which lead us to collocate the episode under Valerian and Gallienus' period of joint rule.

10. 'Epí ton kathòlou lògon . . . Basiléos' — Dionysius (*apud* Eusebius, *Hist. eccl.* vii. 10. 5); for Marcus Fulvius Macrianus' status and position see Stein, *Paulys Real-Encyclopaedie der classischen Altertumswissenschaft (RE)* vii (1912) under 'Fulvius', no. 82, 259 ff.

11. M. Besnier, Histoire romaine, 4, 1, L'empire romain de l'avènement des Sévères au Concile de Nicée, *Histoire ancienne 3* (Paris, 1937), p. 172.; P. Paschini, 'La persecuzione di Valeriano', *Studi Romani*, 6 (1958), p. 131; S. I. Oost, 'The Alexandrian Seditions . . .', pp. 7 ff. G. Bardy, commentary on Eusebius, *Hist. eccl.* vii. 10. 4 ff. Molthagen, in his 'Der römische Staat', p. 86, disagrees radically on this point. P. Keresztes, in his 'Two Edicts of the Emperor Valerian' (*Vigiliae Christianae*, 29 (1975), pp. 81 ff.), admits the influence of Macrianus but excludes his having planned to fill the state coffers with the confiscated goods.

12. On this subject see also S. I. Oost ('The Alexandrian Seditions', pp. 8 ff.) and

Gagé ('Commodien et le mouvement millénariste', pp. 372 ff.), who, independently from each other, both point out that Dionysius calls Macrianus 'Rabbi' and Master of the Magicians of Egypt.

13. When Cn. Domitius Philippus (ex-prefect of the guards and father of the martyr Eugenia) was martyred in Rome in 257, his condemnation and death followed precisely this course. (See M. Sordi, 'Un martire romano', *Rivista di Storia della Chiesa in Italia*, 33 (1979), pp. 3 ff.)

14. For the probability that Salonina was a Christian there is the inscription 'Augusta in pace' on a coin, see M. Mattingly and E. A. Sydenham, *Roman Imperial Coinage* (*RIC*), v. 1 (London, 1927, republished 1962), p. 28; S. L. Cesano, 'Salonina Augusta in pace', *Atti della Pontificia Accademia di Archeologia*, 25/26 (1949/50 and 1950/51), pp. 105 ff.

15. Among the friends of Gallienus killed by the senate before Claudius II (Gothicus) intervened, there were probably some Christians. This would explain the reference made by certain Passionari (of dubious authority) to martyrdoms which took place only in Rome and Italy during the reign of Claudius II (see Sordi, *Il cristianesimo*, p. 315).

16. Eusebius, *Hist. eccl.* VII. 17.

17. On the episode of Elias in Commodianus (*Carmen Apologeticum*, 833 ff.) and the analogies between this and Eusebius' account of the miracle of Asturius, see M. Sordi, 'Dionigi di Alessandria', pp. 136 ff. and also A. Salvatore, *Commodiano, Carme Apologetico* (Turin, 1977), ad locum.

18. Dionysis, (*apud.* Eusebius, *Hist. eccl.* VII. 10. 4); cf. M. Sordi, 'Dionigi di Alessandria' pp. 139 and *Il cristianesimo* 290 ff.

19. Cf. *Carmen apologeticum*, 833 ff., 854 ff. (Martin). For Commodianus' mention of the senate and the Jews, see Gagé, 'Commodien et le mouvement millénariste, pp. 370 ff.

20. For the part played by the senate, see Sordi, *Il cristianesimo*, pp. 294 ff. and 441 (with bibliography). In any case, it is certain that the second persecutory edict was in the form of a *senatus consultum* (Cyprian, *Epistles* 80).

21. It is possible to reconstruct accurately the edicts of Valerian from reliable contemporary sources. For the first, see the *Acta Cypriani*, I with the interrogation of Cyprian at Carthage by Aspasius Paternus, proconsul of Africa, on 30 August of the year 257; see also Dio (*apud.* Eusebius, *Hist. eccl.* VII. 11. 3–11), the letter to Germanus with the interrogation of Dionysius before the prefect of Egypt, L. Mussius Aemilianus.

From the identical form of the two interrogations, it is clear that the first edict contained a general call to the Christians to return to the obligations of state religion, as well as containing the dispositions relative to the exile of ecclesiastics and the confiscations of cemeteries and churches: 'eos qui romanam Religionem non colunt debere Romanas caerimonias recognoscere' *Acta Cypriani*, Eusebius, *Hist. eccl.* VII. 11. 7.

According to Commodianus (*Carmen apol.* lines 875–6), the edicts, as well as putting a stop to the *oblatio* to Christ, 'praecipiunt quoque simulacris tura ponenda, et ne quis lateat, omnes coronati procedant'. We find information on the second edict in Cyprian's 80th letter, in which he writes of his second trial, celebrated before the proconsul Galerius Maximus on 14 September 258 (*Acta Cypriani*, III ff.). Information also comes to us from the trials of Montanus and Lucius at Carthage immediately after that of Cyprian (see G. Lazzati, *Gli Sviluppi della letteratura sui martiri*. (Milan, 1956), pp. 201 ff.), the trial of Marianus and James (ibid. pp. 191 ff.) and the trial of Fructuosus (ibid. pp. 160 ff.). A papyrus published in 1975 by Rea (*Pap. Oxy.* 3119. 1. 11) tells of an enquiry into the Christians conducted by one Saiticus on the orders of the prefect of Egypt in 259/60. This shows that the persecution had by this time spread to include the lay brethren, thus confirming Dionysius' report (*apud* Eusebius, *Hist. eccl.* VII. 11. 20 ff.) cf. Sordi, 'Dionigi di Alessandria', pp. 292 ff.

22. See below, Part Two.

23. Baus, 'Von der Urgemeinder zur fruhchristlichen Grosskirche' in the *Handbook of Church History* (Freiburg, 1965), p. 434 and Molthagen, 'Der römische Staat', pp. 98 ff. and also L. De Blois, *The Policy of the Emperor Gallienus* (Leiden, 1976), pp. 178 ff. On the existence of the edict, see P. Keresztes 'The Peace of Gallienus', *Wiener Studien*, 9 (1975), pp. 174 ff. F. Decret has also reviewed the question in 'Les consequences sur le christianisme en Perse etc.', *Recherches Augustiennes* 14 (1979), pp. 115 ff. (but he does not see an official recognition of the Christian faith; rather, he sees a legalisation of the existence of the Church).

24. The Acts of Maximilian, p. 139 (Lazzati). Despite his repeated profession of the Christian faith, Maximilian was convicted a conscientious objector, not a Christian. Indeed, the judge pointed out that there was no incompatibility between being a Christian and serving in the imperial army: 'in sacro comitatu . . . milites Christiani sunt et militant.' The contrast with Marinus could hardly be more evident; cf. Sordi, *Il cristianesimo*, pp. 315–16. On the 'Passio S. Maximiliani', see P. Siniscalco, Massimiliano: un obiettore di coscienza nel tardo impero (Turin–Milan, 1974).

25. Lactantius, De mort. 34. 4.

26. We find the account in Eusebius (*Hist. eccl.* VII. 30. 19). Aurelian had to arbitrate when Paul of Samosata had taken over the church building in Antioch and had been condemned by a synod of bishops, who deposed him from his bishopric and created Domnus bishop in his place. Other ancient sources confirm this account (Johannes Zonaras, Theodoret of Cyrrhus, Malthaeus Blastares). Aurelian decided to refer the matter to the Bishop of Rome and this decision may have been a result of Gallienus' edict; on this question see Sordi, *Il cristianesimo*, pp. 322 ff. and 444 with bibliography, and also A. Baldini, 'Il ruolo di Paolo di Samosata', *Rivista di Storia dell'antichità*, 5 (1975), pp. 70 ff.

27. Dionysius' agreement with Gallienus' propaganda and with the images and inscriptions on the coins of the reign: see Sordi, Dionigi di Alessandria', p. 146 n. 45 (with bibliography).

28. Eusebius, *Hist. eccl.* VIII. 1. 1 on the exemption of Christian functionaries and magistrates from taking part in religious rites. For the Christians' loyal collaboration with the empire, see also the interesting episode which took place at the siege of Bruchion (Sordi, *Il cristianesimo*, pp. 318 ff.).

29. Plotinus, for example, while certainly quarrelling with Christianity, never overstepped the limits of scholastic debate; neither does he seem to have had a political role or to have exerted political influence (cf. G. Pugliese Caratelli in *La Parola del Passato*, 12, 2 (1957), pp. 69 and 70 n. 2); Porphyry too, publishing in or around 270 his attack against the Christians, does not call for persecution (see E. R. Dodds, *Pagans and Christians*, pp. 107–8).

8 Diocletian's Restoration of Ancient Traditions, and the Great Persecution

With Gallienus' peace, the religious concept of solar syncretism had at last reached the goal towards which it had been working for so long. It had at last succeeded in finding a formula which would guarantee peaceful cohabitation among the many different religious groups of the empire: the *summus deus* of the many names, a deity in whom each group could to some extent recognise its own god or gods, and one to whom the empire itself could appeal for protection in the troubled times through which it was passing. From this time onwards, in fact, the selection of the strongest god became the empire's most immediate political problem.

Throughout the whole of the third century and the beginning of the fourth, the sun had been the symbol of the religious tolerance which the emperors had tried to foster, from the Severi to Gallienus and from Constantius Chlorus to Constantine himself (until his confrontation with Maxentius). And in fact even the Christians were prepared to use solar symbols in their icons and religious paintings, seeing Christ as the *Sol Justitiae*.[1] Tertullian himself, writing to confute the pagans' misconceptions of the Christian God, defined as 'plane humanius ac verisimilius' the error of taking the word 'Sunday' — *dies Solis* — as proof of the fact that the Christians worshipped the sun.[2]

When Diocletian reinstated the ancient Roman gods (in particular 'Juppiter, conservator Augusti'), and traditional forms of worship were re-established as the foundations on which the tetrarchy's political structure was built, it was almost inevitable that tolerance would collapse and that the Christians would once again find themselves the victims of pagan intransigence and persecution. It is true that the actual confrontation was postponed for more than ten years after the tetrarchan reform (286 AD) and that more years passed between the first signs of tension (the 'purging' of Christians from the army and the imperial service) and the final publishing of the persecutory edicts which broke Gallienus' peace. The reason for this delay is not that Diocletian was originally in sympathy with the

Christians and was later influenced by Galerius or others; it is that Diocletian believed persecution to be politically dangerous and had enough political sense to understand the serious consequences of taking action against a strong minority group which was by now integrated into the life of the empire at all significant levels.

In fact, ever since the end of Marcus Aurelius' reign the presence of Christians in the ruling classes of the empire had either been tacitly accepted under the Severi and explicitly and legally permitted and even encouraged under Gallienus. As a sign of the benevolence with which the Christians were treated, Eusebius reminds us (*Hist. eccl.* VIII. 1. 2) that, on the very eve of the great persecution, Christian governors and magistrates were exempted from the worship of the gods. This dispensation was something more than a simple declaration of the legality of a religious cult (indeed, not until Septimius Severus did Judaism attain the same status, despite having been a *religio licita* since the time of Caesar). Its aim was, in effect, to remove any last remaining obstacle from the path of those Christians who were prepared to accept official positions, and was planned to stimulate and encourage political co-operation. The fact that the Church did, indeed, co-operate loyally with the state can be seen from what occurred during the siege of the Bruchion in Alexandria, where the Christian priests played a decisive part in recapturing the district for the Rome of an emperor who might have been Claudius the Goth.[3]

The case of Maximilian (in 295, certainly before Diocletian first took action against the Christians) shows that the Christians were widely represented in the armed forces and even in the Imperial Guard. What is more, it is clear that their presence was looked on without any kind of suspicion. When Maximilian made the objection that, as a Christian, he could not fight, the proconsul Dio replied 'in the army of our lords . . . there are Christian soldiers and they do their job as soldiers' (Lazzati, p. 140). Maximilian was condemned not for being a Christian but for insubordination, and in the formulation of his sentence Christianity is not even mentioned among the accusations made against him: 'Because, through lack of discipline he has refused military service' (Lazzati, p. 140). When we compare this formula with those used in the past against Christian soldiers (like Marinus in 253), we find a direct confirmation of how different the legal status of Christians was after Gallienus.

The episode of Maximilian is significant because it shows clearly that in some African Christian circles there were still traces of the rigid stance of the Montanist doctrine embraced by Tertullian and Cyprian and kept alive by Arnobius and Lactantius.[4] However, we can dismiss the idea that it was episodes of this kind — and they were fairly isolated — which led to the military purges or which forced Diocletian to 'realise the dangers inherent in the polemical pacifism of the Christians'.[5] In fact, the purges happened some years later, and the Christians who were 'purged' from the army were not those who refused to take up arms; they were those who were quite prepared to fight, but who were forced to resign from the army against their will because they would not offer sacrifices to the gods — a practice from which they had been exempt for some time. Both Lactantius and Eusebius mention this reapplication of an old regulation as marking the beginning of the persecution, although it was still, at this stage, bloodless. They give the date as corresponding with the Persian campaign (particularly clear in Jerome's translation of Eusebius' *Chronicle*), and, more precisely, between Galerius' defeat by Narsetes in the spring of 297 and his victory at the end of the same year.[6]

According to Lactantius, the regulation was made in answer to a declaration of the *haruspices*, who claimed that the presence of the Christians prevented the gods from giving their responses through the entrails of the sacrificial victims. Angered by this, Diocletian ordered that all those present should sacrifice to the gods, going on to extend the order to include all palatines and all soldiers. Anyone who refused to obey the order would have to leave the army. Eusebius is rather more circumspect and vague on the subject of the origins of the regulation, but he agrees with Lactantius on its nature. He adds that a large number of Christian soldiers paid for their refusal to deny their faith with loss of rank and forced retirement from the army.

Lactantius knew Diocletian well, having been employed by him to teach Latin in Nicomedia. He was therefore undoubtedly right when he attributed the initiative for the first step taken against the Christians to Diocletian[7] and the inspiration for it to the *haruspices*,[8] strongly tied as they were to traditional paganism. As with Valerian, so now with Diocletian, the accusation which sparked off the persecution was religious and came from the pagan ministry. This time, however, it was far more serious and determined, coming as it did, not from the provincial worshippers of some oriental deity, but from the custodians of the most ancient Etrusco-Roman religious tradition. What is more, this happened at a time when religious restoration had assumed a political significance in the structure of the newly divided empire, with loyalty to tradition taken as the absolute criterion of truth, morality and social order. The edict against the Manichees was issued in the same year, 297, at the beginning of the Persian war. Apart from the real differences which existed between Manichaeism and Christianity, and, apart from the fact that there was good reason to be suspicious of a Persian sect at that time, it is nevertheless true that the edict contained arguments which had also been used against the Christians in the past and which must still have seemed valid to the traditional pagan: 'It is a grave fault to challenge what, having been defined and established once and for all in ancient times, by now follows the course fixed for it.'[9]

In the edict against the Manichees, as in the anti-Christian polemics of Celsus and Porphyry, the antiquity of a religion becomes the criterion by which orthodoxy is judged. A *vetus religio* cannot be supplanted or called into question by a *nova religio*. By adopting this mental attitude (incidentally, typical of him and reflected in all his reforms), Diocletian was in fact faithfully following the ancient traditions of Rome. (Livy attributed the same attitude of hostile mistrust of anything new to the consul encharged with putting down the Bacchanals in 186 BC.) It is not surprising, then, to find that the reasons for persecuting the Manichees should have been used also in the case of the Christians, and that the refusal to practise the *vetus religio* should have been the decisive factor in the decision to eliminate the Christians from public service.

Unlike the edict against the Manichees, the text ordering all palatines and all soldiers to offer sacrifice to the gods has not come down to us. For all we know, the Christians may not even have been mentioned by name, as was the case at the time of Decius' edict (and in fact, Decius and his times were being re-evaluated with great interest during this period[10]). It is possible that the order to sacrifice concerned *all* soldiers and *all* palatines with *no exception made for the Christians*, despite the fact that they had been exempt from this practice since the time of Gallienus. For the moment, Christianity was still a *religio licita*, but its adherents were in reality excluded from holding public office and found themselves left on the margins of society and the official life of the state.

The measures were put into effect in different degrees in different parts of the empire, and in many areas the purges never even began. Palatines like Gorgonius, Petrus and Doroteus, well known to be

Christian and among the first to be martyred in 303 (Eusebius, *Hist. eccl.* VIII. 6. 1 ff.), continued to frequent the palace of Nicomedia and to enjoy Diocletian's trust, which would seem to indicate that, after an initial burst, the edict was actually applied very loosely. The same can be said for the army, as we see from the fact that there are records of Christian soldiers even after 297.[11] In fact, Diocletian himself was well aware (Lactantius, *De mort.* 11.3) that the purge had yet to be put into effect. In the famous talks which took place in the winter of 302/3, he tried to convince Galerius (who was determined to arrive at a final solution with regard to the Christians) that it would be dangerous 'to upset the whole world' by shedding blood and that it would be enough to put the existing edict into effect in a more efficient way: 'it was sufficient to forbid this religion to soldiers and palatines.' Despite his basic antipathy towards the Christians and his deep attachment to traditional paganism, Diocletian's behaviour between 297 and 303 seems to indicate that he was not entirely sure of himself on this question and that he felt an instinctive repugnance not only for bloody persecutions but even for over-drastic purges.

It was Galerius who, in 303, finally put an end to Diocletian's vacillation between the intransigence dictated by his traditionalist sympathies and the tolerance suggested by political discretion.

A native of Dacia, son of a priestess of the gods of the mountains, Galerius was Diocletian's Caesar and his successor in the East. Lactantius presents him to us as a man bestial in both body and spirit, as a barbarian whose cruelty 'a Romano sanguine aliena' (*De mort.* 9, 2), was animated by a fanatical and ruthless hatred for the Christians. Even allowing for the distortions inevitable in polemic and apologetic writing (in which '*Romanitas*' is now synonymous with *humanitas* and *Christianitas* and the persecutor persecutes because he is not really a Roman), Lactantius portrays exactly the tone of religious fanaticism that survives powerfully in Galerius' own most important document: the edict with which, in 311, he puts an end to the persecution. Tormented by an unpleasant and humiliating mortal disease, he accuses the Christians of having misunderstood his intentions and of having brought the wrath of their God down on his head. At the same time, he begs them to intercede with their God on his behalf. In Galerius, in the Roman from the frontier regions, the passionate cult of the *mos maiorum*, of the *leges veteres* and of the *publica Romanorum disciplina* becomes a religion in itself, to be defended with rabid fanaticism against those who 'following their own will and according to their own pleasure' have denied the religion of their forefathers.[12] A disciple of Diocletian's as far as the ideal of religious restoration was concerned, Galerius did not share his leader's hesitancy; he overrode all Diocletian's resistance and, taking anti-Christian prejudices to their extreme conclusion, brought about the open and bloody persecution which Diocletian would have preferred to avoid.

The choice of the day of the *Terminalia* (23 February) of the year 303 with its symbolic and auspicious significance for the proclamation of the first edict (Lactantius, *De mort*. 12. 1) clearly reveals the influence of the *haruspices* and the pagan conservatives. On the basis of the edict (Eusebius, *Hist. eccl.* VIII. 2. 4; Lactantius, *De mort*. 13. 1), the churches were to be destroyed, the holy scriptures consigned to the flames and those of the *honestiores* who were Christians were to be accused of *infamia*, deprived of their right to resort to the law, subjected to any legal action brought against them and, if found guilty, subjected to punishments which were designed to degrade and humiliate them.

The first edict thus picked up the basic ideas behind Valerian's first and second edicts and aimed above all at damaging the church as an organisation and the Christians of the ruling classes. Capital punishment was not yet envisaged for those professing the Christian faith and not all Christians were forced to offer sacrifices to the gods. In effect, therefore, the edict reflected both Diocletian's intentions (to purge all imperial organs of all non-traditionalist elements without actually shedding blood) and those of Galerius himself, who openly charged the Church and the Christians with being foreign bodies which had to be eliminated from the state. The condition laid down by Diocletian, 'to keep a moderate line . . . so that the problem may be solved without spilling blood' (Lactantius, ibid. 11. 8) was both utopian and illusory as, indeed, the first edict of Valerian had proved to be. In Nicomedia, using the excuse of arson attempts[13] in the palace after the publication of the edict, priests and deacons were arrested and put to death without trial and the infuriated Diocletian let fly 'not only against those of his household, but against everyone' (Lactantius, ibid. 15. 1). Even the Emperor's wife and daughter, Prisca and Valeria, were made to sacrifice to the gods, while 'the judges present in all the temples forced everyone to offer sacrifice' (ibid. 15. 4). Thus it was Diocletian himself who ended up frustrating his own plans for moderation, and the persecution started on its bloody escalation. News of other edicts comes to us through Eusebius; the second and third edicts were issued in the same year, and forced all ecclesiastics to make sacrifice to the gods. The fourth edict of 304 extended this order to include all Christians in all parts of the empire, without exception. From now onwards, all Christians had to offer sacrifices and libations to the gods.[14] There were many martyrs; Eusebius, a contemporary source and eyewitness to much of what he reports, tells us that the provinces in which the persecution was most fierce were Africa, Mauritania, Egypt with the Thebaid and Palestine. He recalls with horror the atrocities he saw committed and with amazement and admiration the serenity and heroism with which the Christians went to meet their deaths.

The edicts were also enforced in Italy, under Maximian.[15] Only Gaul and Britain, under the Caesar Constantius, were safe from the violence of persecution. Faithful to solar syncretism and well disposed towards the Christians (as seems apparent from his choosing the name Anastasia for his daughter), Constantius was only concerned with not jeopardising the tetrarchy and limited himself to enforcing the first edict only to the extent of destroying church property, while taking no action against the Christians themselves (Lactantius, ibid. 15. 7). The moment he himself became Augustus, after the abdication of Diocletian and Maximian on 1 May 305, he put a stop to the persecution in all its forms. In the period following Diocletian's abdication and the setting up of the second tetrarchy, persecution followed different paths in the East and the West. In the West, where the idea of the tetrarchy was put on one side in favour of a dynastic succession, persecution came to an end immediately, at least in Italy and Rome. In Rome, where Maximian's son Maxentius was elected Augustus by the troops, freedom of worship was restored to the Christians in 306 and by 311 all confiscated church property had been restored. In the states ruled by Constantius, persecution had already come to an end, as we have seen, by the time of his death in York on 25 July 306, and his son, the young Constantine, probably did not even need a formal edict to restore to the Christians their right to worship, contenting himself with simply continuing his father's benevolent policy towards them.[16] Thus Rome, Italy, Gaul, Britain, Africa (which had changed hands many times between Maximian, Maxentius and various usurpers) and Spain (which Constantine took from Maxentius between 308 and 310), all regained religious peace.

In the East, on the other hand, persecution continued. Following the decision taken at the congress of Carnuntum in 308, Galerius now shared his rule with another Augustus, his close friend Licinius, as well as with his nephew Caesar (later Augustus) Maximinus (Daia). In the states ruled by Galerius (Thrace, Greece, Macedonia and Asia Minor as far as the Taurus) persecution continued until 311. In the states ruled by Maximinus persecution was prolonged, albeit in an irregular and less obvious way, until as late as 313.

We have already mentioned the edict with which Galerius finally put an end to persecution, but only from the point of view of the spirit which originally inspired him to persecute the Christians. This edict (preserved for us by both Lactantius (*De mort.* 34) and Eusebius *Hist. eccl.* VIII. 17) is called either the Edict of Serdica, from the city where Galerius signed it, or the Edict of Nicomedia, where it was actually published. Written just before his death in May, perhaps on the suggestion of his friend and colleague Licinius, the edict was signed in the name of all the Augusti, as was the practice at that time, although it clearly reflects the split of the dying Galerius himself. It contains echoes of the feelings which induced him to initiate the persecution in the first place, and his sense of outrage at the Christians who abandoned the *veterum instituta* in favour of a freedom of choice which, despite the failure of his persecution, he continued to see as being purely arbitrary and simply the result of stupidity and pride. Disliking intellectuals ('litterae inter malas artes habitas', says Lactantius (*De mort.* 22. 4.) of Galerius), he refused to use intellectual arguments against the Christians, limiting himself to fighting passionately against Christianity in the name of paganism and traditional religion: 'For this reason [he affirms in his edict] we order *ut ad veterum se instituta conferrent.*' Galerius still believes in the validity of his aims, but it is no longer possible to put them into practice. Like all Utopians, Galerius considers reality is to blame for not fitting in with his schemes, and he blames the Christians for forcing him to massacre them (in the edict he speaks euphemistically of 'multi . . . deturbati'). Now that he sees that 'plurimi' (and the admission of failure could not be clearer) persevere in their course, not rendering due worship to the gods and not even honouring their own God, prompted by a spirit of clemency he has decided to pardon them and allow them 'to be Christians once again and to resume their meetings, as long as they do nothing to disturb the public peace'. With these words, much discussed by scholars in recent years, Galerius *restores* ('denuo' clearly refers to the legal situation after Gallienus' peace and before Diocletian's edicts) to the Christians their freedom to worship and to associate,[17] but at the same time he adds a condition, which he takes the trouble to underline in several successive circulars sent out to governors, 'ne quid contra disciplinam agant.' It is a vague formula which, like that in the ancient rescript of Hadrian, possibly meant that the only exception to the concessions granted to the Christians would be cases of infringement of public order or public morals, which would be punished according to the law. As in the time of Hadrian, this clause made it easy for anyone to find a pretext for bringing charges against the Christians, should they want to do so. However, the fact that Maximinus managed to find all sorts of loopholes and excuses to circumvent the meaning of Galerius' edict does not necessarily mean that duplicity was in the mind of the dying Emperor when he made this stipulation.

Galerius was forced to restore freedom of worship to the Christians by circumstances beyond his control. He bowed to these circumstances against his will, and for this very reason his capitulation was sincere. The conclusion of the edict, with its plea to the Christians to pray for his health and the safety of the empire, is a dramatic and even pathetic cry from a man, fanatically but authentically religious, who knew he had been fighting against God and had been beaten. This is a far cry from Maximinus' approach to persecution in the states under his dominion. Since first coming into power as Caesar in 306, he had put the fourth edict into practice, forcing everyone to offer sacrifice to the gods. Instead of imposing the death penalty, however, he tended to condemn defaulters to mutilation or forced labour in the mines in order to avoid the unpopularity and disgust with which even the pagans now regarded the crueler forms of persecution. In 308, after a brief respite, Maximinus renewed his anti-Christian activities with the so-called fifth edict. From now onwards, all foodstuffs were to be consecrated to the gods before being put on sale and whoever attended the public baths was to sacrifice to the gods upon entering. Then, in 311, after having temporarily abided by Galerius' edict, he went on to instigate a new wave of persecution on his own account, making use of the clause 'ne quid contra disciplinam agant' and encouraging petitions and denunciations of presumed immorality to be brought against the Christians.[18]

The method used by Maximinus in his persecution was very different from that used by other emperors. It was deceitful, subtle and in a certain sense modern, and was aimed at eliminating Christianity without making any martyrs. His main weapon was defamation; infamous slanders were spread with the utmost publicity, and, forging the Acts of Pilate, full of blasphemies against Christ, according to Eusebius (*Hist. eccl.* IX. 5. 1) and obliging them to be taught in the schools, he slandered the very foundations of the Christian religion. He also sent out his own emissaries with instructions to make the cities of Nicomedia, Antioch and Tyre and the provincial assemblies of Lycia and Pamphylia send in petitions against the Christians. The use of propaganda to combat Christianity reminds us to a certain extent of the times of Decius and is also a foretaste of what was to come under Julian. In any case, this use of propaganda, together with the attempt that was being made to create a pagan 'church', are clear signs that the persecutors were beginning to be aware of the irreversible change that had taken place in public opinion. During the first centuries it had been public opinion itself which had called for persecution and the state which had hesitated or even refused to go along with the demands of the populace. Now, the two great state persecutions — that of Valerian and that, far more serious, of Diocletian, Galerius and Maximinus — saw the progressive and increasingly determined dissociation of the pagan masses from the persecutions organised by their leaders. Eusebius repeatedly refers to pagan dissent Lactantius reports the criticism that was levelled in pagan circles against the intellectuals who supported the persecutors, Athanasius remembers having heard from his parents that many pagans in Egypt actually hid Christians who were being searched for, at great risk to themselves. By now, tolerance was popular, a fact demonstrated both by the measures Maxentius took immediately on becoming Augustus and by the efforts made by Maximinus himself not to appear too cruel.[19]

Notes

1. On this question, see L. De Giovanni, *Costantino e il mondo pagano* (Naples, 1977), p. 122

2. Tertullian *Apol.* XVI. 8.

3. Eusebius, *Hist. eccl.* VII. 32. 7 ff. Cf. Sordi, *Il cristianesimo e Roma* (Bologna, 1965), pp. 318 ff.

4. Cf. P. Siniscalco, *Massimiliano, un obiettore di coscienza del tardo impero* (Turin-Milan, 1974), p. 102 (to whom I refer readers for a recent and balanced re-examination of the whole question).

5. A. Pasqualini. *Massimiano Erculio* (Rome, 1979), p. 135.

6. Lactantius, *De mort*. 9. 12 and 10. 1; *Divin. inst.* iv. 27. 4; Eusebius, *Hist. eccl.* viii. 4. 1 ff. and viii; *Chron. Hieron*: (Helm) p. 227; cf. Sordi, *Il cristianesimo*, pp. 334 ff. and 446, and also, Siniscalco, *Massimiliano*, p. 107. Pasqualini, on the other hand, puts the date between 298 and 301 (*Massimiano Erculio*, p. 135) and excludes the year 297 because 'if the regulation went back to 297 . . . the case of the military martyrs (i.e. of 298) would clearly be evidence of the edict's not having been applied . . . Maximian would have adhered unconditionally to his (i.e. Diocletian's) dispositions'. But this begs the question; and the edict was not in fact ever wholly implemented, even by Diocletian himself (see above p. 125).

7. Lactantius consistently tends to attribute the persecution to Galerius. It is thus particularly interesting that in this case he attributes the military purges to Diocletian. On Lactantius' thinking, see F. Amarelli 'Il de mortibus persecutorum nei suoi rapporti con l'ideologia coeva', *Studia et Documenta Historiae et Iuris*, 36 (1970 pp. 207 ff. and in *Vetustas e Innovatio* (Naples, 1978), pp. 45 ff.

8. On the renewed importance of the haruspices in the third century and on their deep-rooted connections with Roman traditionalist thinking, see De Giovanni, *Costantino e il mondo pagano*, pp. 29 ff.

9. For the text of the edict against the Manichaeans, see 'Fontes Iuris Romani Anteiustiniani' (Florence, 1940), ii, pp. 580–81; cf. Sordi, *Il cristianesimo*, pp. 338 ff. and 447; Siniscalco, *Massimiliano*, pp. 105 ff.

10. For the topicality of Decius' reign at the time of Diocletian, see Sordi, 'La data dell'editto', p. 459; cf. above, p. 99.

11. The case of the centurion Marcellus in 298 is typical (Lazzati, *Gli sviluppi*, pp. 141 ff.); cf. above, note 6.

12. For the text of the edict of 311 (called the Edict of Serdica or Nicomedia), see Lactantius, *De mort*. 34.

13. There were two fires (on this question, see Sordi, *Il cristianesimo*, pp. 347–8).

14. Eusebius, *Hist. eccl.* viii. 2. 5; 6. 8 and 10; *De martyribus Palaestinae* pr. 2 and 2. 4 and ii. 1; cf. Sordi, *Il cristianesimo*, pp. 349 ff.

15. On Maximian's persecution, see Lactantius, *De mort*. 15. 6; cf. Pasqualini, *Massimiano Erculio*, pp. 136 ff.

16. Lactantius, *De mort*. 24. 9; *Divin. inst.* i. 1. 13; Eusebius, *Hist. eccl.* viii. 13. 14; cf. Sordi, *Il cristianesimo*, pp. 355 ff.

17. Not, however, the restitution of the confiscated goods. On this question, see Sordi, *Il cristianesimo*, pp. 366 ff.

18. On the policies of Maximinus Daia and anti-Christian propaganda, see Sordi *Il cristianesimo*, pp. 358 ff.

19. On the gradual change in public opinion towards the Christians, see Sordi, *Il cristianesimo*, pp. 371 ff. On Maxentius' measures, see Eusebius, *Hist. eccl.* viii. 14. 1; Optat., i. 18.

9 Constantine: The Turning-point

When, during his campaign against Maxentius, Constantine first started using the mysterious sign on his shields and banners (a cross, a monogram of Christ or a monogrammed cross seen by him in a dream or vision); and then attributed his victory to the God of the Christians, the feeling that the time had come to put an end to persecution and re-establish religious peace in the empire was strong among pagans and Christians alike. The more fanatical persecutors now had to search for support and consent from a public opinion which had become tired of the blood-letting of the past. Maxentius who, as a usurper, had more need than anyone of public support, understood the situation perfectly. From the moment of his taking power, he tried to go one better than the legitimate emperors as far as tolerance was concerned, even if as governor of Rome (the centre of official paganism) and Italy (where the Christians were a small minority, as they were throughout the West), his propaganda was aimed mainly at his pagan subjects. If the turning-point of 312 and the so-called edict of Milan had only been a return to the edict of Serdica, as some modern scholars have claimed, then it would be perfectly legitimate to infer with these historians that Constantine was not himself the author of the great change of 312/13 which was, instead, the work of Maxentius and Licinius. Constantine's 'conversion' to Christianity in 312 would thus have been an expedient invention on the part of the Christian apologists of his court, Eusebius and Lactantius, to which Constantine would have found it convenient to give his backing in the years of his final conflict with Licinius. The mysterious sign used by Constantine in 312 would thus be a solar symbol rather than a Christian one, and Constantine himself would have been a sun-worshipper still for some years to come. This, in brief, is the famous 'Constantinian question' which was originally raised in the 1930s by Gregoire and has since then been kept alive by his school. In 1955 this question was honoured with being the subject of a general report of the Xth International Congress of Historical Studies. Debate went on for many years, along with that on the authenticity of Eusebius' *Vita Constantini* and that on the older, but constantly recurring question of whether Constantine's conversion should be seen in political or religious terms and to what extent it should be considered 'sincere'.[1]

Today, this way of looking at the question is no longer generally accepted, and the traditional chronology of events, with the change to Christianity dated in the year 312, is no longer seriously doubted by most historians. Likewise, the accounts of the contemporary Eusebius and Lactantius are taken to be reliable when they attribute the conversion to Christianity to Constantine rather than to Maxentius and Licinius, and when they inform us that the famous sign on the shields and standards was, indeed, a Christian symbol. Most people would also agree that the *Vita Constantini* is authentic even if, given the nature of the biography, we cannot count on all the information contained in it as being entirely trustworthy. In other words, it is now generally accepted that the year 312 does mark a turning-point, even if many historians prefer to concentrate on the conditions which made this change of policy possible and the varied religious situations within the empire rather than on Constantine's personal convictions or the sincerity of his conversion to the Christian religion.[2]

I believe that we can only approach the question of this extraordinary moment of change, this volte-face which in a few years transformed Christianity from a persecuted minority sect into the official religion of the empire, if we first clear the ground of the modern prejudice which holds that religion was simply an instrument in the hands of political expediency. What we must bear in mind instead is that, from the third century onwards, the religious question of the choice of a deity to whom to entrust the empire, the need for an *alliance with the strongest God*, became a political question of the utmost importance. If political expediency had been the only question at stake, a declared alliance with the Christian God and the choice of a Christian sign under which to fight would be completely incomprehensible; the majority of Constantine's troops in Gaul were, after all, pagan, as were the Italic and Roman peoples whom Constantine was planning to win from his rival.

Religious tolerance was now popular, but Constantine did not use it as the grounds on which to fight Maxentius. Maxentius had, in fact, never been a persecutor and no one could accuse him of having been intolerant towards the Christians. Constantine offered himself as the 'liberator' of Rome from the 'tyrant' and as the saviour of the empire by divine inspiration and with the help of God (*instinctu divinitatis* is inscribed on his arch). He placed the salvation of the empire in the hands of his God with a gesture as decided as that of Aurelian and Diocletian but which differed from theirs dramatically. Not only was his decision taken suddenly, in the middle of a military campaign, but unlike their decision (made in the interest of religious continuity) Constantine's constituted a complete break with all the traditions of the empire. The fact that this break was complete was made clear from the start, when Constantine refused to offer thanks for his victory to Jupiter Optimus Maximus on the Capitol in Rome.[3] Even before the Christian authors took note of it, the extraordinary, revolutionary nature of Constantine's decision was put into words by the anonymous pagan rhetorician who pronounced a panegyric on the subject before the Emperor during the celebrations at either Treves or Autun, in 313.[4]

The panegyric of 313 was written in praise of Constantine's victory over Maxentius and in celebration of the divine origin of this victory; indeed, both the haruspices and the Emperor's advisers had been opposed to Constantine's undertaking the expedition in the first place. The orator asks 'which god and which *praesens maiestas*' had guided him. Certainly, he says, Constantine must have a secret relationship with this 'divine mind' which, having delegated the care of lesser mortals *diis minoribus*, deigned to appear only to Constantine himself (ibid. 2. 5). In the orator's detailed account of the military campaign in Italy, the deity constantly inspires the Emperor who, at Aquileia, models his actions on the merciful example of the 'deus ille mundi creator et dominus' (ibid. 13. 2) and turns the prisoners' swords into chains to disarm them and save them from acts of desperation. In the field before Rome, Constantine faces an adversary from whom the 'mens divina' has taken his senses, so that his army is beaten and he himself overcome by the waters of the Holy Tiber (ibid. 16. 2; 18. 1). The panegyric ends with a prayer to the 'summe rerum sator' (ibid. 26. 1 ff.) 'who desires to have as many names as there are tongues of nations and of whom we may not know by which name he would be called', a prayer to the 'mens divina' immanent in the world, to the transcendental (*extrinsicus*) author of every movement, to the supreme power placed above all the heavens, who from on high watches over his creation, that Constantine may be saved from the world and he and his progeny ('divina suboles tua') preserved to rule.

It has been pointed out that this prayer shows 'evident Stoic–Platonic matrices'. However, if we leave on one side the question of the nature of the supreme divinity (permeating world soul for the Stoics, transcendental power, orderer of the universe for the Platonists and Aristotelians, or even creator of all things for the Judaeo–Christian tradition), this prayer is clearly attempting to establish some kind of meeting-point for all the empire's different philosophies and monotheistic (or increasingly monotheistic) religions. What strikes us in particular, however, is the circumspection and evident embarrassment with which the author, certainly a pagan, speaks of traditional polytheism and of what had been — indeed, officially still was — the religion of the empire. In the panegyric, Constantine is directly inspired by God; he takes no notice of the *haruspices* (although they accompany him), he disregards the gods of paganism which are either not mentioned at all (except for political or geographical personifications like Rome and Tiber, which were acceptable to the Christians), or are referred to as 'minor gods' who look after 'us' lesser mortals. Constantine himself is protected directly by the supreme God; a pious and elegant way of justifying the Emperor's by now evident repudiation of the old gods.

After having read this speech, it is difficult to see how it could be claimed that nothing had happened, that there had been no change in Constantine's religious outlook. All we need do is compare the language used by this orator with that of the official panegyrists of 307 and 310, whose speeches are full of references to the old gods, each one duly called by his own name (Jupiter, Apollo, Victory, Mercury, Liber), and equally full of references to Constantine's devotion to temples and sanctuaries.[5]

The supreme deity with their many different names, the central figure of the panegyrist's speech, has a lot in common not only with the divine spirit of the philosophers but also, indeed particularly, with the *summus deus* of the solar religion, and in fact is not incompatible with the image of this deity which was circulating in the empire during the third century. However, in the speech of 310, the theme of which is Constantine's devotion to this god, we find that the sun is referred to by the traditional names of the Greek and Roman religions ('Apollinem tuum . . . ' (ibid. 21. 4) 'Apollo noster' (ibid. 7)). Together with Apollo, the names of Ceres, Liber, Mercury, Juno, Victory and, above all, Capitoline Jove are all invoked without the least sign of hesitation or reticence, because they were by no means incompatible with the solar religion's idea of a *summus deus*. In contrast, the mysterious *divinitas* of the panegyric of 313 is deliberately given no name and the author insists on the fact that He has as many names as there are nations, though it is impossible to know by which name He wants to be called. If the God to whom Constantine gave credit for his victory in 313 were simply the sun, it is hard to explain why the rhetorician should have been at such pains to avoid being specific.

In short, even if there were no Christian references to the campaign of 312 and we had to depend solely on the anonymous panegyrist of 313, we would still have to admit that something new and extraordinary had happened in Constantine's religious life during the course of the year. Whatever it was that had occurred, it had made him abandon pagan traditions and make it clear that he did not want the old gods to be mentioned in his hearing, to the extent that the panegyrist avoids using their names in his speech. It had apparently made him turn to a mysterious Supreme God, creator and provider of all things, in whom the deity of the philosophers and even the sun god could be recognised to a certain extent, but who could certainly not be identified either with any of the theories currently circulating among the philosophers, nor with the by now well-known god of the solar religion.

This atmosphere of discretion, this deliberate desire to avoid identifying Constantine's deity with any of the traditional gods, whether the ancient ones or the newer solar deity, is evident in the images inscribed on the triumphal arch which the senate and people of Rome dedicated to Constantine in 315.[6] It is also, above all, to be found in the so-called edict of Milan. Lactantius' version of the edict (*De mort*. 48) 'comes from the rescript published by Licinius in Nicomedia on 14 June 313, while Eusebius' version (*Hist. eccl.* ix. 5) is the same text published shortly afterwards in Palestine. Both versions record the agreement reached in the negotiations between Licinius and Constantine in Milan in February 313, together with their decision to include the provinces won from Maxentius in the outcome of their agreement. This document is clearly the result of a compromise between Licinius' paganism and Constantine's new religious beliefs, with its search for a language which would be acceptable to both the increasingly monotheistic areas of paganism (whether philosophical or solar), and the genuinely monotheistic religion of Constantine. In the necessarily concise language of official documents, the 'whatever deity may be seated in heaven' of Lactantius (*De mort*. 48. 2) corresponds with the series of philosophical–theological hypotheses which the unknown panegyrist of 313 offered on the nature of the deity who had led Constantine to victory. Characteristic of Constantine himself, however (and in fact typical of the mentality of the whole empire at this period) is the 'idea of an alliance with the deity'. In the meeting which was to solve the principal political problems of the empire, the decisions to be taken first ('in primis ordinanda') appear to have been those concerning the 'divinitatis reverentia', so that 'whatever deity is seated in the heavens may be placated and be propitious towards us and all those placed in our power' (ibid.).

What is, instead, exclusively Constantine's contribution, the condition on which he personally insists if an agreement is to be reached with his pagan colleague, is the concept of religious freedom, the right of the *divinitas* to be worshipped as He wishes, a right which endows each individual with the 'free prerogative to follow the religion which he chooses' (ibid. 44. 2). This is a far cry from the idea (formulated by Galerius with Licinius' help in the edict of Serdica) that religious tolerance was conceded by the emperor as a sign of his forgiveness for an arbitrary and mistaken deviation: 'pro arbitrio suo atque ut isdem erat libitum' (Lactantius, ibid. 34. 2). Constantine's condition also reverses the traditional order of precedence of the various religions of the empire, and does so in favour of the Christian religion; precisely in order to ensure the support of the deity, the emperors concede 'to the Christians and all others' the freedom to practise whatever religion they desire. Thus, by isolating the Christians from the rest and by putting them first, the so-called edict of Milan takes away from traditional paganism its position as state religion and clearly prepares the way for Christianity to take its place.[7] In fact, Constantine was already thinking along these lines when, in the winter of 312/13, before the meeting in Milan, he wrote to the governor of Africa, Anulinus, and to the Bishop of Carthage to say that the property confiscated from the Christians was to be returned to them and damages paid, and a gift from the state was to be offered 'for the expenses of those who serve the catholic religion, lawful and most holy . . . Indeed, if these worship God in the highest degree, immense benefits will accrue to public affairs.'[8] In 319 Constantine went so far as to forbid, on pain of severe penalties, the private practice of divination and, while he did not yet forbid its public exercise, he contemptuously defined it as 'praeteritae usurpationis officia'.[9]

That most traditional of all Roman religious practices, the one that according to Lactantius, had sparked off Diocletian's great persecution, is now a superstition of the past, barely tolerated in public religious functions.

Constantine was not, however, quite so rigid as far as the solar religion was concerned, at least up to the time of his final victory over Licinius. He allowed solar symbols on the arch dedicated to him by the senate and people of Rome in 315, and the same symbols also appeared on coins minted up to the year 320.[10] I personally do not believe this was a question of opportunism on the part of Constantine, that is that he preferred to avoid a direct break with the bureaucratic classes and the army on whose support he counted, knowing that sun-worship was particularly widespread among these classes and among the municipal oligarchies from whose ranks the panegyrists sprang. If we judge by what Constantine himself told Eusebius — who by now had become his adviser for religious affairs — and Eusebius revealed, after the Emperor's death, in his *Vita Constantini*, Constantine's failure to make an immediate break with the symbols of sun-worship had a far deeper significance than mere political expediency. Its roots are to be found in the fact that Constantine felt his 'conversion' to be a question of proceeding beyond, of defining and refining, the solar religion which had been his and his father's before him. Thus, he did not see his 'conversion' in terms of renouncing one religion in favour of another. According to Constantine (as reported in the *Vita*, 1. 27), at the start of his campaign Maxentius, he had been extremely worried by the use of magic employed by his enemy, a magic he felt would be impossible to defeat without some kind of divine assistance. He had therefore started on a search for a god who would be able to help him, knowing that the gods of the tetrarch, Jove and Hercules, had been of no help to Severus and Galerius when they had fought Maxentius. Only his own father, who had all his life honoured the Supreme God (*tón ólōn theón*) had received protection and allegiance throughout his reign. Constantine had, therefore, decided not to waste his time on gods who would not, or could not, help him, but to dedicate himself forthwith to the worship of the God of his father.

Up to this point there is no discrepancy between this version — told to Eusebius shortly before the Emperor's death, so many years after the campaign — and the impression given by the panegyrist of 313. Constantine leaves the minor gods to others and dedicates himself to the worship of the same *Summus Deus* his father had worshipped before him; and there can be no doubt that this was the sun. But Constantine's story goes further: in his prayers, he calls upon his father's god, begging him to reveal himself and to stretch out his right hand to help him. While he is praying, an extraordinary vision appears to him, a vision — says Eusebius — that 'had it been told me by anyone other than Constantine himself, I would not have believed'. As the day was on the wane, he saw above the sun a trophy in the form of a cross made of light, and writing which said 'With this, conquer'. He was utterly amazed, as was the whole army which was marching with him and which — it is still Constantine speaking — had also seen the vision. Full of doubts, he asked himself what this vision could possibly mean. Night came, and God's Christ appeared to him in a dream with the same sign as had appeared in the sky, exhorting him to make a similar one and to use it as defence against his enemies. The next day, Constantine discussed the affair with all his friends, had the sign constructed (Chapter 31 gives a description of the famous *labarum*) and took the decision to 'honour no other god than the One he had seen' (this coincides once again with the panegyrist of 313 and explains his reticence). He then called for the 'initiates of that doctrine' — the Greek word here is *mystai*, and the allusion may be to Ossius of Cordoba — and asked them who this God was and what was the meaning of the words of the vision. They answered that he had seen the only begotten Son of the one and only God and that the sign was a sign of immortality and a trophy of victory over death. This, in brief, is the story Constantine told Eusebius.

One of the reasons we can be sure that Eusebius' testimony is authentic, that he has faithfully reported both the words and the meaning of the story told him by Constantine, is that it ties up so exactly with what emerges from the words of the panegyrist of 313. There is also a small detail in Constantine's account which a Christian would have no reason to invent: on the eve of his battle against Maxentius, Constantine was still a sun-worshipper and, in becoming converted to Christianity, he felt he was leaving behind an incomplete religion, not renouncing a false one. In the vision, the god of many names had assumed a single name, and the symbol of Christ had appeared above the setting sun.

The historian is obviously not obliged to believe in the reality of Constantine's vision, especially since an earlier event shows that he was naturally prone to seeing 'supernatural' visions (the panegyrist of 310 tells of his having seen Apollo in a temple in Gaul). But an unprejudiced historian would be hard put to deny that in 312

Constantine went through some kind of profound religious experience, an experience so extraordinary that it completely changed his attitude to traditional religion, even to sun-worship (which was not incompatible with traditional paganism). Whatever form his experience may have taken, it convinced him he had an exclusive relationship with the supreme God, who had only now revealed Himself to be the one God, identifiable with the God of the Christians.

This relationship is centred round the idea of having God as an ally, and from now onwards it conditions Constantine's behaviour towards colleagues and rivals, troops and subjects alike. The idea is, of course, the same one that motivated Aurelian and Diocletian: that of the search for the strongest god, the god who would be capable of successfully taking on the defence of the empire. The religious feeling behind this idea is undoubtedly sincere and authentic in its belief in Man's total dependence on the deity, but it is not yet capable of understanding the interior nature of the Christian religion and it does not lead to any changes in behaviour or outlook. The religious attitude of the converted Constantine remains, at least in the years immediately following 312, the typical attitude of the Roman, for whom religion is closely tied to the interests of the state. It concerns Constantine as Emperor rather than Constantine the man, and it takes the form of a committed gratitude to the God who brought him victory over his enemies.

In his own way, Constantine is completely loyal to his new alliance. In Milan in 313, for the first time in the history of the empire, the religious question, indeed the Christian question, became a test case for future relations among the emperors. In order to guarantee Constantine's support in his struggle against Maximinus, Licinius was prepared to put his signature to a document which would undo the work he himself had done at Serdica with his old friend and colleague Galerius, the most fanatical of all persecutors. What is more, he found it expedient to follow Constantine's example and, on the eve of his decisive battle against his Eastern rival, he had a vision of an angel whose task was to teach him a prayer to recite with his troops (Lactantius, *De mort.* 46. 3). *In extremis* after losing the battle, Maximinus himself, forger of the Acts of Pilate, tried to gain Constantine's support by issuing an edict — at Nicomedia or Cappadocia in May 313 — giving total freedom to the Christians and restoring church property (Eusebius *Hist. eccl.* IX. 10. 7). (Incidentally, he was base enough to blame his subordinates for the persecutions of the past (Lactantius, *De mort.* 49. 6).

Although in reality it added nothing to the edict of Milan, we can say that the publication of Maximinus' edict finally marked the end of the conflict between Christianity and the Roman Empire. Maximinus himself died shortly after its publication, perhaps in September 313. It was, however, the decision taken in Milan which had such a profound influence on the history of the empire. From now onwards, Christianity was not simply a legally recognised and tolerated religion, as it had been under Gallienus; now it occupied an equal, even a favoured, position among the other religions of the empire, side by side even with traditional paganism which, as we have already seen, from now onwards ceased to be the official religion of the Roman state.

The situation of total religious freedom which came into being after the agreement of Milan represents a kind of ideal balance, almost impossible to sustain in the face of all the concrete, external factors which condition the course of history. The picture is of a state which chooses to define itself as religious and which, indeed, considers its relationship with the deity as one of the fundamental realities of its political life. At the same time, however, it is non-sectarian. This refusal to choose any one particular creed does not derive from sceptical rationalism, but rather from an honest admission that the state as such is not competent to decide on the theological question of the nature of the deity, the 'quicquid est divinitatis in sede caelesti' of an empire in which the relationship between religion and state originates in unwritten rather than written laws. The right of the deity to be worshipped as he pleases establishes the right of the individual freely to practise his own religion according to his own conscience.

The frailty of this ideal equilibrium soon became evident. In fact it disintegrated as soon as the balance of power was upset between Constantine and Licinius, one of whom had seen the agreement as the minimum requirement for religious legislation while for the other it had been the maximum concession he was prepared to make.

In his 'policy towards God', Constantine looked more for the salvation of the empire than the salvation of the soul. For him, the agreement reached in Milan constituted a kind of intermediate phase, during which the possibilities that he and his pagan colleague would be able to coexist could be explored. At the same time, he would be giving time for the balance of power to evolve, in the hope that it would leave him as sole emperor. At that stage, whatever religion he chose would become the official religion of Rome.

This attitude was characteristic of all the emperors of the third and fourth centuries, and in fact characteristic of the ancient Roman concept of *pietas*: religion was, above all, an alliance between Rome and the deity, an alliance whose object was the salvation of Rome and its empire.

Notes

1. For the Constantinian question, I refer readers to the presentation I myself gave in my book *Il cristianesimo e Roma* (Bologna, 1965), pp. 377 ff. and 450–1, and to the more recent and ample study of the subject made by P. Keresztes, *Constantine, a Great Christian Monarch and Apostle* (Amsterdam, 1981), pp. 9 ff. Sources are: Lactantius, *De mort.* 44; Eusebius, *Hist. eccl.* IX. 9; *De Vita Constantini*, I. 26 ff.

2. For a confirmation of the traditional view, see Keresztes, *Constantine*, pp. 27 ff. On the whole question, see S. Calderone, 'Da Costantino a Teodosio' in *Nuove Questioni di Storia Antica* (Milan, 1968), pp. 625 ff. and 676 ff.; see also, L. De Giovanni, *Costantino e il mondo pagano*, (Naples, 1977), pp. 22 and 15 n. 1. On the symbol adopted by Constantine, see M. Guarducci, 'Le acclamazioni a Cristo e alla croce e la visione di Costantino' in *Mélanges . . . offerts à P. Boyancé* (Rome, 1974), pp. 375 ff. and in *La capella eburnea di Samagher* (Trieste, 1978), pp. 45 ff.; also Keresztes, *Constantine*, p. 29.

3. On this refusal, see J. Straub, 'Konstantins Verzicht auf den Gang zur Kapitol', *Historia*, 4 (1955) pp. 297 ff. and also Keresztes, *Constantine*, pp. 30 ff. G. Bonamente calls for a reappraisal of the subject in his 'Eusebius, Historia ecclesiastica IX. 9 etc.' in *Scritti in Memoria F. Grosso* (Rome, 1981), pp. 55 ff. In agreement with P. Paschoud ('Zosime II, 29 etc.', *Historia*, 20 (1971), pp. 334 ff. and in *Cinq études sur Zosime* (Paris, 1975), pp. 24 ff.), Bonamente insists on the importance of Zosimus II. 29. 5, despite the evident chronological confusion in the text, because of its reference to Constantine's participation in pagan sacrifices on the Capitol in the year 312 (for fear of the soldiers). He attempts at the same time to show how Christian writers have since worked to give a different ideological interpretation. But Zosimus is a later and extremely tendentious source (see G. Zucchelli, 'La propaganda anti-Costantiniana e la falsificazione storica in Zosimo, *CISA* IV (1976), pp. 229 ff.). The silence of the pagan panegyrist of 313 and the triumphal arch of 315 (see p. 135 ff.) seem to me far more telling than Zosimus' confused report.

4. This is the anonymous Panegyric XII (IX), which I cite here and hereafter from R. A. B. Mynors' Oxford edition. On the significance of the testimony offered by the panegyric, see Sordi, *Il cristianesimo*, pp. 378 ff and, also De Giovanni, *Costantino e il Mondo pagano*, pp. 183 ff.

5. Cf. Panegyric VII (VI) to Maximian and Constantine in 307: 'imperatore et semper Herculii' (2. 5); 'ad Capitolini Iovis gremium . . .' (8. 7); Panegyric VI (VII) to Constantine in 310: 'Iovis . . . nutu . . . pinnis Victoriae (8. 5); 'Cereris et Liberi' (9. 2); 'Sic Mercurius . . . sic Liber' (9. 4) 'in Capitolini Iovis templo' (15. 6); 'Apollinem tuum comitante Victoria coronas tibi laureas offerentem . . .' (21. 4).

6. On the subject of the arch, see J. Ruisschaert, 'Unità e significato dell'arco di

Costantino', *Studi Romani*, 11 (1963), pp. 1 ff.; cf. Sordi, *Il cristianesimo*, pp. 382 ff. and 451 ff. and also Keresztes, *Constantine*, pp. 35 ff.

7. On the so-called edict of Milan and its novelty compared with the edict of Serdica, I refer readers to what I wrote in *Il cristianesimo*, pp. 398 ff.

8. For these texts, see H. Doerries, *Das Selbstzeugnis Kaiser Konstantins* (Gottingen, 1954), pp. 16 ff. and also Keresztes, *Constantine* . . . pp. 38 ff.

9. *Codex Theodosianus*, 9. 16. 1 and 2. For the questions raised by these texts, see De Giovanni, *Costantino e il Mondo pagano*, pp. 22 ff.

10. On Constantine and sun-worship, see De Giovanni, *Costantino e il Mondo pagano*, pp. 105 ff. (for the coins, p. 126).

Part Two
The Christians and the Roman World

Introduction

In the first part of this work I made claims which can be summarised more or less as follows: that the conflict between the Roman Empire and Christianity was religious rather than political; that Christianity was persecuted first as a religion and then as an institution and was recognised first as an institution and then as a religion; that Constantine's conversion was a religious conversion, even if it belongs to the Roman tradition of 'policy towards the deity', that is, of an alliance made with god (a concept which is, after all, by no means foreign to the Judeo–Christian religion).

When we pass from the examination of the relationship of Christianity with the State to an examination of its relationship with the Roman world, the society of the times, we immediately come up against the question of how this new religion managed to penetrate society, break down its barriers and become part of it. In other words, how did Christianity make the kind of contact with society that Melito and Tertullian saw as 'natural' and which, as soon as Constantine's peace had been established, led Lactantius to equate 'Roman' with 'Christian'. Obviously there is no single answer to this question. On one hand we can suggest that the Romans and the Christians, albeit in different ways and from different points of view, both represented a way of overcoming the Graeco-Barbarian and Graeco-Jewish antinomy which the Hellenic culture, despite all its ecumenical claims, actually contained within itself.[1] We might also suggest that the Roman soul suffered from a perennial nostalgia for the stern moral code and the virtues on which their culture had been founded and that a religion which called for rigorous moral commitment and the practice of personal and domestic austerity would have attracted many of those who were disgusted by the corruption they saw around them.[2] Equally attractive to those who longed for the security of the group was, probably, the Christians' strong community feeling and their capacity for mutual assistance in times of need; and in fact this kind of solidarity would be recognisable to the Romans as their own *collegia*, enlarged and enriched with new ideas and with a deeper sense of human values.[3]

In this second part of my book I will be dealing, if only partially, with some of these aspects of the meeting of Roman with Christian.

But I would like to say from the start that I believe the conversion of the pagan world to Christianity was first and foremost a religious conversion and that the immense attraction the new religion exerted on the greatest of the empires of antiquity and its cosmopolitan capital grew from the fact that it answered the deepest needs and aspirations of the human soul. And at the moment of Christianity's appearance on the scene, these needs and aspirations were also those of the Roman world.

Periodically during the course of their history, the Romans suffered from the premonition that the end was at hand. But, whereas Hellenic thinking had always seen the end in terms of natural phenomena based on the concept of the corruption of the human constitution and the exhaustion of the earth itself, the Romans rarely saw things in these terms. For the Romans, even before the advent of Christianity, the concept of decadence was closely linked to morality and religion, so that the end tended to take on apocalyptic overtones. This concept was to emerge in full force during the great crisis of the third century, at the time of Decius and Valerian, but Augustan writers had already diagnosed it in Rome's first great crisis, the Gallic catastrophe of 386 BC, and it was equally present in the first century before Christ. In all three cases, but particularly in the period preceding Augustus' accession, the crisis was felt to be the consequence of a sin which had contaminated the roots of the Roman state and had caused the gods to hate it. For example, in the first century the civil wars symbolic of the *scelus* of Romulus' fratricide, were thought to be the cause. Equally in all three cases but particularly in the first century BC it seems that the Romans were convinced that the sin could be expiated, the punishment postponed and Rome renewed. With Augustus, the celebration of the return of the golden age follows punctually on the heels of the crisis, as will happen again under Gallienus.

This religious concept of history with its sequence of sin, expiation and redemption, was part of the inheritance handed on to the Romans by the Etruscans. According to ancient Etruscan beliefs, every human being and every nation had been given a fixed period of life, divided into periods (*saecula* for nations), and marked by moments of crisis which could be postponed by means of the expiation of the sin which had originally caused them. The only exception was the supreme crisis, the last and fatal one, for which there was no remedy. The *haruspices* of the first century, however, perhaps influenced by Pythagorean philosophy, overlaid the idea of the end with the concept of the conclusion of a cycle of the great year, which would bring the beginning of a new cycle, to be foretold by signs and portents. At this point, Etruscan theory took over once more from the Greek: the portents would reveal to the *haruspices* that 'men were born into the world more or less loved by the gods than they were with different characters and a different way of life from previous ones,' (Plut. *Sull.* 7. 3 ff.). The possibility that the men of the new cycle were more or less loved by the gods actually broke the cycle of eternal renewal: by introducing the concept of sin, expiation, postponement and end, they left room for the unexpected and therefore substituted linear time for the cyclic theory characteristic of Greek and Pythagorean philosophy. Thus the linear concept of time which we think of as being typically Christian was actually already in existence in the ancient Roman world.[4] In fact, this concept of history influenced the whole of the period of the great crisis of the first century before Christ, and its echo is to be heard in the works of the more aware and sensitive of the Roman writers of the time.

Poetry often expresses the secret aspirations of an epoch better, and more profoundly, than any other form of intellectual production. It is therefore not coincidental that from the time of Constantine onwards,[5] throughout the last period of antiquity and into the Middle Ages, a Christian interpretation was given to Virgil's Fourth Eclogue. Prophecies of the incarnation and redemption were seen in it, and, when a link between Christianity and the greatest Roman poet was found, some kind of continuity was sought between the intuitions of the greatest spirits of the Roman world (where these had not succumbed to superstition), and the new religion.[6] In reality, the Etrusco-Roman belief in the *saecula* is by itself enough to explain the meaning in Virgil's eclogue of the birth of the mysterious child and the expectation of the new era to which this birth would lead. There is no need to search for possible contacts with the Jewish world to provide an explanation, even though contact may well have existed through Antony's confederate Asinius Pollio. However that may be, I personally believe that, even if the eclogue neither presupposes nor needs a knowledge of Messianic prophecies, even if its meaning can be fully explained by the cultural traditions of the Italic and Roman peoples, by the concept of the *saecula* and by the meaning behind Catullus' sixty-fourth poem, the fact still remains that it is precisely in its deep and innate reflection of the Roman soul that the eclogue reveals its genuinely anticipatory significance and makes of it the highest expression of the pagan sense of Advent.

One of the works which undoubtedly influenced the Fourth Eclogue was the sixty-fourth poem of Catullus.[7] The theme of this ode is the mythical marriage of gods with humans, and the spirit is one of great yearning for a past in which such marriages were possible. As a backdrop to the marriage of Peleus and Thetis, a man and a goddess, is depicted the marriage of a god and a woman, Dionysus and Ariadne, who has been betrayed by Theseus. In this poem, constructed according to pure Hellenic models, the gods have descended from Olympus to take part in the marriage feast of Peleus and Thetis and the poem ends with the chorus of the Fates, sung to the child who will be born of the marriage. What makes this ode particularly interesting and particularly poignant is its tone of deep regret for the passing of a golden age, and it is this which gives us a key to how the poem should be interpreted. Catullus grieves for the loss of an age of heroes, seen as having been an age of happiness for humanity (lines 22 ff.):

> O nimis optato saeculorum tempore nati
> Heroes salvete deum genus, o bona matrem progenies

The regret for its passing introduces the theme of the marriage and appears again, with the past compared to the present, in the wonderful finale in which we hear the longing for a return to an uncorrupted world, a world still visited by the gods (lines 384 ff.):

> Praesentes . . . ante domus invisere castas
> heroum . . . caelicolae nondum spreta pietate solebant

In its turn, this world is contrasted with the injustice and cupidity, the sin and civil strife which characterise the world of the present day:

> postquam tellus scelerest imbuta nefando,
> iustitiamque omnes cupida de mente fugarunt,
> perfundere manus fraterno sanguine fratres

a world in which the values and affections of the family are perverted and trampled underfoot:

Destitit extinctos natus lugere parentes,
optavit genitor primaevi funera nati,
liber ut innuptae poteretur flore novercae,
ignaros mater substernens se impia nato
impia non veritast divos scelerare parentes

A world in which lawful and unlawful, good and evil, turned upside-down and mixed with ungodly violence, have alienated the 'iustificam . . . mentem . . . deorum'. The gods will no longer debase themselves by visiting this guilt-ridden and depraved humankind, and neither will they allow humanity to see them in the light of the day:

nec se contingi patiuntur lumine claro.

The poem ends with Catullus lamenting the loss of the light, a light which has been extinguished by the sins of mankind. But he also invokes the possibility that the 'mens iustifica' of the merciful deity, capable of restoring justice, will in the end grant salvation to erring humanity.

The mythological images of the marriage and the banquet of the gods thus reveal their spiritual significance,[8] and we find we are dealing with the timeless symbols so dear to men of all ages. There is no need to assume a direct derivation if we say that these are the same images, albeit with a different conception of the divine promise, as those to be found in the Messianic prophecies of the Old Testament. The Catullus of poem sixty-four is not simply a poet wistfully longing for a mythical golden age, neither is he simply searching for a refuge from the arid truth of the present in the primordial springtime of fairy-tales. He is a religious human being for whom human happiness is to be found in communion with the deity and for whom sin, both individual and collective, is the original and deep-rooted cause of the breakdown of this communion. He is a man who believes in the power of the deity to restore justice, and who therefore aspires to salvation. And, indeed, the Catullus of the sixty-fourth poem, who cares for the fate of humanity, is the same as the Catullus of the seventy-sixth poem, who asks the merciful deity to grant peace to his soul and freedom from the passions which have disrupted his life:

> O di, si vestrumst misereri, aut si quibus umquam
> extremo iam ipsa in morte tulistis opem
> me miserum aspicite et . . .
> . . . eripite hanc pestem perniciemque mihi . . .[9]

In these lines we have what can perhaps be called the only truly existential prayer of classical literature.

The motif of the golden age, a motif which was to become so common in the works of post-Catullan poets, thus reveals its value as both a cypher and a symbol in the sixty-fourth poem. It is both nostalgia and hope; it offers a way out of the existential crisis from which the whole Roman world was suffering during the last years of the Republic, a crisis caused by the experience of the civil war and the collapse of traditional moral codes.

The coming of the golden age is the dominant theme of Virgil's Fourth Eclogue: ('ac toto surget gens aurea mundo' (line 9)), written some time around 40 BC. This was a period of great fear, when Perugia, having welcomed L. Antonius, fell into the hands of Octavian and was put to the flame. This gigantic pyre seemed to the Romans to be a forewarning that the end was near. Etruscan prophecies had established that the end would coincide with the tenth *saeculum*, and in 44 BC a diviner, Volcacius, had announced that the ninth age was ended (in fact the civil wars had made this age extremely short — from 88 to 44 BC) and the last age beginning. It would last, according to the *haruspices*, for one generation.[10] In the minds of the people of that time, Etruria's destiny and that of Rome were so closely linked that the imminent doom of the *nomen Etruscum* seemed to apply equally to the *nomen Romanorum*. Horace's seventh and sixteenth epodes are vivid examples of this generalised feeling. The second generation to be destroyed in the civil wars (*Epode*, XVI. 1) coincides with the tenth and last age of the Etruscan prophecies (according to official reckoning, the civil wars had started in 88 BC, that is at the beginning of the eighth Etruscan age) and Horace, aware of imminent danger, exhorts the 'pars melior' of the Romans to flee the 'litora etrusca', doomed to extinction, and to search for the possibility of survival along the fabled coasts of the West, where the Ocean lies. As far as Horace is concerned, the roots of the fatal curse which has fallen on the fatherland are to be found in the impiety and evil of the civil war: ('godless generation of cursed blood' (ibid. 9)), an evil which actually reaches back to the origins of Rome itself and Romulus' fratricide (the 'scelus' of epode VII, 17 ff.), the same evil, in fact, which had made the 'mens justifica' of the gods of Catullus' poem turn their faces from humankind.

Virgil's Fourth Eclogue belongs to the same period as Horace's seventh and sixteenth epodes and for Virgil, too, the 'ultima aetas' of the Cumaean Sybil: ('Ultima Cumaei venit iam carminis aetas' (line 4))[11] coincides with the tenth and last age of the Etruscan prophecies. But Virgil was closer than Horace to the Etruscan world and was more immediately aware not only of the general atmosphere of foreboding but also of the secret hopes of that world. He glimpses signs that the great crisis may be overcome and, choosing the alternative left open in the prophecies of the *haruspices* of 88 (Plut. *Sull.* 7. 4), he foretells the advent of a new race, dearer to the gods than the one preceding it. A 'gens aurea' are coming into the world, the new age is about to appear and the sign of its coming will be — in accordance with Etruscan tradition — the birth of an individual who will symbolise the new generation: the *puer* of the Eclogue, whose physical growth will go hand in hand with the progressive liberation of the world and nature from all evil (line 13):

> si qua manent sceleris vestigia nostri
> inrita perpetua solvent formidine terras[12]

In agreement with the invocation of Catullus' poem, the sign of this new birth will be the gift of a new relationship with the deity (line 15 ff.):

> Ille deum vitam accipiet divisque videbit
> permixtos heroas, et ipse videbitur illis[13]

The happiness of the golden age whose return Virgil foresees with the birth of the *puer* as its mysterious symbol, the happiness of the new era awaited with so many hopes and fears by earth and heaven alike, is not only a miraculous idyll unfolding in the midst of flowering nature, among plants, animals and human beings (line 21 ff.):

> ipsae lacte domum referent distenta capellae
> ubera, nec magnos metuent armenta leones.
> Ipsa tibi blandos fundent cunabula flores[14]

It is the direct consequence of *pietas* found once more in family relations (line 62) and, above all, it is the gift of the divine life which Catullus portrayed in the feasting and marriage of the gods: 'nec deus hunc mensa, nec dea dignata cubili est' (line 63).

With the insight of true poets, Catullus and Virgil were both extremely sensitive interpreters of the sufferings and fears of their fellow men in the last years of the Republic. Their cry from the soul for some kind of divine salvation is one that can never be fully answered and, indeed, was not wholly quieted either when Augustus finally put an end to the civil wars or when the new era of the *princeps* brought peace to the empire. The yearning for a new relationship with the deity, the hopes fed by ancient rites and mysteries adopted from the East, the sacred concept of the history of the Etruscans and Romans, the deep-felt need for liberation from sin and death and from the fatigues and difficulties of human life, all these come together in this invocation of the living God. And the God who is invoked is He who visits human beings and makes them worthy of communion with him, in Catullus' image of the wedding feast, the God who renews mankind and mysteriously makes him a participant in His own life.

Christianity 'in the fullness of time' provided the response to this passionate cry and conquered the ancient world.

Having attempted to show that the main reason for the triumph of Christianity is to be found in the most profound and authentically religious aspects of the Gospel message, I will now give a brief account of the relationship between Christianity and the world of culture in the Roman Empire (Chapter 10), the attitudes of the Christians to imperial ideology (Chapter 11) and some of the features of the meeting of church and society and the blending of one with the other (Chapters 12 and 13).

Notes

1. See below, Chapter 10, pp. 156 ff.
2. The Christians' fortitude in the face of death was not the only virtue respected by the pagans (and on this subject, I refer readers to my remarks in *Rivista di Storia della Chiesa in Italia*, 16 (1962), pp. 6 ff.). The pagans also sincerely admired the Christians' temperance, their cult of virginity and their self-control, worthy of true philosophers. This opinion is clear from the surviving fragment of the writings of Galen, Marcus Aurelius' doctor (Abulfida, *Historia Anteislamica*, ed. Fleischer, p. 109, cf. W. Den Boer, *Scriptorum Paganorum de Christianis Testimonia* (Leiden, 1965), pp. 781 ff.).
3. See below, Chapter 12.

4. For the Etrusco-Roman concept of history, see M. Sordi, 'L'idea di crisi e di rinnovamento etc.', *ANRW* I. 2 (1972), pp. 781 ff.

5. *Oratatio ad Sanctorum Coetum* 19 ff. The authenticity of this oration of Constantine's, recorded by Eusebius in his *Vita Constantini* (IV. 32), has been doubted in the past (see I. A. Heikel in *Die griechischen christlichen Schriftsteller der ersten (drei) Jahrhunderte*, VII (1902), XCI ff.), but is now generally considered to be genuine and is dated as having been written between 313 and 325. See S. Mazzarino, 'Antico, tardoantico ed era costantiniana', p. 115; De Giovanni, *Costantino e il mondo pagano*, (Naples, 1977) pp. 174 ff.

6. For an Etruscan interpretation of Virgil's Fourth Eclogue, see J. Carpocino, *Virgile et le mỳstere de la IVme eclogue*' (Paris, 1930), pp. 75 ff.; Sordi, 'L'idea di crisi', pp. 785 ff.

7. For a comparison between the Fourth Eclogue, and Catullus' sixty-fourth poem, see J. Perret, *Virgile* (Paris, 1952), p. 45; Sordi, 'L'idea di crisi', p. 786 n. 18.

8. On the mystical and religious significance of the sixty-fourth Poem, see E. V. Marmorale, *L'ultimo Catullo* (Naples, 1952), pp. 63 ff.

9. 'Ye gods, if mercy is your attribute, or if ye ever brought aid to any at the very moment of death, look upon me in my trouble, and if I have led a pure life, take away this plague and ruin from me' (trans. F. W. Cornish, Loeb Classical Library).

10. On the conception of the haruspices and its immediacy during the years of the Perusine War see Sordi, 'L'idea di crisi', pp. 783 ff.

11. 'Now is come the last age of the song of the Cumae' (Loeb).

12. 'Under thy sway, any lingering traces of our guilt shall become void, and release the earth from its continual dread' (ibid.).

13. 'He shall have the gift of divine life, shall see heroes mingled with gods, and shall himself be seen of them . . .' (ibid.).

14. 'Uncalled, the goats shall bring home their udders swollen with milk, and the herds shall fear not huge lions; unasked, thy cradle shall put forth flowers for thy delight' (ibid.).

10 Christianity and the Culture of the Roman Empire*

When Christianity first appeared in history, the known world was united by the two traditions of Greek culture and Roman political theory. The meeting of these two civilising traditions, themselves the fruit of other meetings, other ancient inheritances, led the people of the times to feel they were participating for the first time in a truly universal experience. This feeling is evident in the preface to the *Bibliotheca historica* written half a century before the Christian era by Diodorus Siculus. According to him, human affairs guided by providence had evolved into a unity and were closed, as in a circle, so that history could no longer be the history of a single city or a single nation or a particular age, but 'of all the world as if it were a single city' (I. 1. 3).

This cosmopolitan consciousness was fostered in the public mind by Hellenic philosophy, in particular that of the Stoics. If we look below the surface, however, we immediately see that many ancient divisions and rivalries were alive in this so-called 'unity'. In the text already quoted (and I use it because Diodorus, simple compiler as he was with no pretensions to artistic genius, seems to be the ideal mouthpiece for the dominant culture of his times), Diodorus attributes various virtues to history 'the metropolis of every philosophy', but above all, he says, the virtue of reinforcing the *logos* (understood as word and rational thought) 'by which the Greeks are superior to the barbarians and the cultured to the uncultured' (I. 2. 5–6). Likewise, Dionysius of Halicarnassus, a contemporary of Augustus, did his best to prove that the Romans were descended from the Greeks in order to justify, by their 'Greekness', their right to rule over the barbarians.

The Jewish world from which Christianity sprang was equally sure that the world could be divided into two camps. But of course the Jews were convinced of their own superiority to the Greeks, who were lumped together under the blanket-term 'Gentiles'.

St Paul was well aware of these divisions when he wrote in his

* This chapter first appeared as an article in *Vetera Christianorum*, 18 (1981), pp. 129–42.

Epistle to the Galatians (3: 28) that in Christ there is 'no more slave and freedman, no more male and female'; and again, to the Colossians (3: 11) there is 'no more Gentile and Jew, no more circumcised and uncircumcised, no one is barbarian or Scythian, no one is slave or free man; there is nothing but Christ in any of us' (see also Romans 10: 12). Now when St Paul writes about the Greek–barbarian or Jewish–Greek divisions, he is obviously not simply talking about ethnic distinctions or the question of having been born in one country rather than another, or of belonging to this cultural background instead of that (and, of course, Christianity abolishes none of these differences, as it does not abolish those of sex or social position). He is talking about the situation which arises when these differences become accepted as absolutes, so that, for example, faith in the One True God becomes the exclusive heritage of one nation, which then demands signs of membership from its people (in the case of the Jews, circumcision, the keeping of the Sabbath, worship in the temple, and so on); or alternatively, in order to acquire a certain kind of intellectual training based on critical rationalism, it is necessary to invent an entirely fictitious 'descent' from a particular ethnic group. In other words, Paul is writing about what happens when a simple difference, whether ethnic–religious or ethnic–cultural, first becomes an absolute and then goes on to become a mark of the intrinsic superiority of one human being to another. At this stage, the unique relationship of the single individual with the one God, creator and redeemer, becomes permanently lost.

When the New Man overcomes ancient antinomies he does not, as a consequence, overcome or dispense with cultural differences, which are, after all, unique and unrepeatable manifestations of each separate national experience. In the process of assuming the perennial values of the new faith, purified from materialistic egoism and polytheistic paganism, he simply overcomes the ethno-centric sense of the exclusiveness of his own particular group. This is the discovery of the seminal *logos* that Justin was talking about when he said 'every truth spoken by any man belongs to us Christians, because we . . . worship and adore the Word which proceeds from God' (II *Apol.* 13); it is the 'testimonium animae naturaliter christianae' of Tertullian (*Apol.* xvii. 6), which calls on the good and great God, which is heard in the common language of everyday life, the *vox omnium* and which puts its trust in the providence and omniscience of this God: 'Deus videt, deo commendo, deus mihi reddet.'

The first to suggest that the Christians should approach classical culture in these terms was St Paul in his sermon before the Areopagus (Acts 17: 22). Taking as his cue the altar with the inscription 'To the Unknown God' which he had seen while walking through the streets of Athens, he announces to the Athenians that he is revealing to them the God they already venerate even though they do not know his name. As Tertullian was to do later, he appeals to his listeners' souls as 'naturaliter christianae', spontaneously orientated towards God. Having won their attention, Paul goes on to quote and interpret from a Jewish–Christian point of view the first nineteen lines of Aratus of Soli's *Phaenomena*, a work with which he would have been very familiar, coming as he did from nearby Tarsus.[1] (Incidentally, it seems certain that it is to Aratus, rather than to Cleanthes of Assos in his *hymn to Zeus*, that the direct quotation of line 5 of the *Phaenomena* should be attributed — 'For indeed we are his children' (Acts 17: 28) — and the same must be said for the image of a provident God who fixes pre-established cycles for mankind — see Aratus, lines 10 ff., whose subject is the stars and signs of the skies which mark the course of the years and the seasons.)

Having established a point of contact with his listeners on a rational level, on the grounds of the *logos* which the Greeks thought of as being particularly their own, Paul goes on to take his reasoning a step further. Rational man, he says, child of God, must necessarily refuse idols made of gold, silver and stone. Now this postulate is basically part of the Hebrew tradition, but it was by no means foreign to Athenian thinking, especially that of the Epicurean school.[2] At this point, however, Paul introduces an entirely new element — he speaks of the need for *metanoia*, and the judgement that is to come through a man whom God has accredited by raising from the dead. As we know, his sermon was interrupted at this stage; on hearing about the resurrection, 'some of his listeners mocked while others said "we must hear more from thee about this"'.

I started by saying that Paul's speech to the Areopagus provides us with a model of the Christians' approach to Greek culture, and this pattern was to be followed throughout the first Christian centuries, not only in its initial respect for the timeless values of that culture — thus, *naturaliter* Christian — but also for the precise limit beyond which this respect was not prepared to go. Thus, when Paul found himself facing the Athenians' refusal to accept the resurrection, the central and wholly new element in the Christian message, he made no attempt to rationalise it or to transform it into a symbolic representation of Christ's moral survival through his teachings or the lives of his disciples, although this approach would have been perfectly acceptable to the pagans (as we see from the writings of Mara Bar Serapion, a Syrian Stoic probably also writing in the first century). Instead, Paul simply accepted the derision of the majority of his listeners, and continued his teaching with those who, like Dionysius and Damaris, were prepared to make the necessary leap of faith.

It appears that in Rome, Paul picked up the threads of his discussion with the philosophers which had been so brusquely interrupted in Athens. In Rome, Stoicism as a moral and political doctrine rather than a theoretical explanation of reality, was the philosophy of the ruling classes and seems to have been particularly congenial to the traditional mentality of the ancient Romans. In fact, the Christians of the second century had an extremely high opinion of the Stoics of the first, as we see from the writings of Justin, who speaks of Musonius Rufus as being unwittingly a Christian martyr, and Tertullian who writes of Seneca, 'saepe noster'. Justin also points out several times in his *Apologia* that Stoicism and Christianity agree closely on moral questions. The First Epistle of St Peter, and Chapter 13 of Paul's Epistle to the Romans both speak of the similarity between the Stoics' approach to politics and their concept of *libertas*, and the Christians' attitude to the state and all it stood for. Putting these facts together, it is tempting to believe that there is some foundation for the tradition of Paul and Seneca's meeting and consequent friendship, a tradition which comes to us through the apocryphal correspondence attributed to them in the fourth century.[3] In fact, Paul certainly had dealings with Seneca's brother Gallio in Corinth, and Seneca himself was a friend of Burrus, the praetorian prefect during Paul's imprisonment who was responsible for the Apostle's lenient treatment (the Acts emphasises the *parresia*, and freedom of speech with which Paul was allowed to preach the gospel while still in prison). In all probability, the same Burrus was also responsible for Paul's pardon. Through these two, Seneca would almost certainly have met Paul and had a means of being in contact with him. Scarpat's recent observations on Seneca's use of the term *caro*[4] — close as it is to the word, probably of Judeo-Hellenic origin, which Paul uses for 'flesh' — could lead to a systematic re-evaluation of the whole question. This is particularly interesting when we bear in mind that another of Paul's contemporaries, the poet Persius, also gives the same meaning to the 'pulp scelerata' (*Satires*, II. 63) which prevents men from living a pure and upright life, and in other passages seems to echo some of the concepts and images of Christianity. A graffito in Pompeii, written before 62 AD defines the Christians as 'saevos Solones'; in one of Persius's satires (III. 79), also written before the year 62, the uneducated masses call the Stoics 'aerumnosi solones', 'dark-faced know-alls' who, with their austerity and moral severity, condemned the dissolute life of the court and the widespread corruption of the times.[5] During the same years, the First Epistle of St Peter (4: 4) reports that the pagans found it strange that, when their compatriots were converted to Christianity, they gave up taking part in the 'lawless disorder' of the times.

It is no coincidence that precisely in these years (in 64 for the Christians and 65/6 for the Stoics), both Christians and Stoics became unpopular with the masses, who completely misunderstood them, and both were persecuted by Nero.

The interest and sympathy with which Christianity seems to have been regarded during the first century, particularly in Roman Stoic circles, are no longer apparent in the second century. From Pliny to Tacitus, from Suetonius to Apuleius, Fronto and Marcus Aurelius, from Aelius Aristides to Celsus, all the representatives of Greek and Roman culture are now either hostile or contemptuous towards the Christians, while aggression and prejudice are becoming steadily more widespread among the increasingly fanatical masses. The second century is, in fact, an age of contrasts. On the one side it is an age of enlightenment, in which philosophy, now a title of honour, ascends the throne in the person of Marcus Aurelius. On the other side, we see a decline in the spirit of research and of faith in reason. Where reason had been a calm and dispassionate instrument for the critical exploration of truth, we now find it re-exploring philosophies with a bias towards mysticism, theosophy and magic like those of Pythagoras and Plato. Christianity comes under fire from both the fideists and the rationalists; the first see the Christians as guilty of bringing down the wrath of the gods by teaching atheism and impiety, the second accuse them of being irrationally dogmatic.[6] Occasionally, the two positions become confused, as when Celsus blames the Christians for their fideistic outlook in the name of rationality, but then reveals that he himself believes in oracles and prodigious signs. A few remain uninfected by the general sense of aversion for the Christians. Epictetus, for example, observed dispassionately but not hostilely the Christian *ethos* in the face of death,[7] but he died at the beginning of the second century, and was therefore linked to the Stoic outlook of the first. The sceptic Lucian mocked the credulity of the Christians in a superficial and sarcastic style, but he did the same by the fanatical masses who wanted to see the Christians sentenced to death for atheism. Galen, a doctor with a scientific turn of mind, trained as an Aristotelian, gives us an acute and not un-admiring analysis of the high moral conduct of the Christians and their strength of character in the face of death, even while he reproves them (but without rancour) for their dogmatism.

The hostile atmosphere gradually wore down the basically tolerant position of the emperors, and encouraged them to intervene in some way against the Christians; and it is at this point that the first Christian *apologiae* are born. The first *apologia* to come down to us is that of Justin, those of Aristides and Quadratus having perished. Justin addresses the Emperors Antoninus Pius and his sons as one philosopher to others, as one man who loves the truth to other men who love the truth. Christianity is presented to them as a philosophy, as it was in other *apologiae* of the second century (and I am thinking in particular of the fragment of Melito of Sardis quoted by Eusebius). Without stopping to stress the significance the word 'philosophy' had for the Christians of the second century (love of knowledge, love of truth), there is no doubt that the apologists' decision to present Christianity in these terms was also dictated by the historical situation of the times.

In a pluralistic culture such as that under the 'enlightened' Antonines, a culture in which so many often contrasting philosophies enjoyed rights of citizenship, the Christians should also have the right to state their case in public, to teach the concept of God, the world and life which their particular faith gave them. While explaining and teaching their doctrine, the Christians would also be comparing and contrasting their concept with the other ideas of God, the world and man which were circulating in the classical world at that time. We must immediately note, however, that Justin was not prepared to confront, or debate with *all* the other ideologies, even if he only refuses explicitly to do so at the end of his Second *Apologia*. Throughout the rest of his work, Epicureanism and Cynicism are consistently excluded as being doctrines which either denied the existence of religious questions, or proclaimed a complete indifference to them, and ended up using elaborate pretences of virtue and theories of spiritual independence to transform moral licence into a theory of life. It may seem to us that Justin is over-simplistic and tends to generalise in his criticism of these particular philosophies, but all the Christian writers of antiquity seem to have shared his views. As far as the Christians were concerned, there was never any possibility of dialogue with the Epicureans or the Cynics, and, because they were aware of the basic incompatibility of their philosophies, no Cynic or Epicurean concepts or systems of thought were ever incorporated into Christian doctrine.[8] And yet it is interesting to note that, because of their common denial of the existence of the gods, the Epicureans and the Christians were often confused in the minds of the ignorant masses, to the extent that the cry of 'death to Epicureans and Christians' was interchangeable with 'death to the atheists', as Lucian tells us. It is also interesting to note on the subject of the Epicureans that they never wanted or encouraged anti-Christian persecution.

If Justin avoids references to the Epicureans and Cynics, he makes up for it by constantly comparing and contrasting Christianity with Stoicism and Platonism, the two philosophies which, meeting and overlapping, permeated the eclectic culture of the times. Justin's approach to these doctrines is complex. He shows a profound respect for individual philosophers (Heraclitus, Socrates and the near-contemporary Gaius Musonius Rufus — I. 5; I. 46; II. 7–8), whom he calls unconscious witnesses to the Word, men who offered themselves as mouthpieces through which the Word could refute the errors of demons. He is careful to point out the areas of agreement and disagreement between Christianity and the Stoic and Platonist schools. Lastly, while he is prepared to admit that Christianity has some points in common with the ancient philosophies, and he concedes that these philosophies expressed some important truths and reflected some aspects of the divine Word, he is nevertheless convinced that Christianity is superior to these in every way and that, compared with them, his own faith is entirely original. Justin quotes his own personal experience to back up what he says; in II 13 he says: 'I confess I have even given up Plato's doctrine, not because it is alien to that of Christ, but because it is not like it in every way, as can also be said of Stoicism.'

The theme of Christian superiority over paganism, over the insights of the philosophers and the poets of antiquity, is examined from two points of view. To begin with, Justin brings out the Hebrew theory according to which the Greeks had imitated Moses and the prophets, a theory which was to be much used by later Christian writers and which led to the Christian preoccupation with the study of chronology. The second, characteristic of Justin, concerns the concept of the seminal *logos*: because the truth sensed by the pagan philosophers proceeds from the Word which lies in each individual, it follows that 'every truth expressed by any man belongs to us Christians because, after God, we worship and love the Word which comes from God, innate and ineffable, who became man for our sake, to cure our ills by participating in them with us' (II 13).

Although possibly less so than in the past, it is still difficult for us to realise fully the force and courage of Justin's affirmation. On behalf of a small, and hated, religious minority, he was facing the dominant culture of the times, a culture rich in prestige and tradition. Against him he had the violent prejudices and ferocious attacks of the masses and the irritated contempt of the intellectuals (who some years after Justin's death in the person of Celsus derided the ignorance of thé uneducated Christians, presumptuous in their dogmatism, eloquent only when talking to women and children, but dumb before the master of the house). In this situation, he could not even count on the help of the state, which at most treated his group with a kind of offhand tolerance, prepared to ignore what appeared to be politically innocuous, but equally prepared to yield to pressure and persecute, when resistance to public opinion seemed impolitic or threatened to upset the peace. For this small minority and for its religion, Justin not only asks to be granted rights of association and worship, he also claims the right to express freely and publicly what his group stands for, the right to propagate the truths of his religion in open and uncensored debate and publication (II 14).

By the end of the second century and the beginning of the third, freedom of expression for the Christians had become a reality, even if the Christian religion itself was not yet legally recognised as existing. Two elements had contributed to this new situation: (1) the birth and growth of the catechism school of Alexandria, in which the theological and philosophical study of the Christian faith reached a high cultural level and gained considerable prestige among the pagan ruling classes and even at the imperial court; (2) the coming to power of an Afro-Syrian dynasty, that of the Severi, which was less attached than that of the Antonines to the traditional religion of the empire and was more open to the influence of oriental religions. Also, of course, it was dedicated to the ideals of syncretism in which the sun, the god of many names, was a unifying and catalysing element.

In this syncretistic atmosphere of religious pluralism and general tolerance, with positions of power now in the hands of men from the Eastern provinces, Christian theology suddenly became fashionable. The prestige of Origen was so great that, in the reign of Caracalla, the governor of Arabia in 215 asked permission from the bishop of Alexandria and the prefect of Egypt for Origen to be sent to him to hold a course of lectures. Equally, in 232, at the time of the Parthian wars, the Empress Julia Mamaea, mother of Alexander Severus, herself summoned the great teacher to Antioch to hear his enlightened theological disputation. Julia Mamaea also had a treatise on the resurrection dedicated to her by Hippolytus. And another Christian writer, the Armenian Bardesanes, dedicated a treatise on destiny to one of the Severan emperors, either Caracalla or Elagabalus. Again, Origen carried on a friendly correspondence with the Emperor Philip the Arab and his wife, Otacilia Severa.

It was in this climate of cordial esteem and evident appreciation that the construction and organisation of the Pantheon library were entrusted in 227/8 to the Christian writer Sextus Julius Africanus. Although certainly not of Jewish extraction, he came from Aelia Capitolina, the ancient Jerusalem, and was a friend of Bardesanes. He was also an expert on oriental questions having been, among other things, tutor to the hereditary prince of the vassal state of Armenia Mannus, son of Abgar IX, the first Christian King of history.

Now the Pantheon library was an important organ of the official culture of the times and was situated at the very heart of the empire. From the fact that its construction and organisation were put in the hands of a Christian, I believe we can deduce that the Christians by now occupied an eminent position in the cultural and political life of the times and were fully integrated into society. Sextus Julius Africanus was also, interestingly enough, the first Christian writer of profane works and the only one to appear before the time of Constantine. His *Kestoi*, written some time after 227-8, possibly during the preparations for the Parthian war, were dedicated to the Emperor Alexander Severus. From the ample fragments which have come down to us, it seems that the work was a kind of encyclopaedia of varied information with military affairs as the unifying element (camp sanitation, treatment for sick soldiers and animals, 'chemical' warfare). The author's treatment of the pagan gods is significant; without being at all polemical, he uses the names of the gods in a completely objective way, simply as words to indicate the fruits or phenomena of nature, so that Pan denotes panic and Bacchus wine. At most he adopts a tone of ironical scepticism as when, when preparing for a cavalry charge, he firmly asserts that a drug of which he has the recipe, injected by means of a syringe into the horses' nostrils, will be far more efficacious than any prayer to Poseidon.[9]

At the same time that Christianity was being peacefully absorbed into the culture of the society of the times, Christians were also rising to positions of power in the ruling classes, culminating in the accession to the throne of the Christian Philip. As we have already seen, this whole process is closely linked to the strengthening of the Severan dynasty and the steadily growing influence of the oriental elements introduced into the empire by the dynasty's Syrian princesses.

However, in response to the steady advance of indigenous Eastern rulers, the Severan age also saw the reawakening of traditional Greek nationalism with its atavistic contempt for Syrians, vilest of all barbarians. The result was the volt-face of the second half of the century. Racial and religious intolerance go hand in hand. In cities like Alexandria, it was extreme Hellenism and the usual anti-Semitism which gave rise to the barbed arrows which were constantly launched at Alexander and to the bursts of fierce anti-Christian feeling which marked the reign of Philip, both Arab and Christian. The *Europaioi* whom the Greek writers of the third century (in particular Dio and Herodian) liked to compare so favourably with the faint-hearted *Syroi* were Illyrians, and they came to the throne in the persons of the Thracian Maximinus, the Pannonian Decius, the Dalmatian Diocletian and the Dacian Galerius. These men were proud of having been born into races renowned for their strength and valour, and to this pride they married a rigid religious traditionalism. They summoned the ancient gods of the Capitoline to counteract the orientalising influence of syncretism; they called up the time-honoured prestige of the religious traditions of ancient Italy, the Etruscan discipline which, never wholly dead, now rose again as the last bulwark against encroaching Christianity. The Illyrian Decius, married to Herennia Etruscilla, was deeply tied to the Etruscan world, and gave his children Etruscan names; Valerian was himself of Etruscan extraction; according to Lactantius, Diocletian's persecution of the Christians was sparked off by a response of the Etruscan *haruspices*.

The Greek intellectuals, entering into this political and religious debate, transformed it into an ethnic confrontation. Identifying the Christians with the *Syroi*, they denied Christianity its universal appeal by stamping it as an ethnically separate religion, alien to the rest of the empire. This was the attitude adopted by Maximin Daia during the last persecution of the Christians (in the rescript to Sabinus in 312) and it reappears even after the victory of Christianity, when another emperor — Julian the Apostate, an intellectual of Greek training — revived the name 'Galileans' for the Christians in order to compare them unfavourably with the Hellenes.

In Julian's Galilean–Greek antinomy we find a last flowering (and indeed an overlapping) of the state of affairs we examined at the beginning of this chapter: the Jewish ethnic—religious opposition between Jew and Greek, and the Greek ethnic—cultural opposition between Greek and barbarian. Both tend to fix, to stabilise, human diversity by forcing it into an ethnic framework, so that it is only possible to pass from one group to another by an act of apostasy, by betraying the *ethnos* of the subject's origin. Religion and culture are an inheritance from the forefathers of the race, and neither individuals nor nations can escape from this heritage, or undergo any kind of change of heart or mind.

When nationalism becomes twisted into fideistic racialism the ancient divisions are simply perpetuated and consolidated, as we have seen. Diodorus and Dionysius pointed it out, and St Paul announced that the time had come to put this kind of division on one side. Now, between the times of Julian and that of Zosimus, it is this vision of humanity and history which constitutes the last defence of Greek culture against Christianity.

I think it is worth pointing out the curious fact that neither Diodorus, nor Dionysius, nor Paul, nor Julian makes any mention of the Romans themselves when discussing the divisions to be overcome or perpetuated, despite the fact that the Romans constituted one of the two basic blocs of the ancient world, and easily the most important one politically. The reason is that both Diodorus and Dionysius include them with the Greeks, Diodorus tacitly and Dionysius by giving credence to the ancient traditions of Greek descent. Paul, on the other hand, while calling himself a Jew by birth and a Christian by faith, did not hesitate to call himself a Roman whenever he had dealings with the authorities.

In fact, of course, there is a reason for this. Greek and Jew continued to be thought of in terms of ethnic extraction (even if the Greek *paideia* of the *logos* and the Jewish faith in the one true God gave these names, respectively, cultural and religious connotations); in either case, to be born a Jew or born a Greek meant to inherit the cultural and religious traditions specific to that race. To be a Roman, on the other hand, was basically a juridical and political concept which could, and did, coexist with any and every ethnic origin.

This indifference to ethnic extraction, this potential for true universality, was already a part of Roman culture before the arrival of Christianity, as Cicero, Sallust, Caesar, Livy, Virgil and the Emperor Claudius all show in their writings. Indeed, the idea was that foreign customs could be freely accepted and integrated into the traditions of the Roman world, as long as they were not actually harmful (Sallust, *Coniuratio Catilinae*, 51. 37 ff.), that the culture of Rome thus showed itself capable of renewing itself while keeping faith with its own tradition and that this tradition owed its originality to prudence, to equality before the law and to the *virtus regendi*. In fact, these concepts of anti-racism and universality put the Roman in an analogous position to the Christian, however different their aims might be; both were agents of synthesis and of the overcoming of the ethnic–cultural and ethnic–religious blocs of the times.

For this reason, we can see as wholly contradictory the attempt made by the persecutors from the end of the second century to transport the Greek–barbarian antinomy in to a Roman setting, transforming a religious difference into an ethnic one and putting 'Roman' in opposition to 'Christian' by the theory of the *tertium genus*. Tertullian himself denounced this state of affairs: 'Sed de superstitione tertium genus deputamur, non de natura, ut sint Romani Judei et Christiani' (*Ad nat.* i. 8. 10 ff.; see also *Apol.* xxiv. 9; xxxv. 5; 9; xxxvi. 1). In effect, to set the Romans and Christians against each other meant doing one of two things: either reducing *Romanitas* to being nothing more than a manifestation of a particular *ethnos* (which was contrary to Roman law, policy and tradition), or giving the Christians their own ethnic identity (as Maximinus and Julian tried to do, though in the case of the latter, the confrontation was to be between Christians, Galileans and Hellenes rather than Romans), which would clearly have been out of touch with reality. From the start, the Christian apologists argued against this contradiction. If Tertullian defined as 'ridicula dementia' (*Ad nat.* ibid.) the idea of denying the Christians their Roman status, Lactantius goes so far as to overturn the charge completely, declaring that Galerius and Maximinus were persecutors and enemies of the Christians because, being barbarians, they were enemies of the Romans (*De mort.* 9. 2; 21. 1; 23. 5; 38).

With the Greek world, the Christians used an intellectual approach. With the Roman world, characterised as it was by traditions of universally applied policies and jurisprudence, with practice taking precedence over theory, the Christians' approach was political, legal and moral. Roman traditions had to be separated from their roots in polytheistic paganism and transplanted into the new soil of the Christian faith.

This operation was the first and most important act undertaken by the Christians in the Roman world. It began in the apostolic epistles, where obedience to the Roman state became an obligation of conscience before God. It went on with Clement of Rome (Chapter 37 of the letter to the Corinthians), who recommended to the Christians the example of military discipline furnished by the Roman soldiers. It continued with Melito for whom 'our philosophy' and the empire, born at the same moment, were made to get on together. Tertullian maintains that Caesar is more truly Caesar to the Christians because his authority derives from the Christian God (*Apol.* XXXIII. 1). Lactantius anticipates the identification of 'Christian' with 'Roman', a concept which was to become a characteristic of the Christian empire.

About seventy years after the end of the persecutions, one man stands out as having clearly understood this process of transplanting old traditions into new soil: Ambrose of Milan, ex-consul of the empire and one of the most authoritative bishops of the Christian church. In his letter to Valentinian II in 384 (*Letters*, XVIII. PL 16, 971 ff.) Ambrose answers the pagan Symmachus, who had painted an image of Rome appealing to the emperor on behalf of the ancient forms of worship. Ambrose disputes the affirmation that the *mores* of the forefathers are to be identified with loyalty to the *caerimoniae avitae* and that it had been the ancient rites which had subdued the world. Ambrose, too, gives Rome a voice:

Aliis ergo disciplinis orbem subegi . . . Non in fibris pecudum sed in viribus bellatorum tropea victoriae sunt . . . Militabat

Camillus, qui sublata Capitolio signa, caesis Tarpeiae rupis triumphatoribus, reportavit: stravit virtus quos religio non removit. Quid de Atilio loquar, qui militiam etiam mortis impendit? Africanus non inter Capitolii aras, sed inter Hannibalis acies triumphum invenit (ibid. 7).

Ambrose refuses to identify Rome with its religious traditions and, indeed, says that pagan religion, far from distinguishing Rome from the rest of the world, was the only element it had in common with the barbarians ('Hoc solum [Rome says] habebam in commune cum barbaris, quia Deum antea nesciebam'). By rejecting as anachronistic, vain and not peculiarly Roman the religion of the past, he makes way for the idea of the continuity of Christian Rome, a Rome which 'does not blush' to be converted in her old age and is not ashamed to 'pass to better things', but goes, taking with her the *disciplinae* — that is the *mores* — with which the old Rome had subdued the world: the *virtus* of Camillus, the *militia* of Regulus, the military expertise of Scipio. These are the traditions which Ambrose considers worthy of praise. In fact, as I have tried to show elsewhere,[10] the whole of Ambrose's thinking on the subject of Rome is characterised by his conviction of the need to reject the religious traditions while keeping alive the political, military and civil ones, that is the traditions most typically 'Roman', the true *mos maiorum*.

While claiming that Rome is willing to accept changes ('longaeva converti') as long as they mean 'ad meliora transire', Ambrose reflects far better than his friend and adversary Symmachus what was the purest line of Roman tradition, the line of conduct which already in the second century BC Polybius had called typical of the Romans,'able more than any others before them have ever been to change their customs and to imitate the best' (VI. 25. 11). It is the same line of conduct which Sallust called typical of the *maiores* (*Cat.* 51. 37), which Livy saw as the key to the whole history of Rome (IV. 4. 4) and which the Emperor Claudius, in the footsteps of his master Livy, first made into a political theory and then put into practice in his speech in favour of admitting the Gauls to the Roman senate (*Inscriptiones Latinae Selectae*, 212).

Notes

1. On Stoic culture in Tarsus, see G. Scarpat, *Il pensiero religioso di Seneca l'ambiente Ebraico e Cristiano* (Brescia, 1977), pp. 74 ff.

2. For the Ithyphallic Hymn sung by the Athenians in 307/6 BC, for Demetrius Poliorcetes, see F. Landucci Gattinoni, 'La divinizzazione di Demetrio' in *Religione e politica nel mondo antico*, *CISA* (Milan, 1981), VII, pp. 119 ff.

3. See L. Bocciolini Palagi, *Il carteggio apocrifo di Seneca e Paolo* (Florence,1978), on the correspondence, certainly apocryphal.

4. Scarpat, *Il pensiero religioso di Seneca*, p. 77.

5. For the graffiti at Pompeii and the interpretation given here, see M. Sordi, 'Aerumnosi Solones', *Aquileia Nostra*, XLV-XLVI (1974/5), pp. 277 ff., and also, O. Montevecchi, 'Nomen Cristianum', in *Paradoxos Politeia*, Studi Patristici in onore di G. Lazzati, (Milan, 1979) p. 494.

6. See above, pp. 32 ff.

7. I believe I can confirm here the interpretation of Epictetus' passage (IV. 7. 6) which I offered in my article 'Le polemiche intorno al Cristianesimo nel II secolo' *Rivista di Storia della Chiesa*' XVI, 1962, pp. 6 ff. For a contrary view, see G. Iossa, *Giudei, Pagani e Cristiani* (Naples, 1977) pp. 81 ff. (who, however, did not take into account the contents of my article).

8. For an examination of this attitude to Epicureanism on the part of Dionysius of Alexandria, see W. A. Bienert, *Dionysius von Alexandrien* (Stuttgart, 1977), pp. 16 and 63.

9. J. R. Vieillefond has recently published the fragments of the *Kestoi* in *Les céstes de Julius Africanus* (Paris–Florence, 1970). On this subject, I here follow Rampoldi's thesis published in the *Rendiconti dell'Istituto Lombardo di Scienze e Lettere*.

10. M. Sordi, 'L'attegiamento di Ambrogio di fronte a Roma' in *Ambrosius Episcopus* Vol. I, Milan, 1976, pp. 203 ff.

11 The Christians' Attitude to the 'Political Theology' of the Empire and the Imperial Cult

In two famous passages of the *Hexaëmeron,* Ambrose describes the two 'natural' constitutions, that of the crane and that of the bee (v. 15, 50 ff.; v. 21. 66 ff.), an idea he took in part from Basil of Caesarea but then inverted to reflect the chronological order of the Roman Republic and Empire.

The principles regulating the constitution of the crane are a common sharing of *labor* and *dignitas*, a strict rotation of duties, and complete solidarity between the governors and the governed. *Potestas* and *servitium* equally are put at the service of the common good and command an allegiance which is as loyal as it is free, allowing no possibility of desertion. The Republican ideal that public office should be held briefly and temporarily and should work on a rotation basis combines with the equally republican horror of power being held beyond the established limit. We hear echoes of Sallust in Ambrose's lament for the passing of the 'pulcherrimus rerum status', by now obliterated by the 'dominandi libido'.

The *libertas* which Ambrose, faithful to Roman senatorial tradition, saw realised in the old Republic can be saved in the Empire as long as the latter is prepared to accept the necessary limits to its *potestas*, and to combine *potestas* and *servitium* in the service of the common good. Ambrose sees this state as typical of a constitution 'a natura accepta', that is of a constitution consistent with the aims established by God, whether command of the nation be in the hands of one or many. He provides an example of what he means in the social organisation of bees 'sub rege . . . liberae'. This society is rigorously egalitarian as far as the law is concerned ('what is lawful is lawful for all and what is unlawful is unlawful for everyone') and supreme power is entrusted to a king who is not chosen by chance, or by dynastic succession, or elected by the masses, but who, as Virgil pointed out (*Georgics*, IV. 95 ff.), is selected on the basis of unequivocal signs of nature, size, physical beauty and, above all, 'mansuetudo morum'.

The sign by which the natural and divine choice of king can be recognised is, therefore, 'mansuetudo morum'. The Greek and Hellenistic concept of *Physis basileos*, Romanised in the concept of *clementia*, fuses naturally with the Christian precept of *misericordia*. Founded on the sharing of rights and duties, the *regnum* is at the same time a *res publica*, and is not incompatible with the concept of *libertas*; the laws a king imposes on his people, he also imposes on himself, as Ambrose states clearly in his epistle to Valentinian II in 386 (*Letters*, 21; *Maur*. 9). The king is first and foremost custodian of the laws he makes and his *potestas* finds its own limits in the *potestas* of God, to whom he, too, is *subditus* and to whom he owes his empire.[1]

Roman Imperial Ideology

The vision of the state given by Ambrose in the *Hexaëmeron* and in his letters draws equally on the apostolic tradition of Paul's thirteenth chapter of the Epistle to the Romans, on the second chapter of the First Epistle of St Peter and, without having to make any kind of compromise, on the Roman tradition of the civil principate and *statio principis*, whose ideological matrix was the Stoicism of the first century. This last was, of course, in direct contrast to the theocratic, orientalising ideology imposed by Antony and seen at its height during the aberrant reigns of Caligula and Nero and the autocracy of Domitian, *dominus et deus*. The concept which Ambrose proposes was originally put forward by Augustus. It was then followed faithfully by Tiberius and Claudius, and was kept alive, at least as an ideal, as a declaration of intent and as an expression of the most genuine Roman tradition, throughout the centuries of the Dominate and up to late antiquity, as Ambrose's revival of it demonstrates.

Thus, even the writers of the first century could see that an agreement was possible between the Roman concept of the principate and the Christian idea of the state. Clement of Rome was certainly aware of it when , keeping up the apostolic tradition, he wrote his epistle to the Corinthians. The apologists of Marcus Aurelius' reign took the subject up again powerfully, particularly Melito. Tertullian was its most eloquent spokesman in his *Apologeticum* (XXXIII. 1) when he said 'Caesar is more truly ours (than yours) because he was put into power by our God'. Paradoxically, we could say that the Christian empire, made into reality by Constantine and his successors, was already potentially present in this claim of Tertullian's, a claim which comes at the end of such a deeply committed declaration of loyalty to Rome and its empire that it should surely suffice to disprove the theory that a so-called 'political theology' was the fruit of Constantine's peace. Tertullian says (ibid. xxx. 4) that the Christians pray for the emperors and ask for them 'a long life, a safe empire, a quiet home, strong armies, a faithful senate, honest subjects, a world at peace'. Again (ibid. xxxii. 1), they pray 'for the general strength and stability of the empire and for Roman power' because they know that 'it is the Roman empire which keeps at bay the great violence which hangs over the universe and even the end of the world itself, harbinger of terrible calamities'. The subject here, as we know, was the interpretation given to the famous passage from the second Epistle to the Thessalonians (2 Thess. 2: 6–7) on the obstacle, whether a person or an object, which impedes the coming of the Anti-Christ. Without attempting to interpret this mysterious passage, the fact remains that all Christian writers, up to and including Lactantius, Ambrose and Augustine, identified this restraining presence with the Roman empire and its emperor. I personally take this as indisputable proof that the Christians were not prejudiced in any way against the Roman empire, either as an institution or as an ideology. Through their conviction that the Roman empire would last as long as the world (Tertullian, *Ad Scap.* 2) the early Christians actually renewed and appropriated as their own the concept of *Roma aeterna*. 'While we pray to delay the end' — it is Tertullian speaking again (*Apol.* xxxii. 1) — 'we are helping Rome to last forever.'[2] We have no reason to say, therefore, that the Christians believed that Roman imperial ideology was in any way incompatible with their faith.

The Cult of the Emperor

The situation is obviously very different when we consider the question of worshipping the person of the emperor himself, either during his lifetime or after his death. From the start, the Christians recognised that this cult and their faith were radically incompatible, and Chapter thirteen of the Revelations of St John, with its passage on the Beast and its adorers, makes it quite clear that their opposition on this matter was adamant. However, it was not only the

Christians who expressed fierce opposition to this cult during the first century; their feelings were shared by the best of the Roman ruling classes, those who were most faithful to the political traditions of Rome. Under both Nero and Domitian, persecution of the Stoics of the ruling classes either immediately preceded or immediately followed persecution of the Christians, as I have shown in Part One of this work.[3] In reality, however, the most heartfelt expression of opposition to emperor-worship precedes both Nero and Domitian. It is to be found in the famous speech of Tiberius which Tacitus quotes under the year 25 AD, in which the Emperor refuses the offer of a temple in honour of himself and his mother in Further Spain (Tac. *Ann.* IV. 37–8).

> I, senators [says Tiberius (ibid. 38. 1)] testify before you and wish those who come after to remember, that I am a mortal and that I perform the functions of a mortal and that it is enough that I fulfil the duties of a Prince. Posterity will render homage enough [*satis superque*] to my memory if it believes me to have been worthy of my forebears, careful of your interests, resolute in danger, not fearful of giving rise to rancour against myself when it is for the public good. These sentiments in your hearts will be my temples, the most beautiful and longest living images of me. Indeed, monuments of marble become despised as sepulchres when the judgement of posterity turns to hatred. I therefore beseech the provincials, the citizens and the gods themselves, the last to grant me, to the end of my life: peace of mind and the ability to distinguish between the rights due to a man and those due to the deity [*quietam et intelligentem humani divinique iuris mentem duint*], the first that when I die, they honour my name and my actions with the glory of a good remembrance.

Tacitus certainly reworked Tiberius' speech, as he did the speeches of all the ancient Stoics; but it is equally certain that, in this case, the speech substantially corresponds to what was actually said. We need only compare this speech with the inscription of Gythium, in which the same Emperor refused the worship offered him by the citizens of this Laconian city, saying that for him more modest and human honours are enough (*SEG* XI. 922–3; the Greek *arkoumai* of the inscription corresponds to the 'satis superque' of Tacitus).

After the period of theocracy experienced under Domitian, these ideas became extremely topical once more when Trajan came to the throne. In his panegyric, Pliny the Younger states clearly: 'He considers himself as one of us . . . and he does not forget that he is a man just because he is set to preside over men' (2.3). Again: 'You are eminent, you excel just as honour and power excel, which are above men and yet are of men' (ibid. 24. 4). The *princeps* is not 'above the laws but the laws are above the *princeps*' (ibid. 65. 1). Domitian's deification of the living emperor is now condemned as being sacrilege towards the gods (ibid. 52.3) and tyrannical towards men (ibid. 2. 3).

Even so, unlike the first century, there are signs in the pagan culture of the second century, and in the panegyric itself, that certain attributes, certain divine epithets, can be associated with the figure of the emperor without causing a scandal. According to Pliny, Trajan can be likened to Hercules (ibid. 14. 5) and is similar to those mortals whom the ancients believed 'maritos dearum ac deum liberos'(ibid. 82. 7). He is Jove's rather than Nerva's son (ibid. 23. 4) and the epithets given to Jove, 'optimus' and 'maximus', can legitimately be applied to him, too (ibid. 88. 8).

Thus, even if Trajan himself does not want to be called 'dominus' ('non de domino sed de parente loquimur' (ibid. 2. 3)), Pliny, in his letters to him, always addresses his emperor as 'domine'; and, even if Trajan does not want his *genius* to be honoured, but only Jove (ibid. 52. 6), Pliny forces those accused of Christianity to worship the emperor's image.

Similarly, it is interesting to note the difference in outlook of two historians interpreting Alexander the Great's claim to divinity in two different historical periods. Curtius Rufus, writing in the first century, judges Alexander deeply guilty for having wanted to 'equate himself with the gods and obtain divine honours, and for having believed in the oracles which persuaded him of this, and for having become enraged with those who did not want to adore him' (x.5). Arrian, on the other hand, writing under the Antonines, heatedly defends Alexander from the accusation of having usurped divine honours, declaring that he is not at all shocked by the fact that Alexander 'traced his birth back to the gods'. The claim is justified as an expedient (*sofisma*) aimed at ensuring his subjects' veneration(*Annals*, VII. 29. 3): Alexander, after all, was no less illustrious a king than Minos, than Aeacus, than Rhadamanthus, and no one considered they were guilty of pride for having traced their ancestry back to Zeus.

The difference in attitude between these two pagan authors, both of Stoic disposition, shows to what extent attitudes to the cult of the emperor had, in fact, changed between the first and second centuries. It also reveals that the original religious significance of the worship of the emperor was gradually disappearing, to become primarily a question of political loyalty. As this transformation became clear to everyone, the Christians found that they, too, could tone down their opposition to words and deeds which in the past had been seen as unequivocal expressions of emperor-worship. The use of the word 'dominus' is a case in point. Tertullian now finds he is quite prepared to concede the emperor this title, *more communi*: 'Dicam plane imperatorem dominum sed more communi, sed quando non cogor ut dominum dei vice dicam (*Apol.* xxxiv. 1).

Some years after writing the *Apologeticum* we find Tertullian, now a Montanist, refusing to face the consequences of a principle he himself had stated. In the *De corona* and the *De idolatria* he criticises the African Christians who were prepared to wear crowns on the occasions of the distribution of the *donativa* and to decorate their houses with lanterns and bay branches for the *gaudia publica*. And yet, it was he himself who had been the first Christian apologist to face in a systematic way the whole subject of the cult of the emperor in both its aspects: that of taking oath for the well-being and 'genius' of the emperor, and that of sacrificing to, or for, the emperor. The whole question had actually been somewhat neglected by the Greek apologists of the second century, and in my opinion this had been done deliberately. In fact, the imperial cult had never been imposed formally, or even encouraged, by any of the emperors to whom the Christian apologists from Aristides to Quadratus, from Melito to Athenagoras, were addressing their works. To raise such a delicate and embarrassing question must therefore have seemed both dangerous and inopportune. For this reason, Justin, Melito and Athenogoras preferred to underline the loyalty of the Christians to the state and the fact that they prayed for the empire and the emperor, rather than actually to make the connection between these and the worship of the emperor's person, which they were not able to accept. In practice, however, the problem did exist; as we have seen, at least since the time of Pliny, judges and governors had been trying to keep in step with the widespread adulatory fanaticism and the practice that was by now common throughout the empire, and had asked the Christians to make libations or to offer sacrifice to the image of the emperor, even though, as we know, this was going beyond what the emperors themselves had ordered (as in the case of Trajan, above). If the Christians refused to comply, this transgression naturally took on the meaning and character of a *crimen maestatis*, at least in the public mind.

If the problem was avoided by the apologists, it could hardly be ignored by the martyrs themselves. And, indeed, it was they who, in the act of refusing the cult, were the first to formulate reasons why their refusal had to be made. In the *Acta* of the Scillitan martyrs, in 180, we are told that Donata, on being asked to swear the oath to the genius of the emperor, answered 'Honour to Caesar as Caesar, but homage only to God' (Lazzati, p. 129). Less than five years later, some time between 183 and 185, Apollonius was also to face the same dilemma in Rome when called before Tigidius Perennius, Commodus' praetorian prefect, and the senate. The answer he made constitutes the first real attempt at an apologetic answer to this problem. In the Greek text of the Acts, Apollonius (ibid. pp. 169–70) states that the Christians cannot accept the swearing of oaths for the emperor's Fortuna; indeed, they consider it a vile act because, for them, the truth in the word 'yes' is worth any oath. Mistrust comes from lies and, because of lies, oaths have to multiply. If Perennius wants him to swear that the Christians honour the emperor and pray for his continued power, he is willing to swear to the truth for the sake of the True God, who exists before all ages, whom the hands of man have not fashioned but who has, on the contrary, established on earth one man to rule over all men on earth. As regards Perennius' request that he should sacrifice to the gods and to the image of the Emperor, Apollonius answers that he and all Christians offer to God a pure and bloodless sacrifice through their prayers for those whom Providence has placed to rule over the earth. Indeed, every day they pray to the God who is in the heavens for the Emperor Commodus, knowing that he reigns on earth not because of the action of others, but by the will of the one invincible God.

In giving a precise answer to the question avoided by the apologists of the second century, Apollonius provides one of the strongest arguments that will be used from now onwards to demonstrate the Christians' political loyalty to Rome. When they refuse to worship the emperor, the Christians are not denying him the honour due to him, neither do they refuse to recognise the sacred nature of the empire itself. On the contrary, they are the first to recognise it because they know that the Emperor is emperor by the will of their God, and for this reason they honour him and pray for his salvation. Here we have a clear link with the phrase of Tertullian's from which we started ('Noster est magis Casear, a nostro Deo constitutus'), and in fact not only the conclusion of Apollonius' *apologia*, but also many of his single arguments appear in the *Apologeticum*. As we know, Tertullian based his chapters on the confutation of political accusations (Chapters xxiix–xxxv) on this lost *apologia* of Apollonius which was, according to tradition, the first to be written in the Latin language.[4]

Tertullian develops at some length the subject of prayer for the emperor as a substitute for sacrifices, and, like Apollonius, he insists on the fact that this prayer is made to the God of the heavens, the God who has given the emperor his empire. On the subject of swearing the oath, Tertullian (*Apol.* xxxii. 2 ff.) says that the Christians swear in favour of the health of the emperor, far more sacred than any *genius*. We — he goes on — venerate in the emperors the wisdom of God who has put them at the head of the people: 'We know that they have in them what God wants them to have, and therefore we desire that what God wants saved should be saved, and this, for us, is stronger than any oath' (ibid. xxxii. 3). Speaking in these terms, the Christians were using a language that was both easily accessible to and convincing for the pagans. From the time of Augustus to that of Diocletian, the concept of the emperor 'by the will of God' had coexisted with that of the 'emperor as god' and had actually been considered truer to the genuine Roman traditions. The Christians knew this, and Tertullian explicitly appeals to the Roman tradition which obliged a victor to remember, at the moment of victory which made him similar to Capitoline Jove, that he is a man (ibid. xxxiii. 4). He also explicitly quotes Augustus, 'imperii formator'(ibid. xxxiv. 1), who did not want to be called 'dominus'. It is no coincidence that, in defining the relationship between the emperor and God, Tertullian uses terms which were typical of Augustan propaganda. He affirms that emperors are above everyone else, second only to God: 'they feel that He alone is God, and compared with Him they are in second place, after which they are first, before and above all' (ibid. xxx. 1). At this point we hear echoes of the famous ode (*Odes*, i. 12 lines 51–2) in which Horace, after the decisive events of 27 BC, beseeches Jove, father and guardian of mankind, to protect Augustus, who will reign second only to him: 'You will reign having Casear as your second

. . . who, lesser than you, will rule with justice over the happy world.'

After Tertullian, emperor-worship was no longer a decisive factor in the persecution of the Christians. The great persecutions of the third century (those of Decius and Valerian) and the beginning of the fourth (Diocletian, Galerius and Maximinus) all concentrated on the question of sacrifice to the gods and transgressions against traditional religion rather than transgressions against the emperor.

The great persecutions of the third and fourth centuries were religious, not political, in character. The position of the Christians as far as the emperors were concerned was clear and, ultimately, unassailable.

Notes

1. Cf. M. Sordi, 'L'attegiamento di Ambrogio di fronte a Roma', in 'Ambrosius Episcopus' A.V. (1976), vol. 1, pp. 203 ff.

2. On the inscription 'Roma Aeterna' on Philip the Arab's coins, see Mattingly – Sydenham – Sutherland, *Roman Impérial Coinage* IV. 3 (London, 1949), pp. 54 ff.

3. See above, pp. 33 ff. and 47 ff

4. For a comparison of Tertullian's *Apologeticum* with Apollonius' *Apologia* (the first Latin apologia, according to tradition), see M. Sordi,'L'apologia del martire Apollonio', *Rivista di Storia della Chiesa in Italia*, 18 (1964), pp. 171 ff.

12 Aspects of the Relationship Between Church and Society

From the start, the church took the form of a hierarchy, a society in which each member had his particular function and office within the life of the community. This was true of the very first nucleus in Jerusalem, as we see from Chapter six of the Acts of the Apostles, and it was also true of the communities which were springing up in various cities of the empire during the lifetime of the Apostles, as we know from their various epistles.

Those who maintain that the Christians were seen as a political danger to the state, and who think that the Christians were persecuted first and foremost for illegal association (*collegium illicitum*), should bear in mind that the authorities were aware of the associative nature of Christianity from its very early days. And yet, as I have pointed out in Part One of this book, Christianity was penalised exclusively as an individual religious crime, right up to the times of Valerian. It was only with Valerian's edicts that detailed and discriminatory penalties were worked out for ecclesiastics and laymen, that the right to associate freely was denied and that church property was confiscated. Valerian's edicts were issued in 257 AD; in the space of a very few years, in 260 to be precise, the edicts of Gallienus granted the church the legal right to exist, for the first time in history. It is paradoxical that Christianity should have been condemned as a religion and recognised as a church; and that Valerian's negative recognition of the church as an institution should have been the necessary, if painful, first step towards Gallienus' positive recognition.

However, we should not be too surprised by the fact that Roman society was prepared to recognise Christianity only under the form of an organised religion. After all, the Roman mentality was by nature mistrustful of new doctrines in themselves, even if it was perfectly prepared to accept and assimilate what in practical terms could be seen to be worthwhile or valuable. For people who needed tangible evidence, concrete demonstrations of practical worth, nothing could be more suspect than the thought that there existed an uncontrolled crowd of people, meeting together in total abandonment to the mass hysteria generated by an unknown religion. When the consul for the year 186 BC made his speech on the subject of the bacchanals, the first and most serious danger to the state was seen in the fact that a promiscuous crowd, including many women, met at night to stupify themselves with wine, shrieks and howls and fanatical carryings on (Livy, XXXIX. 15. 8–10).

The pagans did not fail to compare the community life of the Christians with that of subversive secret societies and even with the bacchanals themselves. In his famous letter to Trajan, Pliny (*Ep.* x. 96. 7) applied to the eucharistic assemblies of the early church the Roman concept of the *sacramentum* typical of the *coniurationes* and affirmed that, in the case of the Christians, the *sacramentum* (the *sacrificium* which binds the *foedus*) was not 'in scelus aliquod' as it had been with the bacchanals but, on the contrary, bound those who participated in it to shun all evil deeds. Thus, while he used the terminology appropriate to the *coniurationes* and secret brotherhoods, Pliny insisted at the same time that the aims of the Christians were very different and, he believed, completely innocent.[1] Fronto and Celsus, on the other hand, were convinced of the opposite, and insisted that Christian meetings were secret and illicit. Fronto,[2] like Pliny, used Livy's description of the bacchanals, but to the opposite effect; Celsus (I. 1. Bader) saw the secrecy of the reunions as sufficient proof of unlawfulness and, perhaps speaking for Marcus Aurelius, appealed to the Christians to come out of hiding. As we have seen earlier (p. 70), the church accepted this invitation with alacrity, publishing details of its organisation and hierarchy and assuming full responsibility for its associative life.

In the passage on the bacchanals quoted above, Livy denounced the ills of nocturnal gatherings of uncontrolled crowds, and went on to say: 'Your forefathers did not lightly allow you, either, to assemble [*coire*]; they decreed that whenever a crowd gathered, there should be a legitimate leader of the crowd' (Livy, XXXIX. 15. 11). And indeed, as soon as the Roman government discovered the facts about the hierarchical structure and rigid discipline of the church, the Christians began to be looked on with admiration rather than mistrust. According to the author of the *Historia Augusta* (*Vita Alex*. 45. 7), Alexander Severus actually took the Christian and Jewish method of choosing priests as a model to be imitated by the Roman state itself. And in fact the Hebrew religion had originally been recognised through its hierarchy, with which, despite various revolts and rebellions, the Roman powers always maintained stable and correct relations.

In the case of the Christian religion, too, the authorities managed from quite early on — at least since the times of Marcus Aurelius and Celsus — to distinguish between the main church and the numerous different sects which called themselves Christian. When the state decided to establish relations with the Christians (first unofficially, then officially), they naturally turned to the Great Church, took note of its hierarchical structure and made contact with its *legitimi rectores*, as was their normal practice in these situations. That is, they went straight to the bishops, and in particular the Bishop of Rome who was known to be the most important of them. (When Decius attempted to block the election of a successor to Pope Fabian, he was actually giving a sort of negative proof of the state's recognition of the church hierarchy; Aurelian's arbitration was a positive proof of the same thing.) If from the start Constantine chose to relate to the Catholic Church rather than to the Donatists or any of the other numerous Christian sects, it was not, I believe, simply because he preferred to ally himself with the leaders of the city groups rather than with the new forces emerging in the country.[3] It was because the Catholics, not the Donatists, represented the Great Church, and it was only through them that church and state could successfully come to an agreement.

Studying as we are the relationship between Christianity and the Roman Empire, we do not have to go into the question of how and why the various different denominations and levels of the hierarchy originally came into being, or — a much debated question — when the church came to adopt its system of a monarchical episcopacy. What we must examine, instead, is the question of how the church organised its associative life within the structure of the society of the times.

The Roman 'Collegia' and the Organisation of the Church

In the Roman world, *collegia* were, as we know, associations of private individuals whose members had in common their profession, their religious beliefs or their mutual desire to contribute to a burial fund. *Collegia* were founded on the solidarity and mutual assistance of their members, their leaders (*magistri*) were chosen by election and a monthly contribution was paid into the society's 'bank' (*arca*). Regarded with suspicion whenever they showed signs of turning into factions or disturbing the public peace, they were nevertheless perfectly legal institutions, thanks to a *senatus consultum* of uncertain date (mentioned in an inscription of Hadrian's times (*CIL* xiv. 2112) which allowed them to exist without special permission as long as they were 'associations for the mutual assistance of the poor' (*tenuiores*). Septimius Severus extended this permission from Rome to the whole of Italy and the provinces and added the right to form *collegia religionis causa* (*Dig.* 47. 22. 1). We can probably take it that this was the form chosen by the early church in its attempt to claim from the authorities the right to possess meeting and burial places and to emerge from the semi-clandestine state to which it had been relegated by Trajan's rescript.[4] In any case we know for certain that Tertullian described the organisation of the Christian communities specifically as 'collegia religionis causa' in Chapter xxxix of his *Apologeticum*, underlining the legitimacy of Christian gatherings by quoting the exact terminology of the contemporary Severan rescript. He also made a point of comparing the organisation of the Christian communities with the pagan *collegia* — in both cases meetings are presided over by the *probati seniores* and there is an *arca* for the monthly contribution — and underlined that the differences between the two were moral rather than legal. For example, the *seniores* (that is the presbyters) did not buy their office but were elected on the basis of evidence of moral integrity and, in fact, this was the practice which later so impressed Alexander Severus. Then, the common funds were not used to pay for drinking bouts, banquets and orgies, but went to feed and bury the poor, to help children with no means of support and to sustain widows and orphans.

The emphasis here would seem to reflect the original spirit of the *sentus consultum*, in which a *collegium* was legally acceptable if its objective was humanitarian in general, and in particular if its aim was to provide for funeral expenses. At the same time we hear echoes of the moral austerity of Roman tradition, with its mistrust of the feasting and drunken revels which could so easily lead to outbreaks of violence.[5] Tertullian's choice of terminology, his mention of the forms of worship and mutual help adopted by the Christians — he speaks of the monthly payment of financial contributions (originally weekly, according to Justin i *Apol.* 66) — were clearly intended to show that the associative life of the Christians was in perfect conformity with the law: in the *Apologeticum*, he uses the word 'corpus'; in the *Ad nationes*, he uses 'collegium' (I. 20. 5).

The fact that this type of *collegium* did not need a specific permit (which of course Christianity, *religio illicita*, would not have been able to obtain) certainly made it easier for the church to expand peacefully and to consolidate its property during the long period of religious tolerance from the death of Marcus Aurelius to the second half of the third century. Despite the fact that the Christian religion was still officially illegal, and that upon receipt of privately brought charges the state still had to persecute the Christians, in general the church leaders were able to be in open contact with the authorities. Thus, Marcia could ask Pope Victor in Commodus' name for a list of the Christians who had been deported so that the Emperor could grant them his pardon; thus, under Caracalla, a governor of Arabia could ask permission of Origen's superior, the Bishop of Alexandria, for the celebrated theologian to come to him to hold lectures; thus, Alexander Severus could officially assign to the Christians in Rome some land claimed by the *popinarii*, saying that the religious use to which the land would be put was preferable to the one the tavern-keepers had in mind.

Gallienus' edict put an end to this paradoxical state of affairs by granting the church formal recognition. Between 260 and 303 AD, Christianity was a legally recognised religion, and this was true not only for the Great Church, but also for all the lesser Christian communities — the 'corpus Christianorum' and the 'conventicula' of the so-called edict of Milan (Lactantius, *De mort.* 49. 8–9). Condemned once again during Diocletian's persecution, their right to exist and associate was then 'newly' (*denuo*) recognised in the edict of Serdica of 311 ('ut denue sint Christiani et conventicula sua componant' (Lactantius, ibid. 34. 4)). Finally, in the so-called edict of Milan, the Christians' right to possess places of worship and ecclesiastical property was also restored: ('ad ius corporis eorum, id est ecclesiarum, non hominum singolarum pertinentia' (Lactantius, ibid. 48. 9)). The existence of rights of ownership for the church and churches *as such*, as 'corpus Christianorum, id est ecclesiarum' and not as 'collegium religionis causa' or 'tenuiorum', therefore, goes back to the time of Gallienus, and was then restored and officially recognised, rather than newly created, by the edicts of Serdica and Milan and in Constantine's time.

So far, we have only looked at the organisation of the church and the Christian communities in the periods immediately following the reigns of Marcus Aurelius and Gallienus; that is the periods during which the church emerged first *de facto* and then *de jure* from its condition of semi-clandestinity, progressing from the cover of the *collegia* and *corpora* — using the formulae for 'collegia religionis causa' and 'collegia tenuiorum' which the state could recognise — to emerge into a clear and unequivocal declaration of identity at the time of Gallienus' peace. If this evolution seems perfectly clear, it is less easy to define the position of the Christian communities in the society of earlier periods. The most probable hypothesis is that they depended for the most part on invitations to private homes and the use of private property in general as cover for their activities.

Phrases such as 'the church in the household of Aquila and Priscilla' (Romans 16: 5) and 'those of Narcissus' household' (ibid. 16. 11) and even 'those who belong to the Emperor's household' (Philippians 4: 22) are frequent in the church of apostolic times and are evidence of the widespread use that was made of private chapels in the primitive church. These would, perhaps, have evolved into collegial structures of the kind so common in the Roman world — the 'collegium quod est in domo' or the 'collegium familiae'. This hypothesis seems particularly credible when we remember that from the first century onwards we find members of the rich and powerful ruling classes in close contact with Christianity and that some of the oldest Christian catacombs seem to be linked with these families.

In the light of this hypothesis, a group of inscriptions (mostly Roman) attesting the existence of a *collegium* in the house of the Sergii Pauli becomes particularly significant.[6] There are 23 of these inscriptions (three are brick stamps and useful for dating purposes), in which the *collegium* is mentioned, usually with the wording 'quod est in domo Sergiae L. filae Paullinae (nos. 1–7; 13–14) or 'collegium Luci nostri (no. 20). Epigraphical studies identify the founder of the *collegium* as the son (Lucius) of the proconsul of Cyprus who was converted to Christianity by St Paul. The *collegium* would have been carried on by Lucius' daughter, Sergia Paullina, wife of Cornelius Severus, consul in the year 112 AD. One of the daughters of this marriage in turn married M. Acilius Glabrio, consul in the year 124 and son of the Acilius Glabrio who was executed as a Christian under Domitian. Thus a marriage in the second century united two of the great Roman families which had adopted Christianity in the first. This would certainly seem to confirm the fact that the two senatorial families had continued to practise Christianity — cautiously dissimulated, but no less genuine for that — and that the *collegium* of the inscriptions was in reality a domestic chapel.[7]

The inscriptions dedicated to the *collegium* certainly never mention the pagan deities. At the same time there is no indication to suggest that the *collegium* was a funeral society for the whole *familia* of the Sergii — there are slaves and freedmen in the family but they do not appear to be part of the *collegium*. And, in fact, the only references to pagan deities are to be found in the inscriptions dedicated to these members of the household: the dedication to the god Men of L. Sergius Corinthus in inscription no. 9, and the symbols of the avenging Sun in inscription no. 21, of the home-born slave Tiridates.

The *collegium* has an *arcarius* (no. 1), a *magister* (no. 20), *maiores* and *minores* (no. 7). These last two formulae were previously unknown but are now apparently found in the pagan *collegia* too.[8] The term 'magister', to which the plural of 'maiores' seems to correspond, belongs to pagan terminology, but it was also used by Fronto to designate Christian priests (see Tertullian, *Ad nat.* I. 7), as 'ministrae' was used by Pliny for two deaconesses (*Ep.* x. 96. 7). Tertullian himself in the *De baptismo* (17) used the term 'maiores' to indicated the members of the clergy as opposed to the 'laici'. In fact, the Greek term 'laici' was not adopted by everyone writing Christian Latin at once; Cyprian, writing half-way through the third century, still often prefers to use 'plebaei' or 'plebs'. It was, of course, inevitable that there would be some uncertainty at first as to how traditional Latin should be adapted to the new ecclesiastical circumstances. In any case, if the inscriptions of Paullina are indeed Christian, they are the oldest Christian Latin documents in existence, belonging as they do to the end of the first century and the beginning of the second.

Lastly, the use of the term 'maiores' logically presupposes the existence of 'minores'. The fact that the Christians certainly used the word 'maiores' to indicate members of the ecclesiastical hierarchy leads us to imagine that already during this period (as in later Latin) 'minores' was used to indicate the *privatae personae*, those, that is, without any precise role in the hierarchy, in other words, the laity.

The Role of the Laity in the Associative Life of the Primitive Church

During the first centuries of the Christian church, and in particular during the years when its activity was semi-clandestine, the laity played an important and often indispensible role. We are well informed on their activities during the apostolic period, thanks to that invaluable record of the life of the early church, the Acts of the Apostles. But from the end of the apostolic period up to the time of Constantine's peace, our information is fragmentary and purely fortuitous, with the Acts of the Martyrs providing most of the evidence on which to reconstruct the life and spiritual development of the Christian laity of the times.

While the Apostles were still alive, the role of the laity seems to have been mainly that of providing help and hospitality. The story of Tabitha-Dorcas (raised from the dead by St Peter who was moved by the prayers of the widows 'who showed him the coats and cloaks she used to make while she was among them' (Acts 9: 39)) is typical of the kind of assistance the laity used to provide for the poor, but we are also struck by the help given to the Apostles and the missionaries who travelled around preaching the gospel. There was, of course, nothing new in this kind of collaboration. As we know, during the life of Jesus, the family at Bethany and the unknown owner of the inn behaved in the same way. When, on the instigation of St Paul and the community of Antioch, the Apostles began to travel beyond Palestine and its immediate environs, following the Jewish diaspora into every province of the empire, this kind of assistance became particularly important. Missionaries travelled from city to city, and stayed for longer or shorter periods in each place to consolidate the already existing communities; and these activities called for well-organised facilities for hospitality. On the one hand, houses had to be found where the missionaries could stay and, if necessary, preach and worship when the local synagogues were not prepared to accommodate them. On the other, premises were needed as permanent meeting-places and centres for communication with other communities. The Acts of the Apostles and the Epistles of St Paul are full of references to the generous Christians who provided these facilities: Lydia the seller of purple at Philippi (Acts 16: 5), Jason at Thessalonica (ibid. 17: 5), Aquila and Priscilla, husband and wife, tent-makers in Corinth and then Ephesus (ibid. 18: 2 and 18), Tyrannus, a school teacher at Ephesus (ibid. 19. 9), Mnason, a Cypriot of Caesarea (ibid. 21: 16),

Nymphas at Laodicea (Colossians 4: 15) and Philemon (Philemon 1: 1–2). We have already seen Paul's reference in his letter to some of these collaborators and the 'church which is in their household'.

Collaboration was not limited to offers of hospitality, however. In many cases, substantive help was given in the form of funds for financing missionary expeditions. If it was the Apostles who organised the collection of funds for the church in Jerusalem, it seems that in Philippi the financing of Paul's missionary journeys was an entirely spontaneous initiative of the lay community itself (Phil. 4: 15 ff.). On some occasions members of the lay community actually took part in the missionary journeys, as happened with Aquila and Priscilla, who started by giving hospitality to Paul in Corinth and then went on to accompany him to Ephesus. Here they preached the gospel and explained points of doctrine, as we know from the episode of Apollo, whom they led from John's baptism to Christ's and to whom they 'explained the way of God more particularly' (Acts 18: 26).

As we have seen, hospitality and the setting up of 'domestic chapels' continued to be the work of the lay community after the end of the apostolic period and right through the first and second centuries. The lack of official recognition and the legal ban on the practice of the Christian religion meant that the church could not give any external signs of its organisation or hierarchy, nor could it openly possess or be legally responsible for the premises in which any of its communities worshipped or buried their dead. Communities were, therefore, forced to rely on the use of their members' private property, the houses or other buildings which the richer and more generous of the faithful were prepared to put at their disposal. Some of the oldest church names (*tituli*) in Rome derive from the names of the lay families that lent their homes for Christian gatherings. Perhaps the best example of this is the *titulus* 'Clementis': today known as the church of San Clemente, excavations have revealed its foundations to be the remains of a Roman villa of the Flavian age, probably belonging to T. Flavius Clemens, consul in 95 AD and cousin of Domitian, who died as a martyr in the year of his consulate. The famous catacombs of Domitilla took their name from Flavius Clemens' wife, Flavia Domitilla, who was condemned by Domitian at the same time as her husband. Similarly, the catacombs of Priscilla were probably named after one of the women of the Acilii Glabriones, another great Roman family, one of whose members was condemned for being a Christian in 95

AD. The catacombs are adjacent to the tombs of the Acilius family.

Some time between the end of the second century and the beginning of the third, the situation changed, thanks mainly to the initiative taken by Pope Callistus. He took advantage of the more tolerant atmosphere of the Severan dynasty and, perhaps in an attempt to dispel the doubts still held by public opinion and the authorities, he brought the Christian church out from its semi-clandestine state and openly assumed responsibility for its places of worship and burial. From this time onwards, the domestic churches began slowly to disappear.

The lay community probably continued to be responsible for some of the financial activities which had developed from the original collection of funds for the needy. We have one characteristic example in the bank run by the Christian freedman Carpophorus for the benefit of widows and orphans. Information on its activities and subsequent failure has come down to us in Hippolytus of Rome's account of the life of Callistus, who was at that time a slave of Carpophorus and not yet Pope (Hippolytus, *Philosophumena* IX. 11–12).

During the early centuries, the laity also appears to have played an important, if not exclusive, part in the propogation of the faith and the writing of *apologiae*. While we know that some of the apologists were members of the ecclesiastic hierarchy (Melito, Bishop of Sardis, for example, or Apollonaris, Bishop of Hierapolis), the lack of any clear indication of the status of others probably means that they were simply members of the lay community. In particular, I believe this is true of Justin, the Greek philosopher and apologist, martyred during the reign of Marcus Aurelius, and the Roman senator Apollonius, one of the earliest Latin apologists (according to St Jerome), martyred at the time of Commodus.

It is interesting to see how these two intellectuals, both of them converts from paganism, took pains to assimilate into Christianity the best that the culture and mentality of Greece and Rome had to offer. In the case of Justin, who had opened a school of philosophy in Rome and organised public debates, reason and criticism were the ideals to be pursued, and in his two *Apologiae*, addressed to the Emperor and the senate, he presented his religion in terms of a search for the truth according to the strict rules of logic. Apollonius, on the other hand, emphasised the Roman ideals of the virile life, lived with fortitude and put at the service of society. His arguments, significant above all for their loyalist views on the relationship between the Christians and the state, have come down to us in the Acts of his martyrdom.[9] And, in fact, it is precisely in these Acts of the Martyrs that we find the most interesting of the lay figures, citizens who were aware that their faith elevated them to a super-natural plane, but who were equally aware of their duties to their terrestial home and their rights as free human beings. Typical of these people were Apollonius, whom we have mentioned above; Donata, one of the Scillitans (180 AD) who told the proconsul of Africa, Saturninus, that she honoured Caesar as Caesar but feared only God; Lucius of Rome, mentioned by Justin in his Second *Apologia*; Vettius Epagathus, one of the martyrs of Lyons (177 AD) who at their own personal risk intervened in favour of the Christians who were on trial, calling on the judges to respect the laws and the correct legal procedures; the young African matron Vibia Perpetua (202–3 AD) who together with her companions refused to dress up as a pagan priest during the festivities to which they had been taken, and died in the name of the freedom she claimed for them. Ennobled by martyrdom, these lay figures acquired a particular aura of authority in the early church, an authority which started to make itself felt even during the course of their trials, when their steadfastness in bearing witness to God and their fortitude in adversity were an example to all the Christians.

The figure of Perpetua as it comes to us in the Passion of Perpetua and Felicita, is, in fact, a typical example of this process. Perpetua's faith, her courage, the youthful exuberance of her naturally optimistic nature, her love of fun, all transform this 22-year-old woman into the natural leader of the Christians who were imprisoned with her, and with whom she was eventually tried and sent to a cruel death. When a disagreement broke out between the bishop Optatus and the priest Aspasius, it was natural that Perpetua's acquired authority should make her and her companions the mediators who would reconcile the two and restore peace to the community. Some decades earlier, in the controversies which flourished around the Montanist heresy, the martyrs of Lyons had tried to carry out the same kind of mediation. The behaviour of Perpetua and her companions and the martyrs of Lyons was dictated by true charity and also by a profound respect for the authority of the church. On the other hand, when Decius' perse-cution caused the defection of many Christians (the famous problem of the *lapsi*), the moral authority of the martyrs and confessors was often used to justify all kinds of ill-advised action, including some episodes of open rebellion, forcing the church authorities to intervene.

During Valerian's persecution (257–60 AD) and, later, Diocletian's, a new factor began to emerge in the kind of action taken against the Christians. The state had learned something of the organisation of the church during the years of tolerance and could now make a distinction between clergy and laity. The persecutory edicts of this time were aimed directly at creating divisions within the church by penalising the clergy specifically and with greater severity than the laity (see above, p. 111f). Not unfrequently during this period we find cases mentioned in the *Acta* of Christians confessing to being deacons or priests, while their pagan friends and relations swore to their lay status before the magistrates in order to save their lives. It seems, however, that this attempt to cause a split between clergy and laity had no great success anywhere in the empire. The way in which (according to Cyprian (*Epistles* 60)) the Christians of Rome rallied round Pope Cornelius when he was sent into exile by Trebonianius Gallus in 253, makes it clear that even the controversy over the *lapsi* had failed to make any deep divisions within the church. During both Valerian's persecution and Diocletian's, we find laity and clergy united in resistance and even death when, as happened during Diocletian's persecution, the penalties for certain categories of laymen (government officials, members of the court and army officers) took particularly insidious forms and the threat was not so much loss of life as loss of career, rank, social position and so on.

To sum up this brief account of the activity of the laity in the early church, we can say that their involvement seems more evident and more intense during the first centuries, when the church lived a semi-clandestine existence. The church owned no property during this period and the laity provided the essential link between Church and society. This was the age of household worship and of intimate and direct collaboration. With the arrival of the third century and a more tolerant attitude on the part of the state (only interrupted by brief, if violent, bouts of persecution), the ecclesiastical organisation which had been growing up over the course of the years came out into the open, taking on direct responsibility for itself in the eyes of the world. The figure of the layman as close collaborator began to disappear, while the composing of *apologiae* and the propagation of the faith, activities in which the laity had worked on equal terms with the clergy, began to be undertaken exclusively by the members of the hierarchy, or at least under their direct control. Justin's school of philosophy seems to have been set up on his own initiative, but the catechism school of Alexandria at the time of Caracalla was controlled directly by the Egyptian metropolis. The distinction which had always existed between clergy and layman, but which had been almost imperceptible from the outside, now became so evident that the state could recognise it for what it was and plan its persecutions accordingly.

Notes

1. Cf. M. Sordi, 'Sacramentum in Plinio, Ep. X, 96, 7', *Vetera Christianorum*, 19 (1982), pp. 97 ff.

2. Fronto apud Minuc. Oct. 8, 4, 'Plebem coniurationis . . . nocturnis congregationibus' (on which, cf. P. Frassinetti, 'L'orazione di Frontone contro i Cristiani', *Giornale Italian di Filologia*, III (1949), pp. 283 ff.; also, M. C. C. Cristofari, 'L'orazione di Frontone contro i Cristiani e la persecuzione di Marco Aurelio', *Revista di Storia della Chiesa in Italia* 32 (1978), p. 132).

3. This would seem to be the opinion of L. De Giovanni, *Costantino e il mondo pagano* (Naples, 1977), pp. 197–8: 'Constantine does not rely on the "democratic" or "popular" currents of the new religion, but rather, the well-tried institution of the urban congregations of the Catholic Church . . . Constantine and his court identify . . . with the "bourgeois" image of Christianity, with its substrata of classical cultures, obviously free from superstitious beliefs.'

4. For the legal position of the Christian communities and the question of church ownership of property, see M. Sordi, *Il cristianesimo e Roma* (Bologna, 1965), pp. 468 ff. (with a *status quaestionis*).

5. For Tertullian's text in relation to the laws of the times, see M. Sordi, 'Sergia Paullina e il suo collegium', *Rendiconti dell'Istituto Lombardo, Scienze e Lettere*, 119 (1979), p. 18.

6. For a list of the inscriptions, their texts and the numeration followed here, see M. Bonfioli and S. Panciera, 'Della cristianità del "Collegium quod est in domo Sergiae Paullinae" ', *Atti del Pontificio Accademia di Archeologia*, 44 (1971/2), pp. 185 ff. and ibid. 45 (1972/3) pp. 113 ff.

7. For further arguments in support of this interpretation, see M. Sordi and M. L. Cavigiolo, 'Un'antica chiesa domestica' in *Rivista di Storia della Chiesa in Italia*, 25 (1971), pp. 169 ff. and Sordi, 'Sergia Paullina e il suo collegium', pp. 14 ff.

8. M. Jaczinowska in *Atti Istituto Veneto* 194 (1975/6) 370 ff., quotes two inscriptions, one from Beneventum (ILS 7219) and one from Sitifis in Mauritania (*Année Epigraphique* (AE) (1910), 7). In these, *maiores iuvenum* seems to be the local equivalent of *magistri*. Bonfioli and Panciera, in *Epigraphica*, 37 (1975), pp. 283 ff., completes an extremely corrupt Algerian inscription with the formula 'collegium maiorum et minorum'. The test contains a dedication to Jove Optimus Maximus, of the time of Alexander Severus.

9. On Apollonius, see M. Sordi,'Un senatore cristiano dell' età di Commodo', *Epigraphica*, 17 (1955), pp. 104 ff. and in 'L'apologia del martire romano Apollonio', *Rivista di Storia della Chiesa in Italia*, 18 (1964), pp. 169 ff. On Carpophorus' bank, see S. Mazzarino, 'La democratizzazione della cultura nel "basso impero" ' in *Rapports, XI Congres International des Sciences Historiques* (Stockholm and Uppsala, 1960), pp. 49 ff.

13 Public Opinion and Persecution in the Roman Empire

The importance of public opinion in the ancient world is often underestimated, and yet during the first centuries of the Empire it seems often to have been the decisive factor which sparked off the persecution of the Christians. With the exceptions of Nero and Domitian, who wanted persecution themselves and orchestrated it with propaganda and all the other means at the disposal of an increasingly totalitarian state, none of the emperors before Decius believed that the Christians represented any kind of threat to the state, or showed any desire to search them out (the only exception being Marcus Aurelius during the misunderstanding over the Montanist question). It is true, however, that in different degrees all the emperors allowed charges to be brought against the Christians — as long as the accusations were not brought anonymously — and this can only mean that all the emperors after Nerva feared that too obvious a protection of the Christians would be unpopular with the general public.[1] On this point, the conclusions I reached in my work *Il cristianesimo e Roma* (*Christianity and Rome*)[2] have been confirmed by J. Speigl who, despite his different approach to the subject and despite considerable disagreement on various details, believes that the persecutions of the first centuries were dictated primarily by questions of *Befriedungspolitik*.[3]

As I pointed out earlier, Hadrian's rescript to Minucius Fundanus is an eloquent witness to the two opposing positions: on the one side, the state's lack of interest, in persecuting the Christians, and on the other, the pressures exerted on the central government by an increasingly hostile public opinion. Minucius' predecessor as proconsul of Asia had sent a petition to the Emperor on behalf of the provincials, asking permission to take action against the Christians. In answer to the petition, the Emperor says that, if the inhabitants of the province can produce proof of the legitimacy of their charges, they should refer them to the tribunals, but that there must be no petitions and no riots. 'But in the name of Hercules', the Emperor goes on, 'if anyone brings forward these accusations simply as calumnies, make sure he pays for it' (Eusebius, *Hist. eccl.* iv. 9; see Justin, I *Apol.* 68). Hadrian's 'in the name of Hercules', breaking through the coldly impersonal official language, shows how irritated he was by those who 'upset the people' with their fanatical hostility towards the Christians.

In Trajan's famous rescript to Pliny the same attitude was already apparent, even if Trajan treated the problem in a more detached way, limiting himself to forbidding the official search for Christians on the basis of anonymous charges (Pliny, *Ep.* x. 97). The same attitude is to be found again in Antoninus Pius' repeated admonitions to the Greek and eastern provinces not to 'make any innovations' as far as the Christians were concerned (Eusebius, *Hist. eccl.* iv. 26. 10). As I mentioned earlier, it was only with Marcus Aurelius that an attempt was made to get around Trajan's veto without actually changing the laws, in order to make it possible to search out the Christians whenever the state felt it necessary. We have already examined the reasons for Marcus Auelius' decision: on the one side the pressure of public opinion, especially in the Greek and eastern provinces, united with the authoritative voice of Fronto, Roman senator and teacher of the Emperor; on the other, the spread of Montanism, which was not clearly distinguishable from mainstream Christianity in the public mind, and which appeared to be radically incompatible with the interests of state security. Possibly during the last years of Marcus Aurelius' reign, certainly under Commodus, the situation reverted to *de facto* tolerance; and under the Severi, with their prevailing ideal of syncretism, this tolerance could only be reinforced until, at the time of the last Severan emperors, it turned into open approval. According to the contemporary Tertullian, Septimius Severus had himself had occasion to take the side of the Christians against a mob which was crying out for persecution (Tertullian, *Ad Scap.* iv. 5).

All Christian sources constantly refer to the weight that public opinion could bring to bear on the authorities (' . . . ἐξ ἐπαναστασεως δημων . . . ' says Eusebius (*Hist. eccl.* iii. 32. 1) on the subject of the persecutory movements of Trajan's times, and Tertullian and Hippolytus both testify more than once to this atmosphere during the persecutions of the Severan era). The same intensity of feeling is also confirmed by the Acts of the Martyrs. But, if it is perfectly clear that these public manifestations could and did play a decisive part in the proceedings, the problem remains as to where these pressures came from and what were the internal dynamics behind them. Now, if it is true that the government itself did not encourage or feed public hostility — at least during the Antonine and Severan eras — this does not necessarily mean that anti-Christian feeling simply grew up spontaneously in the public mind. There is always a moving force behind the *fama* and the *rumores* that the Roman mind connected so closely with the forming of public opinion and (to use the expressions current at the time) *consensus* or *invidia*. 'Quod', says Tertullian, analysing the phenomenon of the public's hatred of the Christians, 'ab uno aliquando principe exhorta sit (fama) necesse est' (*Apol.* VII. 9–10). He goes on to say:

> Exinde in traduces linguarum et aurium serpit, et ita modici seminis vitium cetera rumoris obscurat, ut nemo recogitet, ne primum illud os mendacium seminaverit, quod saepe fit aut ingenio aemulationis, aut arbitrio suspicionis, aut non nova sed ingenita quibusdam mentiendi voluptate.

In analysing the phenomenon, Tertullian also attempted to explain its origins, and, as so often happened in the ancient world, he found an explanation in individual characteristics, in moral and psychological motivations — jealousy in some personalities, arbitrary suspicion, an innate predeliction for lying. But, as we shall see later, over and above these motivations (and Tertullian himself is quite prepared to admit the existence of other more complex social reasons for the phenomenon: ('infructuosi negotiis dicimur' (*Apol.* XLII. 1)), the fact remains that, in order to understand the *fama* and the *rumores* which fed anti-Christian feeling, we have to presuppose the existence of some kind of moving force, a group or groups in whose interest it was to create and spread anti-Christian propaganda.

We must not forget that anti-Christian feeling in fact fluctuated considerably, depending on which of the various clearly identifiable outside influences were at work. This state of affairs can be seen for example, in the famous question of the *flagitia*, a blanket-term under which the Christians were accused of all kinds of dark and evil deeds. Tacitus (*Ann.* XV. 44) tells us these rumours were already circulating in Rome in the year 64 AD, when Nero took advantage of them to accuse the Christians of starting the great fire ('quos per flagitia invisos vulgus, Chrestianos appellabat'). In the same period, the First Epistle of St Peter reports that the pagans 'slandered us as malefactors', speaking evil of their former coreligionists (2: 12; 4: 4) and says that the Christians' refusal to take part in the intemperate and dissolute activities of the times was considered to be extremely suspect. It is probable that the rumours grew up from a misunderstanding of some of the practices of Christian worship, in particular the Eucharist, and that this misunderstanding was then used by interested parties to foster fear and hatred among the public. This would certainly appear to have been the situation in Bithynia at the time of Pliny, if in his letter to Trajan he had to ask whether the Christians were to be punished for the *nomen* or for the 'flagitia cohaerentia nomini' (*Ep.* x. 96. 2). As we know, he then went on to report that in fact the *flagitia* were non-existent, as he had discovered when he interrogated the two *ministrae*. The Christians, he says, meet 'ad capiendum cibum, promiscuum tamen et innoxium', and swear oaths not 'in scelus aliquod', but rather to renounce 'furta, latrocinia, adulteria', to keep their promises and to give back what has been left in their custody (ibid. 5).

Once Pliny had made it clear what he thought on the subject, it appears that the accusations of *flagitia* abated for a time. Rumours of *flagitia* certainly continued to circulate among the masses, but the widespread realisation that the authorities were not prepared to take action evidently rendered them innocuous. It is significant that in his *Apologia*, Justin (writing under Antoninus Pius) takes very little trouble to refute accusations of this sort (I *Apol.* 26).

On the other hand, with Athenagoras in 176–7 and the later apologists, Minucius and Tertullian, the whole question suddenly acquires a renewed sense of urgency. The response of the apologists is obviously in direct relation to the importance the authorities, as well as the masses, seem to have attributed to accusations of *flagitia* in the famous trials at Lyons in 177 AD. Certainly in the years immediately preceding 177 the question had become topical once more and accusations of *flagitia* were both widespread and widely believed. The only possible explanation for this revival of interest is that it was sparked off by Fronto's famous oration to the senate on the subject of the Christians. In the fragment preserved for us by Minucius, Fronto uses all the dramatic tricks at the command of an experienced rhetorician to convince his listeners that the Christians are guilty of infanticide and incest. Obviously, Fronto cannot be held responsible for creating hostile public opinion single-handedly; already at the time of Antoninus Pius, the feeling was present at least in the Greek and Asiatic cities, which rose up on more than one occasion against the 'atheists', with whom the Christians were, of course, equated (see the Acts of Polycarp and the pagan Lucian[4]). But it was certainly Fronto, with all the authority and prestige of an ex-consul, a member of the senate and a tutor to the Emperor, who was responsible for reawakening accusations which had lain dormant since the time of Trajan. It was he more than any other who gave the accusations credibility and broadcast them throughout the empire, so that violent anti-Christian fanaticism was no longer confined to Asia but also touched Gaul for the first time (as Melito records). It was thanks to him that charges of *flagitia* were now taken seriously by the authorities, as we can see by the behaviour of the legate of the *Tres Galliae* at the time of the trials of Lyons.

The story of what happened to accusations of *flagitia* during the course of little over a hundred years gives us a classic example of the relationship between public opinion and propaganda. We can see clearly to what extent the spreading of a 'rumour' depended on the influence of precise areas of interest, particular pressure groups, interacting with the unfathomable areas of irrational and emotional impulse. In this case the anti-Christian feeling which had been gradually maturing in the Senatorial class since Domitian's time is closely linked with the cultural and religious conservatism with which part at least of the senate clothed its irrational nostalgia for the days of the ancient republic.

Thus in the second half of the second century, when opposition to Christianity began to take a definite shape in the dominant culture of the times and in some segments of the ruling classes, we can clearly identify which group inspired, or at least encouraged, the hostility and prejudices of the masses.

However, as we have already seen, various forms of prejudice certainly existed in the public mind well before Nero made his accusations in 64 AD. Although he was no doubt delighted to be able to exploit previously existing anti-Christian feeling when looking for a scapegoat to blame for the fire (and the accusations of *flagitia* had already made the Christians unpopular), we must exonerate him from the responsibility of having actually created the feeling himself. This is all the more certain when we remember that until 62 AD the imperial government itself had never given evidence of any kind of preconceived antipathy for the followers of the new religion.[5]

It is, therefore, worth asking what events and what circumstances could have generated so much hostility and prejudice in the minds of the pagan peoples, at a time when neither the imperial government, nor the ruling classes, nor the dominant culture of the times had shown the slightest interest in inciting the masses to anti-Christian revolt.

The records left us in the Acts of the Apostles, together with some observations in the Epistles, give us some idea as to how we might solve this enigma. In the accounts of the spread of the early church beyond Palestine, anti-Christian feeling seems to be a recurrent and constant theme. (Within the strictly Jewish environment of Palestine, hostility is the natural outcome of the religious situation, and needs no explanation.) For each episode of mob violence, the author of the Acts specifies from where the original instigation came. In most cases it was the local Jewish community which incited the pagans to rise against the disciples of Christ, while the pagans themselves were, at least to begin with, either favourable to the preachers of the new doctrine or, at worst, indifferent. In two cases, however, it was the pagans themselves who took the initiative and provoked serious rioting against the Christians. Both aspects of the question deserve to be examined separately.

Jewish Provocation of the Pagan Masses

In the Acts, the phenomenon is strictly linked to St Paul and his teaching missions, but later, especially in some cities of Asia Minor, it becomes a recurrent feature of anti-Christian persecution at the end of the first century and the beginning of the second. A comment in the Revelation of St John (2. 9) and the Martyrdom of Polycarp both go to confirm that this was the case at least in the city of Smyrna.

The first example we have of this phenomenon is the action taken against St Paul by the 'Jews who lived in Damascus' (Acts 9: 22–3), which can be dated as happening around 36 AD.[6] Events repeat themselves in Pisidian Antioch in 48 AD or thereabouts (ibid. 13: 50) when Paul addressed the pagans and the 'Jews used their influence with such women of fashion as worshipped the true God (*sebomenai*, that is followers of the Hebrew religion), and with the leading men of the city, set on foot a persecution against Paul and Barnabas . . . ', The instruments used to excite feeling here were the 'God-fearing' women of high birth, who in their turn exerted their influence on the *protoi* of the city. In this case, the populace

itself was not involved. At Iconium too (ibid. 14: 2 ff.), it was the
Jews who 'stirred up trouble among the gentiles and poisoned their
minds against the brethren'. The 'multitude' comes into the story
for the first time at Lystra, when it was 'won over' by the Jews who
had come all the way from Antioch and Iconium (ibid. 14: 19). At
Thessalonica, it is the Jews again who, jealous of the conversion of
the Greeks (ibid. 17: 5 ff.), stir up the crowd with the help of some
agitators. They break into Jason's house in the hope of finding Paul
and Silas, who were staying there, in order to drag them before the
crowd they had already thrown into an uproar with their words. In
the end the city council is called on to intervene. The same Jews
came to Beroa to 'upset and disturb the minds of the multitude'
(ibid. 17: 13). In Corinth, the Jews unanimously present themselves
before Gallio's tribunal (ibid. 18: 12 ff.) but, after the proconsul's
firm refusal to intervene, the episode ends with the leader of the
synagogue being severely chastised by the pagans who were present
at the time.

For the Christian community in Jerusalem, at least in the year 54,[7]
there was no mystery attached to Paul's troubles with the Jews of the
diaspora. These Christians, all converts from the Hebrew religion
and 'zealous supporters of the Law' (ibid. 21: 20 ff.), had been told
that Paul was teaching the Jews of the diaspora to 'break away from
the laws of Moses'. For this reason, James advised Paul to
demonstrate his loyalty to the law by making a public act of worship
in the Temple. But this had the unforeseen consequence of being
judged an act of provocation by the Asian Jews who were in
Jerusalem at the time. When, eventually, the advocate Tertullus
spoke for the Jews before the governor Antonius Felix, he accused
Paul of being the ringleader of the Nazarenes and a 'pestilential
mover of sedition among the Jews all over the world' (ibid 24: 5).

The alarm felt by the Jews of the diaspora, and their continuing
hostility towards Paul's teaching are thus clearly motivated by their
fear of the Apostle's indiscriminate conversion of Jews and pagans
alike, conversions which took place outside the formal framework
of the Jewish law. The Acts also give us a fairly clear picture of the
instruments used by the local Jewish authorities in their attempts to
influence the pagans: the God-fearing society women who were
able to influence the notables in Antioch; the professional political
agitators in Thessalonica. If the motivation of the Jews themselves is
clear, it is less easy to establish what arguments the agitators might
have used to rouse the pagan masses in Asia Minor and Greece.

There is no direct mention of this in the Acts, but the accusations Tertullus makes before Felix give us an idea of how the Jews might have generated anti-Christian feeling amongst the pagans. The Christians were apparently being accused of causing the sedition and riots of which the Jews themselves had always been accused in the past. And indeed, the reciprocal and atavistic intolerance which had always existed between the Jews and the pagans had given rise to innumerable uprisings in the larger cities of the empire. Caligula's reign saw a dramatic episode of violence in Alexandria, and Claudius, in 41 AD feared a similar episode in Rome and forcefully denounced the situation in his letter to the Alexandrians.[8] It seems to me that when Tertullus refers to Paul as a 'pestilential man' and the prime mover of the *staseis* of 'Jews all over the world', when the agitators in Thessalonica accuse Paul and Silas of 'defying the edicts of Caesar' (Acts 17: 7),[9] the underlying motif is precisely that of trying to transfer to the Christians the prejudices and the hostility of which the Jews of the diaspora had themselves been the victims for so many centuries. The famous accusation of 'hatred of mankind' which Tacitus tells us was levelled against the Christians at the time of Nero would thus be, at least in part, explained—it was the same accusation that the pagans, especially in Greek-speaking countries, had always levelled against the Jews.

Pagan Provocation of the Pagan Masses

The only examples we have of this phenomenon come to us in the accounts the Acts give us of the events at Philippi and Ephesus. However, these accounts are so significant, so symptomatic of what would occur in the future, that I believe we can legitimately take them as models.

In Philippi, a Roman colony decidedly closed to Jewish religious propaganda,[10] St Paul healed a 'girl possessed by a prophesying spirit', who earned good money for her masters with her predictions (Acts 16: 16 ff.). When these men realised that their means of livelihood had been taken away, they dragged Paul and Silas before the magistrates, claiming that 'these men, Jews by origin, are disturbing the peace of our city; they are recommending customs which it is impossible for us as Roman citizens, to admit or observe' (ibid. 20–1). The crowd became excited and the magistrates, exercising *coercitio*, arrested the presumed agitators and had them beaten, having determined to release them the next day (and not without apologies when they discovered that Paul and Silas were Roman citizens).

As I have already said, this episode is extremely significant for several reasons. To begin with, we have what the author of the Acts diagnoses as the basic motivation behind the accusation: the loss of earnings. This diagnosis is based on intentions which are only attributed to the accusers and it could well seem somewhat partial; but I do not believe we should discard it too lightly. Pliny reports how the market for sacrificial meats in Bithynia[11] fluctuated in response to the growth or repression of Christianity, and Tertullian in his *apologia* feels the need to defend the Christians, 'infructuosi negotiis'. Next, there is the accusation which is intended to worry the authorities: the newcomers disturb the public peace. Lastly, there is the accusation of a violation of the *mos maiorum* ('being Jews they . . . are recommending customs which it is impossible for us, as Roman citizens, to admit or observe'). This last accusation is to recur frequently in Roman circles throughout the second century, and, while on a juridical level it had no significance, it carried enormous emotional weight in the public mind. As far as the general public was concerned, people who violated traditional customs were capable of committing any crime, of perpetrating any enormity. It is also interesting to see the ethnic question being raised here; we can, perhaps, take it as further confirmation of the hypothesis I put forward earlier on the subject of the irreconcileable gulf which divided the Jews and the pagans.

Thus, the episode at Philippi would seem from many points of view to foreshadow the trends anti-Christian persecution was to follow throughout the second century, wherever the Latin culture was dominant (in Africa, therefore, and in the Roman West). This Roman brand of intolerance would find its cultured voice first in Fronto's attack, and later in the polemics which continued up to the time of Symmachus.

The episode of Ephesus takes us into a different world — that of a Greek city with Greek traditions, capital of an Asian province. The initiative against Paul and Silas was taken by a certain Demetrius, a silversmith who made his living from selling miniature models of the temple of Diana, a kind of souvenir for the tourists. Seeing his livelihood threatened by the spread of the new doctrine, according to which gods made by the hands of man are not gods at all, he called a meeting of his fellow craftsmen, with the intention of indicting

Paul (Acts 19: 23 ff.). The craftsmen organised a public demonstration and with the cry of 'Great is Diana of Ephesus' soon had the crowds mobilised. Taking over the theatre, they organised a kind of general assembly-cum-trial, with Paul's companions, the Macedonians Gaius and Aristarchus, as the accused. While the Jews contributed to the confusion, the local authorities, on this occasion clearly on the side of Paul and his friends, did their best to calm the waters. The delegates from Asia, friends of Paul, advised him not to appear before the assembled throng, and the *grammateus* with wise words brought the crowd to its senses by threatening them with Roman reprisals. He also openly defended the Christian preachers, saying that they had never spoken ill of the goddess of Ephesus, nor had they committed sacrilege against her: 'these men you have brought here have not robbed the temples, they have not used blasphemous language about your goddess' (ibid. 37).

With the exception of the behaviour of the local magistrates (characteristic of this period and never to be repeated after the events of 62 AD[12]), the episode of Ephesus is a premonitory example of the kind of situation which was to arise in all the Greek and Eastern cities throughout the second century. Now, as later, the accusation brought against the Christians was fundamentally a religious accusation, encapsulated in a slogan which was guaranteed to produce a strong reaction in the public. Paul and his friends were accused of sacrilege. During the trial of Polycarp and on numerous other occasions, the cry is 'death to the atheists'. At Ephesus as at Philippi, it hardly matters that the underlying motive is, as the author of the Acts claims, the economic threat to an individual or a group; the crowd is moved to violence against the Christians by religious fanaticism, by the conviction that the Christians, in offending their divine protectress, will bring down some terrible malediction on the entire city. The episodes at Ephesus and Philippi, with their fear of possible economic losses and their slogans through which the 'message' was transmitted to the masses, both foreshadow in some ways the underlying motives which would compel alike the fanatical masses of the East and the conservative spheres of the West to press for a persecution which the central government itself did not consider necessary and would without doubt have preferred to avoid.

Notes

1. The conclusions I present here, with some variations, first appeared in M. Sordi, 'Opinione pubblica e persecuzioni anti-cristiani nell'Impero romano', *CISA* v (1978), pp. 159 ff.

2. M. Sordi, *Il cristianesimo e Roma*, (Bologna, 1965), pp. 12 and 129 ff.

3. J. Speigl, *Der römische Staat und die Christen*, (Amsterdam, 1970).

4. *Martyrium Polycarpi* III *(Eusebius, Hist. eccl.* IV. 15. 6); *Lucian Alexander* XX and XXXVIII: A. Donini, in his *Storia del cristianesimo* (Milan, 1975), pp. 204–5, attributes this hostility to an 'organised campaign . . . whose inspiration came from the highest spheres of power and even from the sovereign himself, for whom a refusal to worship in the official way meant a weakening of the religious support for his terrestrial power'. This interpretation, however, ignores the evidence of the original sources.

5. Indeed, the trial of James the Less in Jerusalem in 62 AD only took place because the Saduccees who orchestrated it took advantage of the temporary absence of the Roman governor to attack the Christians. For the episode, see above, Part one, pp. 13 and 29 ff.

6. For the date, see M. Sordi in *Studi Romani*, 8 (1960), pp. 393 ff.; and in *Il cristianesimo*, pp. 454 ff.

7. For the date, see M. Sordi, ibid. note 6.

8. Claudius' letter to the Alexandrians; see I. H. Bell, *Jews and Christians in Egypt* (British Museum, 1924), pp. 23 – 6 and above, p. 26.

9. For a discussion of this accusation, I refer readers to my *Il cristianesimo*, pp. 49–51.

10. Ibid. p. 48.

11. See W. Plankl, 'Wirtschaftliche Hintergrunde der Christenverfolgungen in Bithynien', *Gymnasium*, 60 (1953), pp. 54 ff. E. J. Bickerman ('Trajan, Hadrian and the Christians', *Rivista di Filologia e d'Istruzione Classica* (1968), pp. 295 –6) prefers the term *vectigal* to *carne* in paragraph ten. This leads to a completely different interpretation: the Christians would have been accused of damaging the *vectigalia* of the temples. On this question, see P. V. Cova, 'Plinio il Giovane e il problema delle persecuzioni', *Bollettino di Studi Latini*, 5 (1975), p. 295, in which the author defends the traditional reading.

12. See above, note 5.

Index

205